THE PALM AT THE END
OF THE MIND

WALLACE STEVENS

THE PALM AT THE END OF THE MIND

Selected Poems and a Play by

WALLACE STEVENS

Edited by

HOLLY STEVENS

VINTAGE BOOKS

A Division of Random House, Inc. / New York

VINTAGE BOOKS EDITION, FEBRUARY 1990

Copyright © 1967, 1969, 1971 by Holly Stevens

Library of Congress Cataloging-in-Publication Data
Stevens, Wallace, 1879–1955.
The palm at the end of the mind : selected poems and a play / by
Wallace Stevens : edited by Holly Stevens.
p. cm.
ISBN 0-679-72445-1
I. Stevens, Holly.   II. Title.
[PS3537.T4753A6   1990]
811'.52—dc19   75-136350

"Bowl, Cat and Broomstick," a play, was originally published in the
Quarterly Review of Literature, *July 30, 1969, Princeton, New Jersey.*

Manufactured in the United States of America
10 9 8 7 6 5 4 3 2 1

"The palm at the end of the mind,
Beyond the last thought, rises
In the bronze decor . . ."

—*"Of Mere Being"*

PREFACE

The poems included in this selection have been chosen to represent my father not only at his best but also in the full range of his imagination. They have been arranged in chronological order, determined from manuscript evidence, correspondence, or date of publication. It should be noted, however, that poems dated only by publication must have been written earlier; when date of acceptance by a magazine is known, it helps to limit the gap, but is not definitive. The present order can therefore be debated and, hopefully, improved on in the future as further chronological evidence appears. One exception has been made: "First Warmth" and "As You Leave the Room" are printed together for easy comparison. The first appears to be an early version of the second, which Samuel French Morse dates "1947–55?". Neither poem was published during Stevens' lifetime.

Because no manuscript of poems that appeared in earlier books was submitted for *Collected Poems*, and because certain discrepancies in manuscript and magazine publication versions have not been resolved, minor changes have been made in punctuation, spelling, and line spacing without comment. Where more extensive variations occur, brief explanatory notes appear at the back of this book, although limitations of space preclude a full textual apparatus.

That same limitation has made the final choice difficult, and I am grateful to those scholars and teachers of my father's poetry whose generous comments and suggestions have been helpful. And to those others who assisted in the preparation of the manuscript, my sincere thanks.

—HOLLY STEVENS

CONTENTS

THE PALM AT THE END
OF THE MIND

Blanche McCarthy

Look in the terrible mirror of the sky
And not in this dead glass, which can reflect
Only the surfaces—the bending arm,
The leaning shoulder and the searching eye.

Look in the terrible mirror of the sky.
Oh, bend against the invisible; and lean
To symbols of descending night; and search
The glare of revelations going by!

Look in the terrible mirror of the sky.
See how the absent moon waits in a glade
Of your dark self, and how the wings of stars,
Upward, from unimagined coverts, fly.

Cy Est Pourtraicte, Madame Ste Ursule, et Les Unze Mille Vierges

Ursula, in a garden, found
A bed of radishes.
She kneeled upon the ground
And gathered them,
With flowers around,
Blue, gold, pink, and green.

She dressed in red and gold brocade
And in the grass an offering made
Of radishes and flowers.

She said, "My dear,
Upon your altars,
I have placed

The marguerite and coquelicot,
And roses
Frail as April snow;
But here," she said,
"Where none can see,
I make an offering, in the grass,
Of radishes and flowers."
And then she wept
For fear the Lord would not accept.

The good Lord in His garden sought
New leaf and shadowy tinct,
And they were all His thought.
He heard her low accord,
Half prayer and half ditty,
And He felt a subtle quiver,
That was not heavenly love,
Or pity.

This is not writ
In any book.

Tea

When the elephant's-ear in the park
Shrivelled in frost,
And the leaves on the paths
Ran like rats,
Your lamp-light fell
On shining pillows,
Of sea-shades and sky-shades,
Like umbrellas in Java.

Sunday Morning

I

Complacencies of the peignoir, and late
Coffee and oranges in a sunny chair,
And the green freedom of a cockatoo
Upon a rug mingle to dissipate
The holy hush of ancient sacrifice.
She dreams a little, and she feels the dark
Encroachment of that old catastrophe,
As a calm darkens among water-lights.
The pungent oranges and bright, green wings
Seem things in some procession of the dead,
Winding across wide water, without sound.
The day is like wide water, without sound,
Stilled for the passing of her dreaming feet
Over the seas, to silent Palestine,
Dominion of the blood and sepulchre.

II

Why should she give her bounty to the dead?
What is divinity if it can come
Only in silent shadows and in dreams?
Shall she not find in comforts of the sun,
In pungent fruit and bright, green wings, or else
In any balm or beauty of the earth,
Things to be cherished like the thought of heaven?
Divinity must live within herself:
Passions of rain, or moods in falling snow;
Grievings in loneliness, or unsubdued
Elations when the forest blooms; gusty
Emotions on wet roads on autumn nights;
All pleasures and all pains, remembering
The bough of summer and the winter branch.
These are the measures destined for her soul.

5

Jove in the clouds had his inhuman birth.
No mother suckled him, no sweet land gave
Large-mannered motions to his mythy mind.
He moved among us, as a muttering king,
Magnificent, would move among his hinds,
Until our blood, commingling, virginal,
With heaven, brought such requital to desire
The very hinds discerned it, in a star.
Shall our blood fail? Or shall it come to be
The blood of paradise? And shall the earth
Seem all of paradise that we shall know?
The sky will be much friendlier then than now,
A part of labor and a part of pain,
And next in glory to enduring love,
Not this dividing and indifferent blue.

IV

She says, "I am content when wakened birds,
Before they fly, test the reality
Of misty fields, by their sweet questionings;
But when the birds are gone, and their warm fields
Return no more, where, then, is paradise?"
There is not any haunt of prophecy,
Nor any old chimera of the grave,
Neither the golden underground, nor isle
Melodious, where spirits gat them home,
Nor visionary south, nor cloudy palm
Remote on heaven's hill, that has endured
As April's green endures; or will endure
Like her remembrance of awakened birds,
Or her desire for June and evening, tipped
By the consummation of the swallow's wings.

V

She says, "But in contentment I still feel
The need of some imperishable bliss."

Death is the mother of beauty; hence from her,
Alone, shall come fulfilment to our dreams
And our desires. Although she strews the leaves
Of sure obliteration on our paths,
The path sick sorrow took, the many paths
Where triumph rang its brassy phrase, or love
Whispered a little out of tenderness,
She makes the willow shiver in the sun
For maidens who were wont to sit and gaze
Upon the grass, relinquished to their feet.
She causes boys to pile new plums and pears
On disregarded plate. The maidens taste
And stray impassioned in the littering leaves.

VI

Is there no change of death in paradise?
Does ripe fruit never fall? Or do the boughs
Hang always heavy in that perfect sky,
Unchanging, yet so like our perishing earth,
With rivers like our own that seek for seas
They never find, the same receding shores
That never touch with inarticulate pang?
Why set the pear upon those river-banks
Or spice the shores with odors of the plum?
Alas, that they should wear our colors there,
The silken weavings of our afternoons,
And pick the strings of our insipid lutes!
Death is the mother of beauty, mystical,
Within whose burning bosom we devise
Our earthly mothers waiting, sleeplessly.

VII

Supple and turbulent, a ring of men
Shall chant in orgy on a summer morn
Their boisterous devotion to the sun,
Not as a god, but as a god might be,
Naked among them, like a savage source.
Their chant shall be a chant of paradise,

Out of their blood, returning to the sky;
And in their chant shall enter, voice by voice,
The windy lake wherein their lord delights,
The trees, like serafin, and echoing hills,
That choir among themselves long afterward.
They shall know well the heavenly fellowship
Of men that perish and of summer morn.
And whence they came and whither they shall go
The dew upon their feet shall manifest.

VIII

She hears, upon that water without sound,
A voice that cries, "The tomb in Palestine
Is not the porch of spirits lingering.
It is the grave of Jesus, where he lay."
We live in an old chaos of the sun,
Or old dependency of day and night,
Or island solitude, unsponsored, free,
Of that wide water, inescapable.
Deer walk upon our mountains, and the quail
Whistle about us their spontaneous cries;
Sweet berries ripen in the wilderness;
And, in the isolation of the sky,
At evening, casual flocks of pigeons make
Ambiguous undulations as they sink,
Downward to darkness, on extended wings.

Peter Quince at the Clavier

I

Just as my fingers on these keys
Make music, so the selfsame sounds
On my spirit make a music, too.

Music is feeling, then, not sound;
And thus it is that what I feel,
Here in this room, desiring you,

Thinking of your blue-shadowed silk,
Is music. It is like the strain
Waked in the elders by Susanna.

Of a green evening, clear and warm,
She bathed in her still garden, while
The red-eyed elders watching, felt

The basses of their beings throb
In witching chords, and their thin blood
Pulse pizzicati of Hosanna.

II

In the green water, clear and warm,
Susanna lay.
She searched
The touch of springs,
And found
Concealed imaginings.
She sighed,
For so much melody.

Upon the bank, she stood
In the cool
Of spent emotions.
She felt, among the leaves,
The dew
Of old devotions.

She walked upon the grass,
Still quavering.
The winds were like her maids,
On timid feet,
Fetching her woven scarves,
Yet wavering.

A breath upon her hand
Muted the night.
She turned—
A cymbal crashed,
And roaring horns.

III

Soon, with a noise like tambourines,
Came her attendant Byzantines.

They wondered why Susanna cried
Against the elders by her side;

And as they whispered, the refrain
Was like a willow swept by rain.

Anon, their lamps' uplifted flame
Revealed Susanna and her shame.

And then, the simpering Byzantines
Fled, with a noise like tambourines.

IV

Beauty is momentary in the mind—
The fitful tracing of a portal;
But in the flesh it is immortal.

The body dies; the body's beauty lives.
So evenings die, in their green going,
A wave, interminably flowing.
So gardens die, their meek breath scenting
The cowl of winter, done repenting.
So maidens die, to the auroral
Celebration of a maiden's choral.

Susanna's music touched the bawdy strings
Of those white elders; but, escaping,
Left only Death's ironic scraping.
Now, in its immortality, it plays
On the clear viol of her memory,
And makes a constant sacrament of praise.

The Silver Plough-Boy

A black figure dances in a black field.
It seizes a sheet, from the ground, from a bush, as if spread there
    by some wash-woman for the night.
It wraps the sheet around its body, until the black figure is silver.
It dances down a furrow, in the early light, back of a crazy plough,
    the green blades following.
How soon the silver fades in the dust! How soon the black figure
    slips from the wrinkled sheet! How softly the sheet falls
    to the ground!

Disillusionment of Ten O'Clock

The houses are haunted
By white night-gowns.
None are green,
Or purple with green rings,
Or green with yellow rings,
Or yellow with blue rings.
None of them are strange,
With socks of lace
And beaded ceintures.
People are not going
To dream of baboons and periwinkles.
Only, here and there, an old sailor,
Drunk and asleep in his boots,
Catches tigers
In red weather.

For an Old Woman in a Wig

. . There is a moment's flitter
Of silvers and of blacks across the streaking.

. . . a swarming chitter

Of crows that flap away beyond the creaking
Of wooden wagons in the mountain gutters.
. .

The young dogs bark . .

. .
. .   It is the skeleton Virgil utters

The fates of men. Dogs bay their ghosts. The traces
Of morning grow large and all the cocks are crowing
And . .   the sun . .   paces

The tops of hell . . Death, . . . knowing,
Grieves . . our spirits with too poignant grieving,
. . keeps on showing

[*here 3 lines have been completely erased*]

To our still envious memory, still believing,
The things we knew. For him the cocks awaken.
He spreads the thought of morning past deceiving

And yet deceives. There comes a mood that's taken
From water-deeps reflecting opening roses
And rounding, watery leaves, forever shaken,

And floating colors, which the mind supposes
In an imagination cut by sorrow.
Hell is not desolate Italy. It closes

. . above a morrow
Of common yesterdays: a wagon's rumble,
Loud cocks and barking dogs. It does not borrow,

Except from dark forgetfulness, the mumble
Of sounds returning, or the phantom leaven
Of leaves so shaken in a water's tumble.

II

Is death in hell more death than death in heaven?
And is there never in that noon a turning—
One step descending one of all the seven

Implacable buttresses of sunlight, burning
In the great air? There must be spirits riven
From out contentment by too conscious yearning.

There must be spirits willing to be driven
To that immeasurable blackness, or . .
To those old landscapes, endlessly regiven,

Whence, hell, and heaven itself, were both begotten.
There must be spirits wandering in the valleys,
And on the green-planed hills, that find forgotten

Beggars of earth intent
On maids with aprons lifted up to carry
Red-purples home—beggars that cry out sallies

Of half-remembered songs . .   sing, "Tarry,
Tarry, are you gone?" . . Such spirits are the fellows,
In heaven, of those whom hell's illusions harry.

III

When summer ends and changing autumn mellows
The nights . .   and moons glance
Over the dreamers . . and bring the yellows

Of autumn days and nights into resemblance,
The dreamers wake and watch the moonlight streaming.
They shall have much to suffer in remembrance.

They shall have much to suffer when the beaming
Of the clear moons, long afterward, returning,
Shines on them, elsewhere, in a deeper dreaming.

. .   Suns, too, shall follow them with burning
Hallucinations in their turbid sleeping . .
. .

O pitiful lovers of earth, why are you keeping
Such count of beauty in the ways you wander?
Why are you so insistent on the sweeping

Poetry of sky and sea? . Are you, then, fonder
Of the circumference of earth's impounding
Than of some sphere on which the mind might blunder,

If you, with irrepressible will, abounding
In . .   wish for revelation,
Sought out the unknown new in your surrounding?

Domination of Black

At night, by the fire,
The colors of the bushes
And of the fallen leaves,
Repeating themselves,
Turned in the room,
Like the leaves themselves
Turning in the wind.
Yes: but the color of the heavy hemlocks
Came striding.
And I remembered the cry of the peacocks.

The colors of their tails
Were like the leaves themselves

Turning in the wind,
In the twilight wind.
They swept over the room,
Just as they flew from the boughs of the hemlocks
Down to the ground.
I heard them cry—the peacocks.
Was it a cry against the twilight
Or against the leaves themselves
Turning in the wind,
Turning as the flames
Turned in the fire,
Turning as the tails of the peacocks
Turned in the loud fire,
Loud as the hemlocks
Full of the cry of the peacocks?
Or was it a cry against the hemlocks?

Out of the window,
I saw how the planets gathered
Like the leaves themselves
Turning in the wind.
I saw how the night came,
Came striding like the color of the heavy hemlocks.
I felt afraid.
And I remembered the cry of the peacocks.

Six Significant Landscapes

I

An old man sits
In the shadow of a pine tree
In China.
He sees larkspur,
Blue and white,

At the edge of the shadow,
Move in the wind.
His beard moves in the wind.
The pine tree moves in the wind.
Thus water flows
Over weeds.

II

The night is of the color
Of a woman's arm:
Night, the female,
Obscure,
Fragrant and supple,
Conceals herself.
A pool shines,
Like a bracelet
Shaken in a dance.

III

I measure myself
Against a tall tree.
I find that I am much taller,
For I reach right up to the sun,
With my eye;
And I reach to the shore of the sea
With my ear.
Nevertheless, I dislike
The way the ants crawl
In and out of my shadow.

IV

When my dream was near the moon,
The white folds of its gown
Filled with yellow light.
The soles of its feet
Grew red.
Its hair filled
With certain blue crystallizations

From stars,
Not far off.

v

Not all the knives of the lamp-posts,
Nor the chisels of the long streets,
Nor the mallets of the domes
And high towers,
Can carve
What one star can carve,
Shining through the grape-leaves.

vi

Rationalists, wearing square hats,
Think, in square rooms,
Looking at the floor,
Looking at the ceiling.
They confine themselves
To right-angled triangles.
If they tried rhomboids,
Cones, waving lines, ellipses—
As, for example, the ellipse of the half-moon—
Rationalists would wear sombreros.

Inscription for a Monument

To the imagined lives
Evoked by music,
Creatures of horns, flutes, drums,
Violins, bassoons, cymbals—
Nude porters that glistened in Burma
Defiling from sight;
Island philosophers spent
By long thought beside fountains;
Big-bellied ogres curled up in the sunlight,
Stuttering dreams . . .

17

The Worms at Heaven's Gate

Out of the tomb, we bring Badroulbadour,
Within our bellies, we her chariot.
Here is an eye. And here are, one by one,
The lashes of that eye and its white lid.
Here is the cheek on which that lid declined,
And, finger after finger, here, the hand,
The genius of that cheek. Here are the lips,
The bundle of the body and the feet.

. . . .

Out of the tomb we bring Badroulbadour.

In the Carolinas

The lilacs wither in the Carolinas.
Already the butterflies flutter above the cabins.
Already the new-born children interpret love
In the voices of mothers.

Timeless mother,
How is it that your aspic nipples
For once vent honey?

The pine-tree sweetens my body.
The white iris beautifies me.

Indian River

The trade-wind jingles the rings in the nets around the racks by
    the docks on Indian River.
It is the same jingle of the water among the roots under the
    banks of the palmettoes,
It is the same jingle of the red-bird breasting the orange-trees
    out of the cedars.
Yet there is no spring in Florida, neither in boskage perdu, nor on
    the nunnery beaches.

To the Roaring Wind

What syllable are you seeking,
Vocalissimus,
In the distances of sleep?
Speak it.

Valley Candle

My candle burned alone in an immense valley.
Beams of the huge night converged upon it,
Until the wind blew.
Then beams of the huge night
Converged upon its image,
Until the wind blew.

Thirteen Ways of Looking
at a Blackbird

I

Among twenty snowy mountains,
The only moving thing
Was the eye of the blackbird.

II

I was of three minds,
Like a tree
In which there are three blackbirds.

III

The blackbird whirled in the autumn winds.
It was a small part of the pantomime.

IV

A man and a woman
Are one.
A man and a woman and a blackbird
Are one.

V

I do not know which to prefer,
The beauty of inflections
Or the beauty of innuendoes,
The blackbird whistling
Or just after.

VI

Icicles filled the long window
With barbaric glass.
The shadow of the blackbird
Crossed it, to and fro.

The mood
Traced in the shadow
An indecipherable cause.

VII

O thin men of Haddam,
Why do you imagine golden birds?
Do you not see how the blackbird
Walks around the feet
Of the women about you?

VIII

I know noble accents
And lucid, inescapable rhythms;
But I know, too,
That the blackbird is involved
In what I know.

IX

When the blackbird flew out of sight,
It marked the edge
Of one of many circles.

X

At the sight of blackbirds
Flying in a green light,
Even the bawds of euphony
Would cry out sharply.

XI

He rode over Connecticut
In a glass coach.
Once, a fear pierced him,
In that he mistook
The shadow of his equipage
For blackbirds.

XII

The river is moving.
The blackbird must be flying.

XIII

It was evening all afternoon.
It was snowing
And it was going to snow.
The blackbird sat
In the cedar-limbs.

The Plot against the Giant

First Girl

When this yokel comes maundering,
Whetting his hacker,
I shall run before him,
Diffusing the civilest odors
Out of geraniums and unsmelled flowers.
It will check him.

Second Girl

I shall run before him,
Arching cloths besprinkled with colors
As small as fish-eggs.
The threads
Will abash him.

Third Girl

Oh, la . . . le pauvre!
I shall run before him,

With a curious puffing.
He will bend his ear then.
I shall whisper
Heavenly labials in a world of gutturals.
It will undo him.

Gray Room

Although you sit in a room that is gray,
Except for the silver
Of the straw-paper,
And pick
At your pale white gown;
Or lift one of the green beads
Of your necklace,
To let it fall;
Or gaze at your green fan
Printed with the red branches of a red willow;
Or, with one finger,
Move the leaf in the bowl—
The leaf that has fallen from the branches of the forsythia
Beside you . . .
What is all this?
I know how furiously your heart is beating.

Bowl, Cat and Broomstick

Two figures sit in the circle of a spotlight, on a white bench, before a golden curtain. The rest of the stage is obscure. Their shadows are strongly reflected on the curtain. One, at the right, wears a gown falling below his knees. It is black covered with a faded silver pattern. Flat hat. Jewel in the hat. Black stockings. Small silver buckles on his shoes. He is gaunt. He is reading aloud from a book which is bound in yellow paper, like a French book. The other figure is smaller and more supple. Tight green costume. He is listening closely. The floor of the stage has a violet covering.

BOWL (*With finical importance*): She says — m — m — she says — m. (*Patronizing Cat*) I shall continue to translate this for you. Fleurs — des fleurs — full of flowers — full of tawny flowers —
CAT (*A little bored*): Tawny? What is the word for tawny?
BOWL: Rouges.
CAT: But, Bowl, rouges means red.
BOWL (*Coolly*): No doubt, when it refers to something red. But when, as here, it refers to something tawny, then it means tawny.

Broomstick saunters on the stage at the left. Heavily built. Hard-looking. Elderly. He uses a stick. Blue blouse, red sash, white trousers, like a French peasant. Bowl studies his book. Cat is interested in Broomstick's appearance.

BROOMSTICK (*Brusquely*): Bibliophiles!
CAT (*Very politely*): Bowl is reading from the poems of Claire Dupray.
BROOMSTICK: Charming!
He seats himself on the bench.

CAT: What was the line you read last, Bowl?

BOWL (*With chilly diffidence*): Le jardin est si plein de fleurs rouges . . . The garden is so full of tawny flowers.

BROOMSTICK: Remarkable!

CAT: He translates fleurs rouges by tawny flowers.

BROOMSTICK: Why not?

[*at this point a page is missing*]

BOWL: Are incongruous.

CAT: You see.

BOWL: They are incongruous at that age. It is an age when red becomes tawny, when blue becomes aerial — and when a girl, at least, when a girl like Claire Dupray, becomes a poetess.

CAT: Say poet — poet. I hate poetess.

BROOMSTICK: Oh, poetess is just the word at twenty-two! What you are thinking of is forty-two.

CAT: You are right, old Broomstick. May I see the portrait? *Bowl hands him the book.*
You speak of her hair because her head is bare.

BROOMSTICK: It is only the poetess of forty-two that sits for a portrait covered.

BOWL: I speak of her hair because in the case of a poetess, in the sense in which that word is just and beautiful, the speaking of it means so much to the portrait of her.

CAT: More than her nose or her chin? She has a delicate nose. She has a good chin.

BROOMSTICK: She has a good chin! Oh, ho! She has a good chin. Has she?

BOWL: Her hair reveals her. Three things live in the portrait of a poetess: her hair, her eyes and her mouth. These make it possible to discover something of what she is from the image of her. Claire Dupray has black hair. It is arranged simply, but, for all that, it remains full of the long motions of her bare arms. Is not that a part of her? What are we to expect from such a poet-

25

ess? Waxen odes? Skimped meditations? Let me have the book. *Cat hands him the book.*

Take this poem on twilight. What does she see in twilight? Not the commonplace end of daily momentum. She sees the light continuing to burn in stars. She says that the sun burns all night. And, in that, she sees the incessant momentum that tranquillizes because of the knowledge that it is immortal. The sun burns all night. She says that she will love as long as she lives.

CAT (*Fascinated*): She is glorious.

BROOMSTICK: How little it would take to turn the poets into the only true comedians! There's no truer comedy than this hodge-podge of men and sunlight, women and moonlight, houses and clouds, and so on.

BOWL: Nor any truer tragedy.

BROOMSTICK: No one believes in tragedy.

CAT: At twenty-two —

BROOMSTICK: That brings us to her eyes.

BOWL: But her eyes are nothing unless you believe in tragedy.

CAT: I believe.

BROOMSTICK: Poor sensualist! You think you believe. The truth is, you believe in eyes.

CAT: Have you seen the portrait?

He hands Broomstick the book.

Now, we shall have Broomstick on eyes.

BROOMSTICK: I concede that these eyes are capable of tragedy. But that is not the same thing as tragedy itself: and it is tragedy itself that we were speaking of.

BOWL: Then let me amend what I said: and say, instead, that her eyes are nothing unless you believe in eyes.

BROOMSTICK: A very proper amendment. But I am rather old, don't you think, to believe in eyes? I have reached the point where I don't believe in much of anything except legs. And one cannot be too sure even of legs.

CAT: Legs are art, not literature.

BROOMSTICK: They were always intended to be.

CAT: They are still intended to be.

BOWL: All the more reason for saying no more about them. It is a new thing that the eyes of a poetess should bring us to this.

BROOMSTICK (*Drily*): Possibly. And yet it may not be so new, after all. (*He pauses.*) We are not living in the seventeenth century for nothing. (*He pauses.*) Moreover, just as the relations of man and moonlight, women and moonlight, man and mountains, women and waves, and so on, are undefined, so the relations of eyes and legs, lips and cheeks, and that kind of thing, are equally undefined. It is all part of the universal comedy, which the poets ignore, because they continue to believe in tragedy. You see tragedy in these eyes. They are capable of tragedy. Does the voice of tragedy dwell in this mouth?

BOWL: I was not thinking of that. I was thinking merely of the expression it gives to the portrait. That expression is vitally biographical.

BROOMSTICK: Vitally biographical? The book has the usual preface. Is that not biographical enough?

CAT: We shall come to that in time.

BOWL (*Making a point*): We had agreed to skip it, for the moment, and to form our own idea of Claire Dupray from her portrait, and from her poetry. That is what we are doing.

CAT: Bowl is an idealist, you know.

BROOMSTICK: An idealist has nothing to fear from a preface.

CAT: That she has heavy black hair, large eyes, capable of tragedy, as you say, which means, I hope, that they are brilliant and mysterious, for so I see them, and that her mouth is expressive, this seemed preface enough.

BROOMSTICK: It is the kind of preface you yourself would write and that is why you think it preface enough.

CAT (*Offended*): What do you mean?

BROOMSTICK (*Putting him down*): I assume that in what Bowl has been saying of this portrait he has been intending to derive from ink and paper a vivid impression of the sensibility of his poetess. You have seen only her beauty.

CAT (*As if justified*): I make no bones about that. There is a special power in the poetry of a beauty.

BROOMSTICK: For you: yes.

CAT: For you, too.

BROOMSTICK (*Maliciously*): Pathos, perhaps; not power. But Bowl's portrait is a failure.

BOWL: A failure?

BROOMSTICK (*Sarcastically*): You might have been describing one of the many dark-haired and dark-eyed Peloponnesians. And what you say of the expressive quality of the mouth has been trite for a long time.

BOWL: And true for a long time.

BROOMSTICK: If it has been true for a long time, then I doubt if it is true any longer. The fact remains that your young poetess is an old poetess.

BOWL (*Querulously*): Ought her hair to be cropped?

BROOMSTICK: Unquestionably. Something of the sort.

CAT: Adieu, Dupray!

BROOMSTICK: I do not insist on the cropped hair.

CAT: But on something of the sort. Poor Claire!

BROOMSTICK: You judge her poetry by her portrait. Very well. I judge her portrait by her poetry.

BOWL: You are prejudiced by the cant of the moment that she should be of her day.

BROOMSTICK: That is far from being the cant of the moment. It will still be the cant of the moment in the eighteenth century, and in the nineteenth century, too.

BOWL: Broomstick, it galls me to agree with you. If I submit, will you go no farther?

BROOMSTICK: I shall go as far as possible. Take the book again. *He hands the book to Bowl.*
Would it have any effect if she wore black pendants in her ears? It should have. Test her poetry by that. They are wearing black pendants, you know.
Cat snatches the book out of Bowl's hands.

CAT: Would it have any effect?

He laughs heartily.

Confound it, Bowl! What was that poem about? The incessant momentum that tranquillizes because of the knowledge that it is immortal. Tranquillity and long, black pendants!

Bowl recovers the book from him.

BOWL: As you like. My portrait is not a failure. Broomstick is right. A poetess should be of her day. But he is thinking of the poetess of forty-two: the sophisticated poetess. I am thinking of the unsophisticated poetess of twenty-two. If she happens to look like one of the dark-haired and dark-eyed Peloponnesians, that is not a rococo pose. It is an unaffected disclosure of her relationship.

CAT: Dupray returns, a little.

BOWL: And besides, Broomstick, what you mean, no doubt, by being of one's day is being one's self in one's day.

BROOMSTICK: Well, Bowl, I submit to that, provided you, in turn, go no farther.

BOWL: Only to the extent of saying that Claire Dupray is simply herself in this portrait. It is true that she is not of the long, black pendant type. Nevertheless, she is of her day, in the sense in which you used that phrase.

CAT (*Succulently*): And I may be tempted by her again?

BOWL: In the long run, you would have been tempted by her regardless of these, or any other, considerations; so that your question is not honest.

CAT (*Brazenly*): It is honest enough. I am still a little harrowed by the poem on twilight.

BROOMSTICK: It haunts my own mind.

BOWL (*To Cat*): You said that there was a special power in the poetry of a beauty.

CAT (*Alarmed*): I said it. But I am not so certain of the beauty now.

BOWL: Then let me see.

He turns over the pages of the book rapidly.

Banal Sojourn. Old Catamaran — an amazing thing in the way it designs the catamaran on the surface of the sea: one of the poems in which by the description of the thing seen, she makes an image of the greatest intensity. Nothing in nature could have revealed what her imagination and sensibility have revealed. How true that is to my conception of Claire Dupray! She is beautiful. Her poems are beautiful. Here are similar poems: Les Dahlias — The Dahlias — What an extraordinary effect one gets from seeing things as they are, that is to say: from looking at ordinary things intensely!

BROOMSTICK: But to look at ordinary things intensely, is not to see things as they are. However, go on.

BOWL: Here, in another division of her book, is a group of poems in which she studies herself — not the individual Claire Dupray, but the racial Claire —

CAT: Ah! The racial Claire.

BOWL: When you think of what the study of self used to mean, and then read these clear and thoughtful pages —

BROOMSTICK (*Impatiently*): Read them, read them. Please do.

BOWL: I thought you might like me to explain.

BROOMSTICK: I may, bye and bye; but if these pages are as clear as you say they are, then I am content to have you read them first.

BOWL (*Translating à la mode*): In the motion of trees, m — m — that is, in the movement of trees, I find my own agitation. If it be morning, the mood of poplars, filled with sunlight, glistening in the dark west-wind, is already my own. If it be noon, the tossing of the elm trees in the golden sky has an identity with my own exulting. And if it be evening, the forms of trees, moving not at all, defining their beauty through the obscure air, m — m — m — These things are atrociously difficult in English. In French, they seem almost pellucid. Let me see: the forms of trees, moving not at all, outlining their beauty across the dim air, or in the midst of the dim air — the forms of trees are the only images in my mind. She means that the images in her mind are of the forms of trees and that there are no other images there.

Cat takes the book from Bowl, turns to the portrait, looks at it, as if impressed, and then returns the book to Bowl, marking his place.

BOWL: Does not such a poem, so young, so communicative, warrant the definition of the poetess made by her portrait? How new she is!

BROOMSTICK (*Astonished*): New? But read another.

BOWL: One of The Dahlias, this time. Le Bouquet — The Bouquet. She tries to stimulate the sense of color and, therefore, her poem consists of nothing more than the names of colors. You read these rapidly and so produce in the mind a visual impression like that produced by the actual sight of dahlias.

BROOMSTICK: And that is a poem?

CAT (*Apprehensively*): Read just as rapidly as you can.

BOWL: Are you ready?

CAT: I am.

BROOMSTICK: I am ready.

BOWL: Green, green, green — no doubt, this indicates the stalks — green, green, green, green, green, yellow, green, yellow, green, green, gray, green, yellow, yellow, white, white, white, green —

BROOMSTICK: We ought to be getting to the flowers soon.

BOWL: We're right in them now. The white, white, white indicates white flowers, white dahlias.

BROOMSTICK: I am sorry. I was thinking of a white holder. I thought we had come up the stalks and were going around the edge of the holder.

CAT (*Like a knowing person*): This is really very promising; but not for Broomstick, I'm afraid.

BROOMSTICK: There might be some advantage in getting along.

BOWL: Shall I read another?

BROOMSTICK (*Striking the floor with his cane*): Provided I select it.

BOWL: Nothing would please me more.

He hands the book to Broomstick, who refers to the index at the back.

Broomstick (*With the hopeful manner of one consulting an index*): The Shadow in the Trees.

Bowl: That is the one I read you a moment ago, the one beginning, "In the movement of trees, I find my own agitation."

Broomstick (*With disgust*): An index is full of pit-falls.

Cat: Why do you say that? I thought The Shadow in the Trees rather lovely.

Broomstick (*Energetically*): Pshaw! And imagine Bowl's thinking it new. Only because he wanted to think well of his poetess. She is young. Therefore she is new. Or therefore her poetry is young. That is one of the most persistent of all fallacies. Her poetry is young if her spirit is young — or whatever it is that poetry springs from. Not otherwise. This emotional waste, like the first poem, the one about twilight, this stale monism like The Shadow of the Trees, this sophisticated green, green, green — it is all thirty years old at the least. Thirty years at the very least. I might even put it in the last century. But aside from the poems we have actually heard — and I daresay the book is full of others just like them — what I hold against Claire Dupray, above everything else, is just that she is not herself in her day. To be herself she must be free. She looks free (*looking at the portrait*). But she is not free in spirit, and therefore her portrait fails.

Bowl: Free from what? I regarded The Shadow in the Trees as an instance of good seventeenth century work. And Le Bouquet seemed fairly advanced. Such things are not myths.

Broomstick: The most fascinating myths in the world. To be free, Claire Dupray must be as free from to-day as from yesterday.

Cat: Rather difficult.

Broomstick: Indescribably so. Look at people the world over. The extent and degree of imitation is appalling.

Cat: Necessarily, as a matter of convenience.

Broomstick: Oh, but convenience is impossible in poetry. It is bad enough that Claire Dupray imitates at all. But it is fatal that she imitates the point of view and the feelings of a generation ago. Let her portrait be ever so charming. When all is said and done, she is a poetess in the old-maidenly sense of the word, not the brilliant and vivid creature you conceive her to be.

BOWL: In what year was her book published?

Broomstick examines the title page.

BROOMSTICK: In sixteen hundred and sixty.

CAT: If Bowl was right in supposing her to be twenty-two then, she would be twenty-nine or thirty now.

Cat makes a wry face. Bowl seems shocked. Broomstick turns a page or two.

BROOMSTICK (*With zest*): Avant — Propos. You must help me with this, Bowl. My knowledge of French is not absolutely penetrating.

BOWL: Well, avant-propos means preface.

BROOMSTICK (*Imitating Bowl*): Claire Madeleine Colombier Dupray, the writer of the — m — the extraordinary poems gathered together in this volume, was born — m — in Geneva, of French parents. During the first fifteen years of her life she lived with her parents in Geneva, receiving instruction from her mother, a Calvinist, a woman of pronounced devotional character, and of wide reading.

Cat goes behind Broomstick and looks over his shoulder. Bowl paces up and down the stage.

BROOMSTICK: It will interest my readers — What a nice old touch that is! — It will interest my readers to know that Madame Dupray —

BOWL (*With force*): Madame?

Cat puts his finger on the word over Broomstick's shoulder.

CAT: Mademoiselle, mademoiselle.

BROOMSTICK: I always confuse them. It will interest my readers to know that Mademoiselle Dupray still has in her possession some of the books from which she first became acquainted with — m — literature, in her early years.

BOWL (*Protesting*): Still has? Her early years?

CAT: Jeunesse. Youth.

BROOMSTICK: The abbott of Bellozane's translation of Plutarch's

33

Lives, Florio's Dictionary, a volume of Du Bellay . . . There is a list of twenty or thirty in all. I shall skip them.

Bowl is visibly affected.

BROOMSTICK: I gather that the books were selected by her mother. Piquant reading for a young French poetess.

Cat takes the book from Broomstick and runs with it to Bowl.

CAT: Here is something about the portrait. Translate it, Bowl.

Bowl looks at the preface. He seems incredulous. He looks at the portrait and then at the preface, and again at the portrait. He throws the book on the floor.

BOWL: What a fool I have been!

He hurries off the stage. Cat is dumbfounded. Broomstick laughs loudly. Cat picks up the book and returns it to Broomstick.

CAT: What does it say about the portrait?

BROOMSTICK: Well, just here, skipping a few lines, the sentence you saw reads as follows: The frontispiece of this volume was etched in Amsterdam, from life, after Mademoiselle Dupray, at the age of twenty-three, in the year —

He pauses.

CAT: At the age of twenty-three, in the year —

BROOMSTICK: Sixteen hundred and thirty-seven.

CAT: Sixteen hundred and thirty-seven! If she was twenty-three in sixteen hundred and thirty-seven, she was forty-six in sixteen hundred and sixty when her poems were published. She is more than fifty now — fifty-three. She will love as long as she lives.

BROOMSTICK (*Cavalierly*): I think you are right, after all, in your translation of rouges.

CAT: Oh, red, red! Acutely red! Damn all portraits of poets and poetesses.

Cat collapses. Broomstick laughs again, turning over the pages of the book.

BROOMSTICK: One should always read a preface first.

He helps Cat off the stage.

CURTAIN

34

The Death of a Soldier

Life contracts and death is expected,
As in a season of autumn.
The soldier falls.

He does not become a three-days personage,
Imposing his separation,
Calling for pomp.

Death is absolute and without memorial,
As in a season of autumn,
When the wind stops,

When the wind stops and, over the heavens,
The clouds go, nevertheless,
In their direction.

Metaphors of a Magnifico

Twenty men crossing a bridge,
Into a village,
Are twenty men crossing twenty bridges,
Into twenty villages,
Or one man
Crossing a single bridge into a village.

This is old song
That will not declare itself . . .

Twenty men crossing a bridge,
Into a village,

Are
Twenty men crossing a bridge
Into a village.

That will not declare itself
Yet is certain as meaning . . .

The boots of the men clump
On the boards of the bridge.
The first white wall of the village
Rises through fruit-trees.

Of what was it I was thinking?

So the meaning escapes.

The first white wall of the village . . .
The fruit-trees. . . .

Depression before Spring

The cock crows
But no queen rises.

The hair of my blonde
Is dazzling,
As the spittle of cows
Threading the wind.

Ho! Ho!

But ki-ki-ri-ki
Brings no rou-cou,
No rou-cou-cou.

But no queen comes
In slipper green.

Earthy Anecdote

Every time the bucks went clattering
Over Oklahoma
A firecat bristled in the way.

Wherever they went,
They went clattering,
Until they swerved
In a swift, circular line
To the right,
Because of the firecat.

Or until they swerved
In a swift, circular line
To the left,
Because of the firecat.

The bucks clattered.
The firecat went leaping,
To the right, to the left,
And
Bristled in the way.

Later, the firecat closed his bright eyes
And slept.

The Apostrophe to Vincentine

I

I figured you as nude between
Monotonous earth and dark blue sky.
It made you seem so small and lean
And nameless,
Heavenly Vincentine.

II

I saw you then, as warm as flesh,
Brunette,
But yet not too brunette,
As warm, as clean.
Your dress was green,
Was whited green,
Green Vincentine.

III

Then you came walking,
In a group
Of human others,
Voluble.
Yes: you came walking,
Vincentine.
Yes: you came talking.

IV

And what I knew you felt
Came then.
Monotonous earth I saw become
Illimitable spheres of you,
And that white animal, so lean,
Turned Vincentine,
Turned heavenly Vincentine,
And that white animal, so lean,
Turned heavenly, heavenly Vincentine.

Nuances of a Theme by Williams

It's a strange courage
you give me, ancient star:

Shine alone in the sunrise
toward which you lend no part!

I

Shine alone, shine nakedly, shine like bronze,
that reflects neither my face nor any inner part
of my being, shine like fire, that mirrors nothing.

II

Lend no part to any humanity that suffuses
you in its own light.
Be not chimera of morning,
Half-man, half-star.
Be not an intelligence,
Like a widow's bird
Or an old horse.

Le Monocle de Mon Oncle

I

"Mother of heaven, regina of the clouds,
O sceptre of the sun, crown of the moon,
There is not nothing, no, no, never nothing,
Like the clashed edges of two words that kill."
And so I mocked her in magnificent measure.
Or was it that I mocked myself alone?
I wish that I might be a thinking stone.
The sea of spuming thought foists up again

The radiant bubble that she was. And then
A deep up-pouring from some saltier well
Within me, bursts its watery syllable.

II

A red bird flies across the golden floor.
It is a red bird that seeks out his choir
Among the choirs of wind and wet and wing.
A torrent will fall from him when he finds.
Shall I uncrumple this much-crumpled thing?
I am a man of fortune greeting heirs;
For it has come that thus I greet the spring.
These choirs of welcome choir for me farewell.
No spring can follow past meridian.
Yet you persist with anecdotal bliss
To make believe a starry *connaissance*.

III

Is it for nothing, then, that old Chinese
Sat tittivating by their mountain pools
Or in the Yangtse studied out their beards?
I shall not play the flat historic scale.
You know how Utamaro's beauties sought
The end of love in their all-speaking braids.
You know the mountainous coiffures of Bath.
Alas! Have all the barbers lived in vain
That not one curl in nature has survived?
Why, without pity on these studious ghosts,
Do you come dripping in your hair from sleep?

IV

This luscious and impeccable fruit of life
Falls, it appears, of its own weight to earth.
When you were Eve, its acrid juice was sweet,
Untasted, in its heavenly, orchard air.
An apple serves as well as any skull
To be the book in which to read a round,

And is as excellent, in that it is composed
Of what, like skulls, comes rotting back to ground.
But it excels in this, that as the fruit
Of love, it is a book too mad to read
Before one merely reads to pass the time.

v

In the high west there burns a furious star.
It is for fiery boys that star was set
And for sweet-smelling virgins close to them.
The measure of the intensity of love
Is measure, also, of the verve of earth.
For me, the firefly's quick, electric stroke
Ticks tediously the time of one more year.
And you? Remember how the crickets came
Out of their mother grass, like little kin,
In the pale nights, when your first imagery
Found inklings of your bond to all that dust.

vi

If men at forty will be painting lakes
The ephemeral blues must merge for them in one,
The basic slate, the universal hue.
There is a substance in us that prevails.
But in our amours amorists discern
Such fluctuations that their scrivening
Is breathless to attend each quirky turn.
When amorists grow bald, then amours shrink
Into the compass and curriculum
Of introspective exiles, lecturing.
It is a theme for Hyacinth alone.

vii

The mules that angels ride come slowly down
The blazing passes, from beyond the sun.
Descensions of their tinkling bells arrive.

41

These muleteers are dainty of their way.
Meantime, centurions guffaw and beat
Their shrilling tankards on the table-boards.
This parable, in sense, amounts to this:
The honey of heaven may or may not come,
But that of earth both comes and goes at once.
Suppose these couriers brought amid their train
A damsel heightened by eternal bloom.

VIII

Like a dull scholar, I behold, in love,
An ancient aspect touching a new mind.
It comes, it blooms, it bears its fruit and dies.
This trivial trope reveals a way of truth.
Our bloom is gone. We are the fruit thereof.
Two golden gourds distended on our vines,
Into the autumn weather, splashed with frost,
Distorted by hale fatness, turned grotesque.
We hang like warty squashes, streaked and rayed,
The laughing sky will see the two of us
Washed into rinds by rotting winter rains.

IX

In verses wild with motion, full of din,
Loudened by cries, by clashes, quick and sure
As the deadly thought of men accomplishing
Their curious fates in war, come, celebrate
The faith of forty, ward of Cupido.
Most venerable heart, the lustiest conceit
Is not too lusty for your broadening.
I quiz all sounds, all thoughts, all everything
For the music and manner of the paladins
To make oblation fit. Where shall I find
Bravura adequate to this great hymn?

X

The fops of fancy in their poems leave
Memorabilia of the mystic spouts,
Spontaneously watering their gritty soils.
I am a yeoman, as such fellows go.
I know no magic trees, no balmy boughs,
No silver-ruddy, gold-vermilion fruits.
But, after all, I know a tree that bears
A semblance to the thing I have in mind.
It stands gigantic, with a certain tip
To which all birds come sometime in their time.
But when they go that tip still tips the tree.

XI

If sex were all, then every trembling hand
Could make us squeak, like dolls, the wished-for words.
But note the unconscionable treachery of fate,
That makes us weep, laugh, grunt and groan, and shout
Doleful heroics, pinching gestures forth
From madness or delight, without regard
To that first, foremost law. Anguishing hour!
Last night, we sat beside a pool of pink,
Clippered with lilies scudding the bright chromes,
Keen to the point of starlight, while a frog
Boomed from his very belly odious chords.

XII

A blue pigeon it is, that circles the blue sky,
On sidelong wing, around and round and round.
A white pigeon it is, that flutters to the ground,
Grown tired of flight. Like a dark rabbi, I
Observed, when young, the nature of mankind,
In lordly study. Every day, I found
Man proved a gobbet in my mincing world.

Like a rose rabbi, later, I pursued,
And still pursue, the origin and course
Of love, but until now I never knew
That fluttering things have so distinct a shade.

Nomad Exquisite

As the immense dew of Florida
Brings forth
The big-finned palm
And green vine angering for life,

As the immense dew of Florida
Brings forth hymn and hymn
From the beholder,
Beholding all these green sides
And gold sides of green sides,

And blessed mornings,
Meet for the eye of the young alligator,
And lightning colors
So, in me, come flinging
Forms, flames, and the flakes of flames.

Life Is Motion

In Oklahoma,
Bonnie and Josie,
Dressed in calico,
Danced around a stump.
They cried,
"Ohoyaho,
Ohoo" . . .
Celebrating the marriage
Of flesh and air.

Banal Sojourn

Two wooden tubs of blue hydrangeas stand at the foot of the
      stone steps.
The sky is a blue gum streaked with rose. The trees are black.
The grackles crack their throats of bone in the smooth air.
Moisture and heat have swollen the garden into a slum of bloom.
Pardie! Summer is like a fat beast, sleepy in mildew,
Our old bane, green and bloated, serene, who cries,
"That bliss of stars, that princox of evening heaven!" reminding
      of seasons,
When radiance came running down, slim through the bareness.
And so it is one damns that green shade at the bottom of the land.
For who can care at the wigs despoiling the Satan ear?
And who does not seek the sky unfuzzed, soaring to the princox?
One has a malady, here, a malady. One feels a malady.

Anecdote of the Jar

I placed a jar in Tennessee,
And round it was, upon a hill.
It made the slovenly wilderness
Surround that hill.

The wilderness rose up to it,
And sprawled around, no longer wild.
The jar was round upon the ground
And tall and of a port in air.

It took dominion everywhere.
The jar was gray and bare.
It did not give of bird or bush,
Like nothing else in Tennessee.

Fabliau of Florida

Barque of phosphor
On the palmy beach,

Move outward into heaven,
Into the alabasters
And night blues.

Foam and cloud are one.
Sultry moon-monsters
Are dissolving.

Fill your black hull
With white moonlight.

There will never be an end
To this droning of the surf.

Ploughing on Sunday

The white cock's tail
Tosses in the wind.
The turkey-cock's tail
Glitters in the sun.

Water in the fields.
The wind pours down.
The feathers flare
And bluster in the wind.

Remus, blow your horn!
I'm ploughing on Sunday,
Ploughing North America.
Blow your horn!

Tum-ti-tum,
Ti-tum-tum-tum!
The turkey-cock's tail
Spreads to the sun.

The white cock's tail
Streams to the moon.
Water in the fields.
The wind pours down.

The Place of the Solitaires

Let the place of the solitaires
Be a place of perpetual undulation.

Whether it be in mid-sea
On the dark, green water-wheel,
Or on the beaches,
There must be no cessation
Of motion, or of the noise of motion,
The renewal of noise
And manifold continuation;

And, most, of the motion of thought
And its restless iteration,

In the place of the solitaires,
Which is to be a place of perpetual undulation.

The Paltry Nude
Starts on a Spring Voyage

But not on a shell, she starts,
Archaic, for the sea.
But on the first-found weed
She scuds the glitters,
Noiselessly, like one more wave.

She too is discontent
And would have purple stuff upon her arms,
Tired of the salty harbors,
Eager for the brine and bellowing
Of the high interiors of the sea.

The wind speeds her,
Blowing upon her hands
And watery back.
She touches the clouds, where she goes
In the circle of her traverse of the sea.

Yet this is meagre play
In the scrurry and water-shine,
As her heels foam—
Not as when the goldener nude
Of a later day

Will go, like the centre of sea-green pomp,
In an intenser calm,
Scullion of fate,
Across the spick torrent, ceaselessly,
Upon her irretrievable way.

Infanta Marina

Her terrace was the sand
And the palms and the twilight.

She made of the motions of her wrist
The grandiose gestures
Of her thought.

The rumpling of the plumes
Of this creature of the evening
Came to be sleights of sails
Over the sea.

And thus she roamed
In the roamings of her fan,

Partaking of the sea,
And of the evening,
As they flowed around
And uttered their subsiding sound.

Cortège for Rosenbloom

Now, the wry Rosenbloom is dead
And his finical carriers tread,
On a hundred legs, the tread
Of the dead.
Rosenbloom is dead.

They carry the wizened one
Of the color of horn
To the sullen hill,
Treading a tread
In unison for the dead.

Rosenbloom is dead.
The tread of the carriers does not halt
On the hill, but turns
Up the sky.
They are bearing his body into the sky.

It is the infants of misanthropes
And the infants of nothingness
That tread
The wooden ascents
Of the ascending of the dead.

It is turbans they wear
And boots of fur
As they tread the boards
In a region of frost,
Viewing the frost;

To a chirr of gongs
And a chitter of cries
And the heavy thrum
Of the endless tread
That they tread;

To a jangle of doom
And a jumble of words
Of the intense poem
Of the strictest prose
Of Rosenbloom.

And they bury him there,
Body and soul,
In a place in the sky.
The lamentable tread!
Rosenbloom is dead.

The Man Whose Pharynx Was Bad

The time of year has grown indifferent.
Mildew of summer and the deepening snow
Are both alike in the routine I know.
I am too dumbly in my being pent.

The wind attendant on the solstices
Blows on the shutters of the metropoles,
Stirring no poet in his sleep, and tolls
The grand ideas of the villages.

The malady of the quotidian . . .
Perhaps, if summer ever came to rest
And lengthened, deepened, comforted, caressed
Through days like oceans in obsidian

Horizons full of night's midsummer blaze;
Perhaps, if winter once could penetrate
Through all its purples to the final slate,
Persisting bleakly in an icy haze;

One might in turn become less diffident—
Out of such mildew plucking neater mould
And spouting new orations of the cold.
One might. One might. But time will not relent.

The Doctor of Geneva

The doctor of Geneva stamped the sand
That lay impounding the Pacific swell,
Patted his stove-pipe hat and tugged his shawl.

Lacustrine man had never been assailed
By such long-rolling opulent cataracts,
Unless Racine or Bossuet held the like.

He did not quail. A man so used to plumb
The multifarious heavens felt no awe
Before these visible, voluble delugings,

Which yet found means to set his simmering mind
Spinning and hissing with oracular
Notations of the wild, the ruinous waste,

Until the steeples of his city clanked and sprang
In an unburgherly apocalypse.
The doctor used his handkerchief and sighed.

Gubbinal

That strange flower, the sun,
Is just what you say.
Have it your way.

The world is ugly,
And the people are sad.

That tuft of jungle feathers,
That animal eye,
Is just what you say.

That savage of fire,
That seed,
Have it your way.

The world is ugly,
And the people are sad.

The Snow Man

One must have a mind of winter
To regard the frost and the boughs
Of the pine-trees crusted with snow;

And have been cold a long time
To behold the junipers shagged with ice,
The spruces rough in the distant glitter

Of the January sun; and not to think
Of any misery in the sound of the wind,
In the sound of a few leaves,

Which is the sound of the land
Full of the same wind
That is blowing in the same bare place

For the listener, who listens in the snow,
And, nothing himself, beholds
Nothing that is not there and the nothing that is.

Tea at the Palaz of Hoon

Not less because in purple I descended
The western day through what you called
The loneliest air, not less was I myself.

What was the ointment sprinkled on my beard?
What were the hymns that buzzed beside my ears?
What was the sea whose tide swept through me there?

Out of my mind the golden ointment rained,
And my ears made the blowing hymns they heard.
I was myself the compass of that sea:

I was the world in which I walked, and what I saw
Or heard or felt came not but from myself;
And there I found myself more truly and more strange.

Another Weeping Woman

Pour the unhappiness out
From your too bitter heart,
Which grieving will not sweeten.

Poison grows in this dark.
It is in the water of tears
Its black blooms rise.

The magnificent cause of being,
The imagination, the one reality
In this imagined world

Leaves you
With him for whom no phantasy moves,
And you are pierced by a death.

On the Manner
of Addressing Clouds

Gloomy grammarians in golden gowns,
Meekly you keep the mortal rendezvous,
Eliciting the still sustaining pomps
Of speech which are like music so profound
They seem an exaltation without sound.
Funest philosophers and ponderers,
Their evocations are the speech of clouds.
So speech of your processionals returns
In the casual evocations of your tread
Across the stale, mysterious seasons. These
Are the music of meet resignation; these
The responsive, still sustaining pomps for you
To magnify, if in that drifting waste
You are to be accompanied by more
Than mute bare splendors of the sun and moon.

Of Heaven Considered as a Tomb

What word have you, interpreters, of men
Who in the tomb of heaven walk by night,
The darkened ghosts of our old comedy?
Do they believe they range the gusty cold,
With lanterns borne aloft to light the way,
Freemen of death, about and still about
To find whatever it is they seek? Or does
That burial, pillared up each day as porte
And spiritous passage into nothingness,
Foretell each night the one abysmal night,

When the host shall no more wander, nor the light
Of the steadfast lanterns creep across the dark?
Make hue among the dark comedians,
Halloo them in the topmost distances
For answer from their icy Élysée.

The Bird with the Coppery, Keen Claws

Above the forest of the parakeets,
A parakeet of parakeets prevails,
A pip of life amid a mort of tails.

(The rudiments of tropics are around,
Aloe of ivory, pear of rusty rind.)
His lids are white because his eyes are blind.

He is not paradise of parakeets,
Of his gold ether, golden alguazil,
Except because he broods there and is still.

Panache upon panache, his tails deploy
Upward and outward, in green-vented forms,
His tip a drop of water full of storms.

But though the turbulent tinges undulate
As his pure intellect applies its laws,
He moves not on his coppery, keen claws.

He munches a dry shell while he exerts
His will, yet never ceases, perfect cock,
To flare, in the sun-pallor of his rock.

The Comedian as the Letter C

The World without Imagination

Nota: man is the intelligence of his soil,
The sovereign ghost. As such, the Socrates
Of snails, musician of pears, principium
And lex. Sed quæritur: is this same wig
Of things, this nincompated pedagogue,
Preceptor to the sea? Crispin at sea
Created, in his day, a touch of doubt.
An eye most apt in gelatines and jupes,
Berries of villages, a barber's eye,
An eye of land, of simple salad-beds,
Of honest quilts, the eye of Crispin, hung
On porpoises, instead of apricots,
And on silentious porpoises, whose snouts
Dibbled in waves that were mustachios,
Inscrutable hair in an inscrutable world.

One eats one paté, even of salt, quotha.
It was not so much the lost terrestrial,
The snug hibernal from that sea and salt,
That century of wind in a single puff.
What counted was mythology of self,
Blotched out beyond unblotching. Crispin,
The lutanist of fleas, the knave, the thane,
The ribboned stick, the bellowing breeches, cloak
Of China, cap of Spain, imperative haw
Of hum, inquisitorial botanist,
And general lexicographer of mute
And maidenly greenhorns, now beheld himself,
A skinny sailor peering in the sea-glass.
What word split up in clickering syllables

And storming under multitudinous tones
Was name for this short-shanks in all that brunt?
Crispin was washed away by magnitude.
The whole of life that still remained in him
Dwindled to one sound strumming in his ear,
Ubiquitous concussion, slap and sigh,
Polyphony beyond his baton's thrust.

Could Crispin stem verboseness in the sea,
The old age of a watery realist,
Triton, dissolved in shifting diaphanes
Of blue and green? A wordy, watery age
That whispered to the sun's compassion, made
A convocation, nightly, of the sea-stars,
And on the clopping foot-ways of the moon
Lay grovelling. Triton incomplicate with that
Which made him Triton, nothing left of him,
Except in faint, memorial gesturings,
That were like arms and shoulders in the waves,
Here, something in the rise and fall of wind
That seemed hallucinating horn, and here,
A sunken voice, both of remembering
And of forgetfulness, in alternate strain.
Just so an ancient Crispin was dissolved.
The valet in the tempest was annulled.
Bordeaux to Yucatan, Havana next,
And then to Carolina. Simple jaunt.
Crispin, merest minuscule in the gales,
Dejected his manner to the turbulence.
The salt hung on his spirit like a frost,
The dead brine melted in him like a dew
Of winter, until nothing of himself
Remained, except some starker, barer self
In a starker, barer world, in which the sun
Was not the sun because it never shone

With bland complaisance on pale parasols,
Beetled, in chapels, on the chaste bouquets.
Against his pipping sounds a trumpet cried
Celestial sneering boisterously. Crispin
Became an introspective voyager.

Here was the veritable ding an sich, at last,
Crispin confronting it, a vocable thing,
But with a speech belched out of hoary darks
Noway resembling his, a visible thing,
And excepting negligible Triton, free
From the unavoidable shadow of himself
That lay elsewhere around him. Severance
Was clear. The last distortion of romance
Forsook the insatiable egotist. The sea
Severs not only lands but also selves.
Here was no help before reality.
Crispin beheld and Crispin was made new.
The imagination, here, could not evade,
In poems of plums, the strict austerity
Of one vast, subjugating, final tone.
The drenching of stale lives no more fell down.
What was this gaudy, gusty panoply?
Out of what swift destruction did it spring?
It was caparison of wind and cloud
And something given to make whole among
The ruses that were shattered by the large.

Concerning the Thunderstorms of Yucatan

In Yucatan, the Maya sonneteers
Of the Caribbean amphitheatre,
In spite of hawk and falcon, green toucan
And jay, still to the night-bird made their plea,

As if raspberry tanagers in palms,
High up in orange air, were barbarous.
But Crispin was too destitute to find
In any commonplace the sought-for aid.
He was a man made vivid by the sea,
A man come out of luminous traversing,
Much trumpeted, made desperately clear,
Fresh from discoveries of tidal skies,
To whom oracular rockings gave no rest.
Into a savage color he went on.

How greatly had he grown in his demesne,
This auditor of insects! He that saw
The stride of vanishing autumn in a park
By way of decorous melancholy; he
That wrote his couplet yearly to the spring,
As dissertation of profound delight,
Stopping, on voyage, in a land of snakes,
Found his vicissitudes had much enlarged
His apprehension, made him intricate
In moody rucks, and difficult and strange
In all desires, his destitution's mark.
He was in this as other freemen are,
Sonorous nutshells rattling inwardly.
His violence was for aggrandizement
And not for stupor, such as music makes
For sleepers halfway waking. He perceived
That coolness for his heat came suddenly,
And only, in the fables that he scrawled
With his own quill, in its indigenous dew,
Of an æsthetic tough, diverse, untamed,
Incredible to prudes, the mint of dirt,
Green barbarism turning paradigm.
Crispin foresaw a curious promenade
Or, nobler, sensed an elemental fate,

And elemental potencies and pangs,
And beautiful barenesses as yet unseen,
Making the most of savagery of palms,
Of moonlight on the thick, cadaverous bloom
That yuccas breed, and of the panther's tread.
The fabulous and its intrinsic verse
Came like two spirits parleying, adorned
In radiance from the Atlantic coign,
For Crispin and his quill to catechize.
But they came parleying of such an earth,
So thick with sides and jagged lops of green,
So intertwined with serpent-kin encoiled
Among the purple tufts, the scarlet crowns,
Scenting the jungle in their refuges,
So streaked with yellow, blue and green and red
In beak and bud and fruity gobbet-skins,
That earth was like a jostling festival
Of seeds grown fat, too juicily opulent,
Expanding in the gold's maternal warmth.

So much for that. The affectionate emigrant found
A new reality in parrot-squawks.
Yet let that trifle pass. Now, as this odd
Discoverer walked through the harbor streets
Inspecting the cabildo, the façade
Of the cathedral, making notes, he heard
A rumbling, west of Mexico, it seemed,
Approaching like a gasconade of drums.
The white cabildo darkened, the façade,
As sullen as the sky, was swallowed up
In swift, successive shadows, dolefully.
The rumbling broadened as it fell. The wind,
Tempestuous clarion, with heavy cry,
Came bluntly thundering, more terrible
Than the revenge of music on bassoons.

Gesticulating lightning, mystical,
Made pallid flitter. Crispin, here, took flight.
An annotator has his scruples, too.
He knelt in the cathedral with the rest,
This connoisseur of elemental fate,
Aware of exquisite thought. The storm was one
Of many proclamations of the kind,
Proclaiming something harsher than he learned
From hearing signboards whimper in cold nights
Or seeing the midsummer artifice
Of heat upon his pane. This was the span
Of force, the quintessential fact, the note
Of Vulcan, that a valet seeks to own,
The thing that makes him envious in phrase.

And while the torrent on the roof still droned
He felt the Andean breath. His mind was free
And more than free, elate, intent, profound
And studious of a self possessing him,
That was not in him in the crusty town
From which he sailed. Beyond him, westward, lay
The mountainous ridges, purple balustrades,
In which the thunder, lapsing in its clap,
Let down gigantic quavers of its voice,
For Crispin to vociferate again.

III

Approaching Carolina

The book of moonlight is not written yet
Nor half begun, but, when it is, leave room
For Crispin, fagot in the lunar fire,
Who, in the hubbub of his pilgrimage
Through sweating changes, never could forget
That wakefulness or meditating sleep,
In which the sulky strophes willingly

Bore up, in time, the somnolent, deep songs.
Leave room, therefore, in that unwritten book
For the legendary moonlight that once burned
In Crispin's mind above a continent.
America was always north to him,
A northern west or western north, but north,
And thereby polar, polar-purple, chilled
And lank, rising and slumping from a sea
Of hardy foam, receding flatly, spread
In endless ledges, glittering, submerged
And cold in a boreal mistiness of the moon.
The spring came there in clinking pannicles
Of half-dissolving frost, the summer came,
If ever, whisked and wet, not ripening,
Before the winter's vacancy returned.
The myrtle, if the myrtle ever bloomed,
Was like a glacial pink upon the air.
The green palmettoes in crepuscular ice
Clipped frigidly blue-black meridians,
Morose chiaroscuro, gauntly drawn.

How many poems he denied himself
In his observant progress, lesser things
Than the relentless contact he desired;
How many sea-masks he ignored; what sounds
He shut out from his tempering ear; what thoughts,
Like jades affecting the sequestered bride;
And what descants, he sent to banishment!
Perhaps the Arctic moonlight really gave
The liaison, the blissful liaison,
Between himself and his environment,
Which was, and if, chief motive, first delight,
For him, and not for him alone. It seemed
Illusive, faint, more mist than moon, perverse,
Wrong as a divagation to Peking,

To him that postulated as his theme
The vulgar, as his theme and hymn and flight,
A passionately niggling nightingale.
Moonlight was an evasion, or, if not,
A minor meeting, facile, delicate.

Thus he conceived his voyaging to be
An up and down between two elements,
A fluctuating between sun and moon,
A sally into gold and crimson forms,
As on this voyage, out of goblinry,
And then retirement like a turning back
And sinking down to the indulgences
That in the moonlight have their habitude.
But let these backward lapses, if they would,
Grind their seductions on him, Crispin knew
It was a flourishing tropic he required
For his refreshment, an abundant zone,
Prickly and obdurate, dense, harmonious,
Yet with a harmony not rarefied
Nor fined for the inhibited instruments
Of over-civil stops. And thus he tossed
Between a Carolina of old time,
A little juvenile, an ancient whim,
And the visible, circumspect presentment drawn
From what he saw across his vessel's prow.

He came. The poetic hero without palms
Or jugglery, without regalia.
And as he came he saw that it was spring,
A time abhorrent to the nihilist
Or searcher for the fecund minimum.
The moonlight fiction disappeared. The spring,
Although contending featly in its veils,
Irised in dew and early fragrancies,

Was gemmy marionette to him that sought
A sinewy nakedness. A river bore
The vessel inward. Tilting up his nose,
He inhaled the rancid rosin, burly smells
Of dampened lumber, emanations blown
From warehouse doors, the gustiness of ropes,
Decays of sacks, and all the arrant stinks
That helped him round his rude æsthetic out.
He savored rankness like a sensualist.
He marked the marshy ground around the dock,
The crawling railroad spur, the rotten fence,
Curriculum for the marvelous sophomore.
It purified. It made him see how much
Of what he saw he never saw at all.
He gripped more closely the essential prose
As being, in a world so falsified,
The one integrity for him, the one
Discovery still possible to make,
To which all poems were incident, unless
That prose should wear a poem's guise at last.

IV

The Idea of a Colony

Nota: his soil is man's intelligence.
That's better. That's worth crossing seas to find.
Crispin in one laconic phrase laid bare
His cloudy drift and planned a colony.
Exit the mental moonlight, exit lex,
Rex and principium, exit the whole
Shebang. Exeunt omnes. Here was prose
More exquisite than any tumbling verse:
A still new continent in which to dwell.
What was the purpose of his pilgrimage,
Whatever shape it took in Crispin's mind,
If not, when all is said, to drive away

The shadow of his fellows from the skies,
And, from their stale intelligence released,
To make a new intelligence prevail?
Hence the reverberations in the words
Of his first central hymns, the celebrants
Of rankest trivia, tests of the strength
Of his æsthetic, his philosophy,
The more invidious, the more desired.
The florist asking aid from cabbages,
The rich man going bare, the paladin
Afraid, the blind man as astronomer,
The appointed power unwielded from disdain.
His western voyage ended and began.
The torment of fastidious thought grew slack,
Another, still more bellicose, came on.
He, therefore, wrote his prolegomena,
And, being full of the caprice, inscribed
Commingled souvenirs and prophecies.
He made a singular collation. Thus:
The natives of the rain are rainy men.
Although they paint effulgent, azure lakes,
And April hillsides wooded white and pink,
Their azure has a cloudy edge, their white
And pink, the water bright that dogwood bears.
And in their music showering sounds intone.
On what strange froth does the gross Indian dote,
What Eden sapling gum, what honeyed gore,
What pulpy dram distilled of innocence,
That streaking gold should speak in him
Or bask within his images and words?
If these rude instances impeach themselves
By force of rudeness, let the principle
Be plain. For application Crispin strove,
Abhorring Turk as Esquimau, the lute
As the marimba, the magnolia as rose.

Upon these premises propounding, he
Projected a colony that should extend
To the dusk of a whistling south below the south,
A comprehensive island hemisphere.
The man in Georgia waking among pines
Should be pine-spokesman. The responsive man,
Planting his pristine cores in Florida,
Should prick thereof, not on the psaltery,
But on the banjo's categorical gut,
Tuck, tuck, while the flamingos flapped his bays.
Sepulchral señors, bibbling pale mescal,
Oblivious to the Aztec almanacs,
Should make the intricate Sierra scan.
And dark Brazilians in their cafés,
Musing immaçulate, pampean dits,
Should scrawl a vigilant anthology,
To be their latest, lucent paramour.
These are the broadest instances. Crispin,
Progenitor of such extensive scope,
Was not indifferent to smart detail.
The melon should have apposite ritual,
Performed in verd apparel, and the peach,
When its black branches came to bud, belle day,
Should have an incantation. And again,
When piled on salvers its aroma steeped
The summer, it should have a sacrament
And celebration. Shrewd novitiates
Should be the clerks of our experience.

These bland excursions into time to come,
Related in romance to backward flights,
However prodigal, however proud,
Contained in their afflatus the reproach
That first drove Crispin to his wandering.
He could not be content with counterfeit,

With masquerade of thought, with hapless words
That must belie the racking masquerade,
With fictive flourishes that preordained
His passion's permit, hang of coat, degree
Of buttons, measure of his salt. Such trash
Might help the blind, not him, serenely sly.
It irked beyond his patience. Hence it was,
Preferring text to gloss, he humbly served
Grotesque apprenticeship to chance event,
A clown, perhaps, but an aspiring clown.
There is a monotonous babbling in our dreams
That makes them our dependent heirs, the heirs
Of dreamers buried in our sleep, and not
The oncoming fantasies of better birth.
The apprentice knew these dreamers. If he dreamed
Their dreams, he did it in a gingerly way.
All dreams are vexing. Let them be expunged.
But let the rabbit run, the cock declaim.

Trinket pasticcio, flaunting skyey sheets,
With Crispin as the tiptoe cozener?
No, no: veracious page on page, exact.

v

A Nice Shady Home

Crispin as hermit, pure and capable,
Dwelt in the land. Perhaps if discontent
Had kept him still the pricking realist,
Choosing his element from droll confect
Of was and is and shall or ought to be,
Beyond Bordeaux, beyond Havana, far
Beyond carked Yucatan, he might have come
To colonize his polar planterdom
And jig his chits upon a cloudy knee.
But his emprize to that idea soon sped.

69

Crispin dwelt in the land and dwelling there
Slid from his continent by slow recess
To things within his actual eye, alert
To the difficulty of rebellious thought
When the sky is blue. The blue infected will.
It may be that the yarrow in his fields
Sealed pensive purple under its concern.
But day by day, now this thing and now that
Confined him, while it cosseted, condoned,
Little by little, as if the suzerain soil
Abashed him by carouse to humble yet
Attach. It seemed haphazard denouement.
He first, as realist, admitted that
Whoever hunts a matinal continent
May, after all, stop short before a plum
And be content and still be realist.
The words of things entangle and confuse.
The plum survives its poems. It may hang
In the sunshine placidly, colored by ground
Obliquities of those who pass beneath,
Harlequined and mazily dewed and mauved
In bloom. Yet it survives in its own form,
Beyond these changes, good, fat, guzzly fruit.
So Crispin hasped on the surviving form,
For him, of shall or ought to be in is.

Was he to bray this in profoundest brass
Arointing his dreams with fugal requiems?
Was he to company vastest things defunct
With a blubber of tom-toms harrowing the sky?
Scrawl a tragedian's testament? Prolong
His active force in an inactive dirge,
Which, let the tall musicians call and call,
Should merely call him dead? Pronounce amen
Through choirs infolded to the outmost clouds?

Because he built a cabin who once planned
Loquacious columns by the ructive sea?
Because he turned to salad-beds again?
Jovial Crispin, in calamitous crape?
Should he lay by the personal and make
Of his own fate an instance of all fate?
What is one man among so many men?
What are so many men in such a world?
Can one man think one thing and think it long?
Can one man be one thing and be it long?
The very man despising honest quilts
Lies quilted to his poll in his despite.
For realist, what is is what should be.

And so it came, his cabin shuffled up,
His trees were planted, his duenna brought
Her prismy blonde and clapped her in his hands,
The curtains flittered and the door was closed.
Crispin, magister of a single room,
Latched up the night. So deep a sound fell down
It was as if the solitude concealed
And covered him and his congenial sleep.
So deep a sound fell down it grew to be
A long soothsaying silence down and down.
The crickets beat their tambours in the wind,
Marching a motionless march, custodians.

In the presto of the morning, Crispin trod,
Each day, still curious, but in a round
Less prickly and much more condign than that
He once thought necessary. Like Candide,
Yeoman and grub, but with a fig in sight,
And cream for the fig and silver for the cream,
A blonde to tip the silver and to taste
The rapey gouts. Good star, how that to be

Annealed them in their cabin ribaldries!
Yet the quotidian saps philosophers
And men like Crispin like them in intent,
If not in will, to track the knaves of thought.
But the quotidian composed as his,
Of breakfast ribands, fruits laid in their leaves,
The tomtit and the cassia and the rose,
Although the rose was not the noble thorn
Of crinoline spread, but of a pining sweet,
Composed of evenings like cracked shutters flung
Upon the rumpling bottomness, and nights
In which those frail custodians watched,
Indifferent to the tepid summer cold,
While he poured out upon the lips of her
That lay beside him, the quotidian
Like this, saps like the sun, true fortuner.
For all it takes it gives a humped return
Exchequering from piebald fiscs unkeyed.

VI

And Daughters with Curls

Portentous enunciation, syllable
To blessed syllable affined, and sound
Bubbling felicity in cantilene,
Prolific and tormenting tenderness
Of music, as it comes to unison,
Forgather and bell boldly Crispin's last
Deduction. Thrum with a proud douceur
His grand pronunciamento and devise.

The chits came for his jigging, bluet-eyed,
Hands without touch yet touching poignantly,
Leaving no room upon his cloudy knee,
Prophetic joint, for its diviner young.
The return to social nature, once begun,

72

Anabasis or slump, ascent or chute,
Involved him in midwifery so dense
His cabin counted as phylactery,
Then place of vexing palankeens, then haunt
Of children nibbling at the sugared void,
Infants yet eminently old, then dome
And halidom for the unbraided femes,
Green crammers of the green fruits of the world,
Bidders and biders for its ecstasies,
True daughters both of Crispin and his clay.

All this with many mulctings of the man,
Effective colonizer sharply stopped
In the door-yard by his own capacious bloom.
But that this bloom grown riper, showing nibs
Of its eventual roundness, puerile tints
Of spiced and weathery rouges, should complex
The stopper to indulgent fatalist
Was unforeseen. First Crispin smiled upon
His goldenest demoiselle, inhabitant,
She seemed, of a country of the capuchins,
So delicately blushed, so humbly eyed,
Attentive to a coronal of things
Secret and singular. Second, upon
A second similar counterpart, a maid
Most sisterly to the first, not yet awake
Excepting to the motherly footstep, but
Marvelling sometimes at the shaken sleep.
Then third, a thing still flaxen in the light,
A creeper under jaunty leaves. And fourth,
Mere blusteriness that gewgaws jollified,
All din and gobble, blasphemously pink.
A few years more and the vermeil capuchin
Gave to the cabin, lordlier than it was,
The dulcet omen fit for such a house.

The second sister dallying was shy
To fetch the one full-pinioned one himself
Out of her botches, hot embosomer.
The third one gaping at the orioles
Lettered herself demurely as became
A pearly poetess, peaked for rhapsody.
The fourth, pent now, a digit curious.
Four daughters in a world too intricate
In the beginning, four blithe instruments
Of differing struts, four voices several
In couch, four more personæ, intimate
As buffo, yet divers, four mirrors blue
That should be silver, four accustomed seeds
Hinting incredible hues, four selfsame lights
That spread chromatics in hilarious dark,
Four questioners and four sure answerers.

Crispin concocted doctrine from the rout.
The world, a turnip once so readily plucked,
Sacked up and carried overseas, daubed out
Of its ancient purple, pruned to the fertile main,
And sown again by the stiffest realist,
Came reproduced in purple, family font,
The same insoluble lump. The fatalist
Stepped in and dropped the chuckling down his craw,
Without grace or grumble. Score this anecdote
Invented for its pith, not doctrinal
In form though in design, as Crispin willed,
Disguised pronunciamento, summary,
Autumn's compendium, strident in itself
But muted, mused, and perfectly revolved
In those portentous accents, syllables,
And sounds of music coming to accord
Upon his lap, like their inherent sphere,
Seraphic proclamations of the pure
Delivered with a deluging onwardness.

Or if the music sticks, if the anecdote
Is false, if Crispin is a profitless
Philosopher, beginning with green brag,
Concluding fadedly, if as a man
Prone to distemper he abates in taste,
Fickle and fumbling, variable, obscure,
Glozing his life with after-shining flicks,
Illuminating, from a fancy gorged
By apparition, plain and common things,
Sequestering the fluster from the year,
Making gulped potions from obstreperous drops,
And so distorting, proving what he proves
Is nothing, what can all this matter since
The relation comes, benignly, to its end?

So may the relation of each man be clipped.

Bantams in Pine-Woods

Chieftain Iffucan of Azcan in caftan
Of tan with henna hackles, halt!

Damned universal cock, as if the sun
Was blackamoor to bear your blazing tail.

Fat! Fat! Fat! Fat! I am the personal.
Your world is you. I am my world.

You ten-foot poet among inchlings. Fat!
Begone! An inchling bristles in these pines,

Bristles, and points their Appalachian tangs,
And fears not portly Azcan nor his hoos.

The Ordinary Women

Then from their poverty they rose,
From dry catarrhs, and to guitars
They flitted
Through the palace walls.

They flung monotony behind,
Turned from their want, and, nonchalant,
They crowded
The nocturnal halls.

The lacquered loges huddled there
Mumbled zay-zay and a-zay, a-zay.
The moonlight
Fubbed the girandoles.

And the cold dresses that they wore,
In the vapid haze of the window-bays,
Were tranquil
As they leaned and looked

From the window-sills at the alphabets,
At beta b and gamma g,
To study
The canting curlicues

Of heaven and of the heavenly script.
And there they read of marriage-bed.
Ti-lill-o!
And they read right long.

The gaunt guitarists on the strings
Rumbled a-day and a-day, a-day.
The moonlight
Rose on the beachy floors.

How explicit the coiffures became,
The diamond point, the sapphire point,
The sequins
Of the civil fans!

Insinuations of desire,
Puissant speech, alike in each,
Cried quittance
To the wickless halls.

Then from their poverty they rose,
From dry guitars, and to catarrhs
They flitted
Through the palace walls.

A High-Toned Old Christian Woman

Poetry is the supreme fiction, madame.
Take the moral law and make a nave of it
And from the nave build haunted heaven. Thus,
The conscience is converted into palms,
Like windy citherns hankering for hymns.
We agree in principle. That's clear. But take
The opposing law and make a peristyle,
And from the peristyle project a masque
Beyond the planets. Thus, our bawdiness,
Unpurged by epitaph, indulged at last,
Is equally converted into palms,
Squiggling like saxophones. And palm for palm,
Madame, we are where we began. Allow,
Therefore, that in the planetary scene
Your disaffected flagellants, well-stuffed,

Smacking their muzzy bellies in parade,
Proud of such novelties of the sublime,
Such tink and tank and tunk-a-tunk-tunk,
May, merely may, madame, whip from themselves
A jovial hullabaloo among the spheres.
This will make widows wince. But fictive things
Wink as they will. Wink most when widows wince.

O Florida, Venereal Soil

A few things for themselves,
Convolvulus and coral,
Buzzards and live-moss,
Tiestas from the keys,
A few things for themselves,
Florida, venereal soil,
Disclose to the lover.

The dreadful sundry of this world,
The Cuban, Polodowsky,
The Mexican women,
The negro undertaker
Killing the time between corpses
Fishing for crayfish . . .
Virgin of boorish births,

Swiftly in the nights,
In the porches of Key West,
Behind the bougainvilleas,
After the guitar is asleep,
Lasciviously as the wind,
You come tormenting,
Insatiable,

When you might sit,
A scholar of darkness,
Sequestered over the sea,
Wearing a clear tiara
Of red and blue and red,
Sparkling, solitary, still,
In the high sea-shadow.

Donna, donna, dark,
Stooping in indigo gown
And cloudy constellations,
Conceal yourself or disclose
Fewest things to the lover—
A hand that bears a thick-leaved fruit,
A pungent bloom against your shade.

The Emperor of Ice-Cream

Call the roller of big cigars,
The muscular one, and bid him whip
In kitchen cups concupiscent curds.
Let the wenches dawdle in such dress
As they are used to wear, and let the boys
Bring flowers in last month's newspapers.
Let be be finale of seem.
The only emperor is the emperor of ice-cream.

Take from the dresser of deal,
Lacking the three glass knobs, that sheet
On which she embroidered fantails once
And spread it so as to cover her face.
If her horny feet protrude, they come

To show how cold she is, and dumb.
Let the lamp affix its beam.
The only emperor is the emperor of ice-cream.

Hymn from a Watermelon Pavilion

You dweller in the dark cabin,
To whom the watermelon is always purple,
Whose garden is wind and moon,

Of the two dreams, night and day,
What lover, what dreamer, would choose
The one obscured by sleep?

Here is the plantain by your door
And the best cock of red feather
That crew before the clocks.

A feme may come, leaf-green,
Whose coming may give revel
Beyond revelries of sleep,

Yes, and the blackbird spread its tail,
So that the sun may speckle,
While it creaks hail.

You dweller in the dark cabin,
Rise, since rising will not waken,
And hail, cry hail, cry hail.

Stars at Tallapoosa

The lines are straight and swift between the stars.
The night is not the cradle that they cry,
The criers, undulating the deep-oceaned phrase.
The lines are much too dark and much too sharp.

The mind herein attains simplicity.
There is no moon, on single, silvered leaf.
The body is no body to be seen
But is an eye that studies its black lid.

Let these be your delight, secretive hunter,
Wading the sea-lines, moist and ever-mingling,
Mounting the earth-lines, long and lax, lethargic.
These lines are swift and fall without diverging.

The melon-flower nor dew nor web of either
Is like to these. But in yourself is like:
A sheaf of brilliant arrows flying straight,
Flying and falling straightway for their pleasure,

Their pleasure that is all bright-edged and cold;
Or, if not arrows, then the nimblest motions,
Making recoveries of young nakedness
And the lost vehemence the midnights hold.

Floral Decoration for Bananas

Well, nuncle, this plainly won't do.
These insolent, linear peels
And sullen, hurricane shapes

Won't do with your eglantine.
They require something serpentine.
Blunt yellow in such a room!

You should have had plums tonight,
In an eighteenth-century dish,
And pettifogging buds,
For the women of primrose and purl,
Each one in her decent curl.
Good God! What a precious light!

But bananas hacked and hunched . . .
The table was set by an ogre,
His eye on an outdoor gloom
And a stiff and noxious place.
Pile the bananas on planks.
The women will be all shanks
And bangles and slatted eyes.

And deck the bananas in leaves
Plucked from the Carib trees,
Fibrous and dangling down,
Oozing cantankerous gum
Out of their purple maws,
Darting out of their purple craws
Their musky and tingling tongues.

To the One of Fictive Music

Sister and mother and diviner love,
And of the sisterhood of the living dead
Most near, most clear, and of the clearest bloom,
And of the fragrant mothers the most dear

And queen, and of diviner love the day
And flame and summer and sweet fire, no thread
Of cloudy silver sprinkles in your gown
Its venom of renown, and on your head
No crown is simpler than the simple hair.

Now, of the music summoned by the birth
That separates us from the wind and sea,
Yet leaves us in them, until earth becomes,
By being so much of the things we are,
Gross effigy and simulacrum, none
Gives motion to perfection more serene
Than yours, out of our imperfections wrought,
Most rare, or ever of more kindred air
In the laborious weaving that you wear.

For so retentive of themselves are men
That music is intensest which proclaims
The near, the clear, and vaunts the clearest bloom,
And of all vigils musing the obscure,
That apprehends the most which sees and names,
As in your name, an image that is sure,
Among the arrant spices of the sun,
O bough and bush and scented vine, in whom
We give ourselves our likest issuance.

Yet not too like, yet not so like to be
Too near, too clear, saving a little to endow
Our feigning with the strange unlike, whence springs
The difference that heavenly pity brings.
For this, musician, in your girdle fixed
Bear other perfumes. On your pale head wear
A band entwining, set with fatal stones.
Unreal, give back to us what once you gave:
The imagination that we spurned and crave.

Anecdote of the Prince of Peacocks

In the moonlight
I met Berserk,
In the moonlight
On the bushy plain.
Oh, sharp he was
As the sleepless!

And, "Why are you red
In this milky blue?"
I said.
"Why sun-colored,
As if awake
In the midst of sleep?"

"You that wander,"
So he said,
"On the bushy plain,
Forget so soon.
But I set my traps
In the midst of dreams."

I knew from this
That the blue ground
Was full of blocks
And blocking steel.
I knew the dread
Of the bushy plain,
And the beauty
Of the moonlight
Falling there,
Falling
As sleep falls
In the innocent air.

Two Figures in Dense Violet Light

I had as lief be embraced by the porter at the hotel
As to get no more from the moonlight
Than your moist hand.

Be the voice of night and Florida in my ear.
Use dusky words and dusky images.
Darken your speech.

Speak, even, as if I did not hear you speaking,
But spoke for you perfectly in my thoughts,
Conceiving words,

As the night conceives the sea-sounds in silence,
And out of their droning sibilants makes
A serenade.

Say, puerile, that the buzzards crouch on the ridge-pole
And sleep with one eye watching the stars fall
Below Key West.

Say that the palms are clear in a total blue,
Are clear and are obscure; that it is night;
That the moon shines.

The Virgin Carrying a Lantern

There are no bears among the roses,
Only a negress who supposes
Things false and wrong

About the lantern of the beauty
Who walks there, as a farewell duty,
Walks long and long.

The pity that her pious egress
Should fill the vigil of a negress
With heat so strong!

Academic Discourse at Havana

I

Canaries in the morning, orchestras
In the afternoon, balloons at night. That is
A difference, at least, from nightingales,
Jehovah and the great sea-worm. The air
Is not so elemental nor the earth
So near.
              But the sustenance of the wilderness
Does not sustain us in the metropoles.

II

Life is an old casino in a park.
The bills of the swans are flat upon the ground.
A most desolate wind has chilled Rouge-Fatima
And a grand decadence settles down like cold.

III

The swans . . . Before the bills of the swans fell flat
Upon the ground, and before the chronicle
Of affected homage foxed so many books,
They warded the blank waters of the lakes
And island canopies which were entailed

To that casino. Long before the rain
Swept through its boarded windows and the leaves
Filled its encrusted fountains, they arrayed
The twilights of the mythy goober khan.
The centuries of excellence to be
Rose out of promise and became the sooth
Of trombones floating in the trees.

                              The toil
Of thought evoked a peace eccentric to
The eye and tinkling to the ear. Gruff drums
Could beat, yet not alarm the populace.
The indolent progressions of the swans
Made earth come right; a peanut parody
For peanut people.

                    And serener myth
Conceiving from its perfect plenitude,
Lusty as June, more fruitful than the weeks
Of ripest summer, always lingering
To touch again the hottest bloom, to strike
Once more the longest resonance, to cap
The clearest woman with apt weed, to mount
The thickest man on thickest stallion-back,
This urgent, competent, serener myth
Passed like a circus.

                    Politic man ordained
Imagination as the fateful sin.
Grandmother and her basketful of pears
Must be the crux for our compendia.
That's world enough, and more, if one includes
Her daughters to the peached and ivory wench
For whom the towers are built. The burgher's breast,

And not a delicate ether star-impaled,
Must be the place for prodigy, unless
Prodigious things are tricks. The world is not
The bauble of the sleepless nor a word
That should import a universal pith
To Cuba. Jot these milky matters down.
They nourish Jupiters. Their casual pap
Will drop like sweetness in the empty nights
When too great rhapsody is left annulled
And liquorish prayer provokes new sweats: so, so:
Life is an old casino in a wood.

IV

Is the function of the poet here mere sound,
Subtler than the ornatest prophecy,
To stuff the ear? It causes him to make
His infinite repetition and alloys
Of pick of ebon, pick of halcyon.
It weights him with nice logic for the prim.
As part of nature he is part of us.
His rarities are ours: may they be fit
And reconcile us to our selves in those
True reconcilings, dark, pacific words,
And the adroiter harmonies of their fall.
Close the cantina. Hood the chandelier.
The moonlight is not yellow but a white
That silences the ever-faithful town.
How pale and how possessed a night it is,
How full of exhalations of the sea . . .
All this is older than its oldest hymn,
Has no more meaning than tomorrow's bread.
But let the poet on his balcony
Speak and the sleepers in their sleep shall move,
Waken, and watch the moonlight on their floors.
This may be benediction, sepulcher,

And epitaph. It may, however, be
An incantation that the moon defines
By mere example opulently clear.
And the old casino likewise may define
An infinite incantation of our selves
In the grand decadence of the perished swans.

Sea Surface Full of Clouds

In that November off Tehuantepec,
The slopping of the sea grew still one night
And in the morning summer hued the deck

And made one think of rosy chocolate
And gilt umbrellas. Paradisal green
Gave suavity to the perplexed machine

Of ocean, which like limpid water lay.
Who, then, in that ambrosial latitude
Out of the light evolved the moving blooms,

Who, then, evolved the sea-blooms from the clouds
Diffusing balm in that Pacific calm?
C'était mon enfant, mon bijou, mon âme.

The sea-clouds whitened far below the calm
And moved, as blooms move, in the swimming green
And in its watery radiance, while the hue

Of heaven in an antique reflection rolled
Round those flotillas. And sometimes the sea
Poured brilliant iris on the glistening blue.

II

In that November off Tehuantepec
The slopping of the sea grew still one night.
At breakfast jelly yellow streaked the deck

And made one think of chop-house chocolate
And sham umbrellas. And a sham-like green
Capped summer-seeming on the tense machine

Of ocean, which in sinister flatness lay.
Who, then, beheld the rising of the clouds
That strode submerged in that malevolent sheen,

Who saw the mortal massives of the blooms
Of water moving on the water-floor?
C'était mon frère du ciel, ma vie, mon or.

The gongs rang loudly as the windy booms
Hoo-hooed it in the darkened ocean-blooms.
The gongs grew still. And then blue heaven spread

Its crystalline pendentives on the sea
And the macabre of the water-glooms
In an enormous undulation fled.

III

In that November off Tehuantepec,
The slopping of the sea grew still one night
And a pale silver patterned on the deck

And made one think of porcelain chocolate
And pied umbrellas. An uncertain green,
Piano-polished, held the tranced machine

Of ocean, as a prelude holds and holds.
Who, seeing silver petals of white blooms
Unfolding in the water, feeling sure

Of the milk within the saltiest spurge, heard, then,
The sea unfolding in the sunken clouds?
Oh! *C'était mon extase et mon amour.*

So deeply sunken were they that the shrouds,
The shrouding shadows, made the petals black
Until the rolling heaven made them blue,

A blue beyond the rainy hyacinth,
And smiting the crevasses of the leaves
Deluged the ocean with a sapphire blue.

IV

In that November off Tehuantepec
The night-long slopping of the sea grew still.
A mallow morning dozed upon the deck

And made one think of musky chocolate
And frail umbrellas. A too-fluent green
Suggested malice in the dry machine

Of ocean, pondering dank stratagem.
Who then beheld the figures of the clouds
Like blooms secluded in the thick marine?

Like blooms? Like damasks that were shaken off
From the loosed girdles in the spangling must.
C'était ma foi, la nonchalance divine.

The nakedness would rise and suddenly turn
Salt masks of beard and mouths of bellowing,
Would—But more suddenly the heaven rolled

Its bluest sea-clouds in the thinking green,
And the nakedness became the broadest blooms,
Mile-mallows that a mallow sun cajoled.

In that November off Tehuantepec
Night stilled the slopping of the sea. The day
Came, bowing and voluble, upon the deck,

Good clown. . . . One thought of Chinese chocolate
And large umbrellas. And a motley green
Followed the drift of the obese machine

Of ocean, perfected in indolence.
What pistache one, ingenious and droll,
Beheld the sovereign clouds as jugglery

And the sea as turquoise-turbaned Sambo, neat
At tossing saucers—cloudy-conjuring sea?
C'était mon esprit bâtard, l'ignominie.

The sovereign clouds came clustering. The conch
Of loyal conjuration trumped. The wind
Of green blooms turning crisped the motley hue

To clearing opalescence. Then the sea
And heaven rolled as one and from the two
Came fresh transfigurings of freshest blue.

The Sun This March

The exceeding brightness of this early sun
Makes me conceive how dark I have become,

And re-illumines things that used to turn
To gold in broadest blue, and be a part

Of a turning spirit in an earlier self.
That, too, returns from out the winter's air,

Like an hallucination come to daze
The corner of the eye. Our element,

Cold is our element and winter's air
Brings voices as of lions coming down.

Oh! Rabbi, rabbi, fend my soul for me
And true savant of this dark nature be.

Lunar Paraphrase

The moon is the mother of pathos and pity.

When, at the wearier end of November,
Her old light moves along the branches,
Feebly, slowly, depending upon them;
When the body of Jesus hangs in a pallor,
Humanly near, and the figure of Mary,
Touched on by hoar-frost, shrinks in a shelter
Made by the leaves, that have rotted and fallen;
When over the houses, a golden illusion
Brings back an earlier season of quiet
And quieting dreams in the sleepers in darkness—

The moon is the mother of pathos and pity.

Anatomy of Monotony

I

If from the earth we came, it was an earth
That bore us as a part of all the things
It breeds and that was lewder than it is.
Our nature is her nature. Hence it comes,
Since by our nature we grow old, earth grows
The same. We parallel the mother's death.
She walks an autumn ampler than the wind
Cries up for us and colder than the frost
Pricks in our spirits at the summer's end,
And over the bare spaces of our skies
She sees a barer sky that does not bend.

II

The body walks forth naked in the sun
And, out of tenderness or grief, the sun
Gives comfort, so that other bodies come,
Twinning our phantasy and our device,
And apt in versatile motion, touch and sound
To make the body covetous in desire
Of the still finer, more implacable chords.
So be it. Yet the spaciousness and light
In which the body walks and is deceived,
Falls from that fatal and that barer sky,
And this the spirit sees and is aggrieved.

Autumn Refrain

The skreak and skritter of evening gone
And grackles gone and sorrows of the sun,
The sorrows of sun, too, gone . . . the moon and moon,

94

The yellow moon of words about the nightingale
In measureless measures, not a bird for me
But the name of a bird and the name of a nameless air
I have never—shall never hear. And yet beneath
The stillness that comes to me out of this, beneath
The stillness of everything gone, and being still,
Being and sitting still, something resides,
Some skreaking and skrittering residuum,
And grates these evasions of the nightingale
Though I have never—shall never hear that bird.
And the stillness is in the key, all of it is,
The stillness is all in the key of that desolate sound.

The Brave Man

The sun, that brave man,
Comes through boughs that lie in wait,
That brave man.

Green and gloomy eyes
In dark forms of the grass
Run away.

The good stars,
Pale helms and spiky spurs,
Run away.

Fears of my bed,
Fears of life and fears of death,
Run away.

That brave man comes up
From below and walks without meditation,
That brave man.

A Fading of the Sun

Who can think of the sun costuming clouds
When all people are shaken
Or of night endazzled, proud,
When people awaken
And cry and cry for help?

The warm antiquity of self,
Everyone, grows suddenly cold.
The tea is bad, bread sad.
How can the world so old be so mad
That the people die?

If joy shall be without a book
It lies, themselves within themselves,
If they will look
Within themselves
And cry and cry for help,

Within as pillars of the sun,
Supports of night. The tea,
The wine is good. The bread,
The meat is sweet.
And they will not die.

The Pleasures of Merely Circulating

The garden flew round with the angel,
The angel flew round with the clouds,
And the clouds flew round and the clouds flew round
And the clouds flew round with the clouds.

Is there any secret in skulls,
The cattle skulls in the woods?
Do the drummers in black hoods
Rumble anything out of their drums?

Mrs. Anderson's Swedish baby
Might well have been German or Spanish,
Yet that things go round and again go round
Has rather a classical sound.

The Idea of Order at Key West

She sang beyond the genius of the sea.
The water never formed to mind or voice,
Like a body wholly body, fluttering
Its empty sleeves; and yet its mimic motion
Made constant cry, caused constantly a cry,
That was not ours although we understood,
Inhuman, of the veritable ocean.

The sea was not a mask. No more was she.
The song and water were not medleyed sound
Even if what she sang was what she heard,
Since what she sang was uttered word by word.
It may be that in all her phrases stirred
The grinding water and the gasping wind;
But it was she and not the sea we heard.

For she was the maker of the song she sang.
The ever-hooded, tragic-gestured sea
Was merely a place by which she walked to sing.
Whose spirit is this? we said, because we knew
It was the spirit that we sought and knew
That we should ask this often as she sang.

If it was only the dark voice of the sea
That rose, or even colored by many waves;
If it was only the outer voice of sky
And cloud, of the sunken coral water-walled,
However clear, it would have been deep air,
The heaving speech of air, a summer sound
Repeated in a summer without end
And sound alone. But it was more than that,
More even than her voice, and ours, among
The meaningless plungings of water and the wind,
Theatrical distances, bronze shadows heaped
On high horizons, mountainous atmospheres
Of sky and sea.

           It was her voice that made
The sky acutest at its vanishing.
She measured to the hour its solitude.
She was the single artificer of the world
In which she sang. And when she sang, the sea,
Whatever self it had, became the self
That was her song, for she was the maker. Then we,
As we beheld her striding there alone,
Knew that there never was a world for her
Except the one she sang and, singing, made.

Ramon Fernandez, tell me, if you know,
Why, when the singing ended and we turned
Toward the town, tell why the glassy lights,
The lights in the fishing boats at anchor there,
As the night descended, tilting in the air,
Mastered the night and portioned out the sea,
Fixing emblazoned zones and fiery poles,
Arranging, deepening, enchanting night.

Oh! Blessed rage for order, pale Ramon,
The maker's rage to order words of the sea,

Words of the fragrant portals, dimly-starred,
And of ourselves and of our origins,
In ghostlier demarcations, keener sounds.

Lions in Sweden

No more phrases, Swenson: I was once
A hunter of those sovereigns of the soul
And savings banks, Fides, the sculptor's prize,
All eyes and size, and galled Justitia,
Trained to poise the tables of the law,
Patientia forever soothing wounds
And mighty Fortitudo, frantic bass.
But these shall not adorn my souvenirs,
These lions, these majestic images.
If the fault is with the soul, the sovereigns
Of the soul must likewise be at fault, and first.
If the fault is with the souvenirs, yet these
Are the soul itself. And the whole of the soul,
    Swenson,
As every man in Sweden will concede,
Still hankers after lions, or, to shift,
Still hankers after sovereign images.
If the fault is with the lions, send them back
To Monsieur Dufy's Hamburg whence they came.
The vegetation still abounds with forms.

Evening Without Angels

*the great interests of man: air and
light, the joy of having a body, the
voluptuousness of looking.*
　　　　　　　　—MARIO ROSSI

Why seraphim like lutanists arranged
Above the trees? And why the poet as
Eternal *chef d'orchestre?*

　　　　　　　　　Air is air.
Its vacancy glitters round us everywhere.
Its sounds are not angelic syllables
But our unfashioned spirits realized
More sharply in more furious selves.

　　　　　　　　And light
That fosters seraphim and is to them
Coiffeur of haloes, fecund jeweller—
Was the sun concoct for angels or for men?
Sad men made angels of the sun, and of
The moon they made their own attendant ghosts,
Which led them back to angels, after death.

Let this be clear that we are men of sun
And men of day and never of pointed night,
Men that repeat antiquest sounds of air
In an accord of repetitions. Yet,
If we repeat, it is because the wind
Encircling us, speaks always with our speech.

Light, too, encrusts us making visible
The motions of the mind and giving form
To moodiest nothings, as, desire for day
Accomplished in the immensely flashing East,

Desire for rest, in that descending sea
Of dark, which in its very darkening
Is rest and silence spreading into sleep.

. . . Evening, when the measure skips a beat
And then another, one by one, and all
To a seething minor swiftly modulate.
Bare night is best. Bare earth is best. Bare, bare,
Except for our own houses, huddled low
Beneath the arches and their spangled air,
Beneath the rhapsodies of fire and fire,
Where the voice that is in us makes a true response,
Where the voice that is great within us rises up,
As we stand gazing at the rounded moon.

The Reader

All night I sat reading a book,
Sat reading as if in a book
Of sombre pages.

It was autumn and falling stars
Covered the shrivelled forms
Crouched in the moonlight.

No lamp was burning as I read,
A voice was mumbling, "Everything
Falls back to coldness,

Even the musky muscadines,
The melons, the vermilion pears
Of the leafless garden."

The sombre pages bore no print
Except the trace of burning stars
In the frosty heaven.

Like Decorations in a Nigger Cemetery

FOR ARTHUR POWELL

I

In the far South the sun of autumn is passing
Like Walt Whitman walking along a ruddy shore.
He is singing and chanting the things that are part of him,
The worlds that were and will be, death and day.
Nothing is final, he chants. No man shall see the end.
His beard is of fire and his staff is a leaping flame.

II

Sigh for me, night-wind, in the noisy leaves of the oak.
I am tired. Sleep for me, heaven over the hill.
Shout for me, loudly and loudly, joyful sun, when you rise.

III

It was when the trees were leafless first in November
And their blackness became apparent, that one first
Knew the eccentric to be the base of design.

IV

Under the mat of frost and over the mat of clouds.
But in between lies the sphere of my fortune
And the fortunes of frost and of clouds,
All alike, except for the rules of the rabbis,
Happy men, distinguishing frost and clouds.

V

If ever the search for a tranquil belief should end,
The future might stop emerging out of the past,
Out of what is full of us; yet the search
And the future emerging out of us seem to be one.

VI

We should die except for Death
In his chalk and violet robes.
Not to die a parish death.

VII

How easily the feelings flow this afternoon
Over the simplest words:
It is too cold for work, now, in the fields.

VIII

Out of the spirit of the holy temples,
Empty and grandiose, let us make hymns
And sing them in secrecy as lovers do.

IX

In a world of universal poverty
The philosophers alone will be fat
Against the autumn winds
In an autumn that will be perpetual.

X

Between farewell and the absence of farewell,
The final mercy and the final loss,
The wind and the sudden falling of the wind.

XI

The cloud rose upward like a heavy stone
That lost its heaviness through that same will,
Which changed light green to olive then to blue.

XII

The sense of the serpent in you, Ananke,
And your averted stride
Add nothing to the horror of the frost
That glistens on your face and hair.

XIII

The birds are singing in the yellow patios,
Pecking at more lascivious rinds than ours,
From sheer Gemüthlichkeit.

XIV

The leaden pigeon on the entrance gate
Must miss the symmetry of a leaden mate,
Must see her fans of silver undulate.

XV

Serve the rouged fruits in early snow.
They resemble a page of Toulet
Read in the ruins of a new society,
Furtively, by candle and out of need.

XVI

If thinking could be blown away
Yet this remain the dwelling-place
Of those with a sense for simple space.

XVII

The sun of Asia creeps above the horizon
Into this haggard and tenuous air,
A tiger lamed by nothingness and frost.

XVIII

Shall I grapple with my destroyers
In the muscular poses of the museums?
But my destroyers avoid the museums.

An opening of portals when night ends,
A running forward, arms stretched out as drilled.
Act I, Scene i, at a German Staats-Oper.

Ah, but the meaningless, natural effigy!
The revealing aberration should appear,
The agate in the eye, the tufted ear,
The rabbit fat, at last, in glassy grass.

She was a shadow as thin in memory
As an autumn ancient underneath the snow,
Which one recalls at a concert or in a café.

The comedy of hollow sounds derives
From truth and not from satire on our lives.
Clog, therefore, purple Jack and crimson Jill.

The fish are in the fishman's window,
The grain is in the baker's shop,
The hunter shouts as the pheasant falls.
Consider the odd morphology of regret.

A bridge above the bright and blue of water
And the same bridge when the river is frozen.
Rich Tweedle-dum, poor Tweedle-dee.

From oriole to crow, note the decline
In music. Crow is realist. But, then,
Oriole, also, may be realist.

XXVI

This fat pistache of Belgian grapes exceeds
The total gala of auburn aureoles.
Cochon! Master, the grapes are here and now.

XXVII

John Constable they could never quite transplant
And our streams rejected the dim Academy.
Granted the Picts impressed us otherwise
In the taste for iron dogs and iron deer.

XXVIII

A pear should come to the table popped with juice,
Ripened in warmth and served in warmth. On terms
Like these, autumn beguiles the fatalist.

XXIX

Choke every ghost with acted violence,
Stamp down the phosphorescent toes, tear off
The spittling tissues tight across the bones.
The heavy bells are tolling rowdy-dow.

XXX

The hen-cock crows at midnight and lays no egg,
The cock-hen crows all day. But cockerel shrieks,
Hen shudders: the copious egg is made and laid.

XXXI

A teeming millpond or a furious mind.
Gray grasses rolling windily away
And bristling thorn-trees spinning on the bank.
The actual is a deft beneficence.

XXXII

Poetry is a finikin thing of air
That lives uncertainly and not for long
Yet radiantly beyond much lustier blurs.

For all his purple, the purple bird must have
Notes for his comfort that he may repeat
Through the gross tedium of being rare.

A calm November. Sunday in the fields.
A reflection stagnant in a stagnant stream.
Yet invisible currents clearly circulate.

Men and the affairs of men seldom concerned
This pundit of the weather, who never ceased
To think of man the abstraction, the comic sum.

The children will be crying on the stair,
Half-way to bed, when the phrase will be spoken,
The starry voluptuary will be born.

Yesterday the roses were rising upward,
Pushing their buds above the dark green leaves,
Noble in autumn, yet nobler than autumn.

The album of Corot is premature.
A little later when the sky is black.
Mist that is golden is not wholly mist.

Not the ocean of the virtuosi
But the ugly alien, the mask that speaks
Things unintelligible, yet understood.

Always the standard repertoire in line
And that would be perfection, if each began
Not by beginning but at the last man's end.

XLI

The chrysanthemums' astringent fragrance comes
Each year to disguise the clanking mechanism
Of machine within machine within machine.

XLII

God of the sausage-makers, sacred guild,
Or possibly, the merest patron saint
Ennobled as in a mirror to sanctity.

XLIII

It is curious that the density of life
On a given plane is ascertainable
By dividing the number of legs one sees by two.
At least the number of people may thus be fixed.

XLIV

Freshness is more than the east wind blowing round one.
There is no such thing as innocence in autumn,
Yet, it may be, innocence is never lost.

XLV

Encore un instant de bonheur. The words
Are a woman's words, unlikely to satisfy
The taste of even a country connoisseur.

XLVI

Everything ticks like a clock. The cabinet
Of a man gone mad, after all, for time, in spite
Of the cuckoos, a man with a mania for clocks.

XLVII

The sun is seeking something bright to shine on.
The trees are wooden, the grass is yellow and thin.
The ponds are not the surfaces it seeks.
It must create its colors out of itself.

108

Music is not yet written but is to be.
The preparation is long and of long intent
For the time when sound shall be subtler than we ourselves.

It needed the heavy nights of drenching weather
To make him return to people, to find among them
Whatever it was that he found in their absence,
A pleasure, an indulgence, an infatuation.

Union of the weakest develops strength
Not wisdom. Can all men, together, avenge
One of the leaves that have fallen in autumn?
But the wise man avenges by building his city in snow.

Re-statement of Romance

The night knows nothing of the chants of night.
It is what it is as I am what I am:
And in perceiving this I best perceive myself

And you. Only we two may interchange
Each in the other what each has to give.
Only we two are one, not you and night,

Nor night and I, but you and I, alone,
So much alone, so deeply by ourselves,
So far beyond the casual solitudes,

That night is only the background of our selves,
Supremely true each to its separate self,
In the pale light that each upon the other throws.

Lytton Strachey, Also, Enters into Heaven

I care for neither fugues nor feathers.
What interests me most is the people
Who have always interested me most,
To see them without their passions
And to understand them.

Perhaps, without their passions, they will be
Men of memories explaining what they meant.
One man opposing a society′
If properly misunderstood becomes a myth.
I fear the understanding.

Death ought to spare their passions.
Memory without passion would be better lost.
But memory and passion, and with these
The understanding of heaven, would be bliss,
If anything would be bliss.

How strange a thing it was to understand
And how strange it ought to be again, this time
Without the distortions of the theatre,
Without the revolutions' ruin,
In the presence of the barefoot ghosts!

Perception as an act of intelligence
And perception as an act of grace
Are two quite different things, in particular
When applied to the mythical.
As for myself, I feel a doubt:

I am uncertain whether the perception
Applied on earth to those that were myths
In every various sense, ought not to be preferred
To an untried perception applied
In heaven. But I have no choice.

In this apologetic air, one well
Might muff the mighty spirit of Lenin.
That sort of thing was always rather stiff.
Let's hope for Mademoiselle de Lespinasse,
Instead, or Horace Walpole or Mrs. Thrale.

He is nothing, I know, to me nor I to him.
I had looked forward to understanding. Yet
An understanding may be troublesome.
I'd rather not. No doubt there's a quarter here,
Dixhuitième and Georgian and serene.

Sailing after Lunch

It is the word *pejorative* that hurts.
My old boat goes round on a crutch
And doesn't get under way.
It's the time of the year
And the time of the day.

Perhaps it's the lunch that we had
Or the lunch that we should have had.
But I am, in any case,
A most inappropriate man
In a most unpropitious place.

Mon Dieu, hear the poet's prayer.
The romantic should be here.
The romantic should be there.
It ought to be everywhere.
But the romantic must never remain,

Mon Dieu, and must never again return.
This heavy historical sail
Through the mustiest blue of the lake
In a really vertiginous boat
Is wholly the vapidest fake. . . .

It is least what one ever sees.
It is only the way one feels, to say
Where my spirit is I am,
To say the light wind worries the sail,
To say the water is swift today,

To expunge all people and be a pupil
Of the gorgeous wheel and so to give
That slight transcendence to the dirty sail,
By light, the way one feels, sharp white,
And then rush brightly through the summer air.

Waving Adieu, Adieu, Adieu

That would be waving and that would be crying,
Crying and shouting and meaning farewell,
Farewell in the eyes and farewell at the centre,
Just to stand still without moving a hand.

In a world without heaven to follow, the stops
Would be endings, more poignant than partings, profounder,
And that would be saying farewell, repeating farewell,
Just to be there and just to behold.

To be one's singular self, to despise
The being that yielded so little, acquired
So little, too little to care, to turn
To the ever-jubilant weather, to sip

One's cup and never to say a word,
Or to sleep or just to lie there still,
Just to be there, just to be beheld,
That would be bidding farewell, be bidding farewell.

One likes to practice the thing. They practice,
Enough, for heaven. Ever-jubilant,
What is there here but weather, what spirit
Have I except it comes from the sun?

The American Sublime

How does one stand
To behold the sublime,
To confront the mockers,
The mickey mockers
And plated pairs?

When General Jackson
Posed for his statue
He knew how one feels.
Shall a man go barefoot
Blinking and blank?

But how does one feel?
One grows used to the weather,
The landscape and that;
And the sublime comes down
To the spirit itself,

The spirit and space,
The empty spirit
In vacant space.
What wine does one drink?
What bread does one eat?

Mozart, 1935

Poet, be seated at the piano.
Play the present, its hoo-hoo-hoo,
Its shoo-shoo-shoo, its ric-a-nic,
Its envious cachinnation.

If they throw stones upon the roof
While you practice arpeggios,
It is because they carry down the stairs
A body in rags.
Be seated at the piano.

That lucid souvenir of the past,
The divertimento;
That airy dream of the future,
The unclouded concerto . . .
The snow is falling.
Strike the piercing chord.

Be thou the voice,
Not you. Be thou, be thou
The voice of angry fear,
The voice of this besieging pain.

Be thou that wintry sound
As of the great wind howling,
By which sorrow is released,
Dismissed, absolved
In a starry placating.

We may return to Mozart.
He was young, and we, we are old.
The snow is falling
And the streets are full of cries.
Be seated, thou.

Sad Strains of a Gay Waltz

The truth is that there comes a time
When we can mourn no more over music
That is so much motionless sound.

There comes a time when the waltz
Is no longer a mode of desire, a mode
Of revealing desire and is empty of shadows.

Too many waltzes have ended. And then
There's that mountain-minded Hoon,
For whom desire was never that of the waltz,

Who found all form and order in solitude,
For whom the shapes were never the figures of men.
Now, for him, his forms have vanished.

There is order in neither sea nor sun.
The shapes have lost their glistening.
There are these sudden mobs of men,

These sudden clouds of faces and arms,
An immense suppression, freed,
These voices crying without knowing for what,

Except to be happy, without knowing how,
Imposing forms they cannot describe,
Requiring order beyond their speech.

Too many waltzes have ended. Yet the shapes
For which the voices cry, these, too, may be
Modes of desire, modes of revealing desire.

Too many waltzes—The epic of disbelief
Blares oftener and soon, will soon be constant.
Some harmonious skeptic soon in a skeptical music

Will unite these figures of men and their shapes
Will glisten again with motion, the music
Will be motion and full of shadows.

Dance of the Macabre Mice

In the land of turkeys in turkey weather
At the base of the statue, we go round and round.
What a beautiful history, beautiful surprise!
Monsieur is on horseback. The horse is covered with mice.

This dance has no name. It is a hungry dance.
We dance it out to the tip of Monsieur's sword,
Reading the lordly language of the inscription,
Which is like zithers and tambourines combined:

The Founder of the State. Whoever founded
A state that was free, in the dead of winter, from mice?
What a beautiful tableau tinted and towering,
The arm of bronze outstretched against all evil!

Anglais Mort à Florence

A little less returned for him each spring.
Music began to fail him. Brahms, although
His dark familiar, often walked apart.

His spirit grew uncertain of delight,
Certain of its uncertainty, in which
That dark companion left him unconsoled

For a self returning mostly memory.
Only last year he said that the naked moon
Was not the moon he used to see, to feel

(In the pale coherences of moon and mood
When he was young), naked and alien,
More leanly shining from a lankier sky.

Its ruddy pallor had grown cadaverous.
He used his reason, exercised his will,
Turning in time to Brahms as alternate

In speech. He was that music and himself.
They were particles of order, a single majesty:
But he remembered the time when he stood alone.

He stood at last by God's help and the police;
But he remembered the time when he stood alone.
He yielded himself to that single majesty;

But he remembered the time when he stood alone,
When to be and delight to be seemed to be one,
Before the colors deepened and grew small.

Some Friends from Pascagoula

Tell me more of the eagle, Cotton,
And you, black Sly,
Tell me how he descended
Out of the morning sky.

Describe with deepened voice
And noble imagery
His slowly-falling round
Down to the fishy sea.

Here was a sovereign sight,
Fit for a kinky clan.
Tell me again of the point
At which the flight began,

Say how his heavy wings,
Spread on the sun-bronzed air,
Turned tip and tip away,
Down to the sand, the glare

Of the pine trees edging the sand,
Dropping in sovereign rings
Out of his fiery lair.
Speak of the dazzling wings.

Mr. Burnshaw and the Statue

I

The thing is dead . . . Everything is dead
Except the future. Always everything
That is is dead except what ought to be.
All things destroy themselves or are destroyed.

These are not even Russian animals.
They are horses as they were in the sculptor's mind.
They might be sugar or paste or citron-skin

Made by a cook that never rode the back
Of his angel through the skies. They might be mud
Left here by moonlit muckers when they fled
At the burst of day, crepuscular images
Made to remember a life they never lived
In the witching wilderness, night's witchingness,
Made to affect a dream they never had,
Like a word in the mind that sticks at artichoke
And remains inarticulate, horses with cream.
The statue seems a thing from Schwarz's, a thing
Of the dank imagination, much below
Our crusted outlines hot and huge with fact,
Ugly as an idea, not beautiful
As sequels without thought. In the rudest red
Of autumn, these horses should go clattering
Along the thin horizons, nobly more
Than this jotting-down of the sculptor's foppishness
Long after the worms and the curious carvings of
Their snouts.

II

Come, all celestial paramours,
Whether in-dwelling haughty clouds, frigid
And crisply musical, or holy caverns temple-toned,
Entwine your arms and moving to and fro,
Now like a ballet infantine in awkward steps,
Chant sibilant requiems for this effigy.
Bring down from nowhere nothing's wax-like blooms,
Calling them what you will but loosely-named
In a mortal lullaby, like porcelain.
Then, while the music makes you, make, yourselves,
Long autumn sheens and pittering sounds like sounds
On pattering leaves and suddenly with lights,
Astral and Shelleyan, diffuse new day;
And on this ring of marble horses shed

The rainbow in its glistening serpentines
Made by the sun ascending seventy seas.
Agree: the apple in the orchard, round
And red, will not be redder, rounder then
Than now. No: nor the ploughman in his bed
Be free to sleep there sounder, for the plough
And the dew and the ploughman still will best be one.
But this gawky plaster will not be here.

III

The stones
That will replace it shall be carved, *"The Mass
Appoints These Marbles Of Itself To Be
Itself."* No more than that, no subterfuge,
No memorable muffing, bare and blunt.

IV

Mesdames, one might believe that Shelley lies
Less in the stars than in their earthy wake,
Since the radiant disclosures that you make
Are of an eternal vista, manqué and gold
And brown, an Italy of the mind, a place
Of fear before the disorder of the strange,
A time in which the poets' politics
Will rule in a poets' world. Yet that will be
A world impossible for poets, who
Complain and prophesy, in their complaints,
And are never of the world in which they live.
Disclose the rude and ruddy at their jobs
And if you weep for peacocks that are gone
Or dance the death of doves, most sallowly,
Who knows? The ploughman may not live alone
With his plough, the peacock may abandon pride,
The dove's adagio may lose its depth
And change. If ploughmen, peacocks, doves alike

In vast disorder live in the ruins, free,
The charts destroyed, even disorder may,
So seen, have an order of its own, a peace
Not now to be perceived yet order's own.

v

A solemn voice, not Mr. Burnshaw's says:
At some gigantic, solitary urn,
A trash can at the end of the world, the dead
Give up dead things and the living turn away.
There buzzards pile their sticks among the bones
Of buzzards and eat the bellies of the rich,
Fat with a thousand butters, and the crows
Sip the wild honey of the poor man's life,
The blood of his bitter brain; and there the sun
Shines without fire on columns intercrossed,
White slapped on white, majestic, marble heads,
Severed and tumbled into seedless grass,
Motionless, knowing neither dew nor frost.
There lies the head of the sculptor in which the thought
Of lizards, in its eye, is more acute
Than the thought that once was native to the skull;
And there are the white-maned horses' heads, beyond
The help of any wind or any sky:
Parts of the immense detritus of a world
That is completely waste, that moves from waste
To waste, out of the hopeless waste of the past
Into a hopeful waste to come. There even
The colorless light in which this wreckage lies
Has faint, portentous lustres, shades and shapes
Of rose, or what will once more rise to rose,
When younger bodies, because they are younger, rise
And chant the rose-points of their birth, and when
For a little time, again, rose-breasted birds
Sing rose-beliefs. Above that urn two lights

122

Commingle, not like the commingling of sun and moon
At dawn, nor of summer-light and winter-light
In an autumn afternoon, but two immense
Reflections, whirling apart and wide away.

VI

Mesdames, it is not enough to be reconciled
Before the strange, having wept and having thought
And having said farewell. It is not enough
That the vista retain ploughmen, peacocks, doves,
However tarnished, companions out of the past,
And that, heavily, you move with them in the dust.
It is not enough that you are indifferent,
Because time moves on columns intercrossed
And because the temple is never quite composed,
Silent and turquoised and perpetual,
Visible over the sea. It is only enough
To live incessantly in change. See how
On a day still full of summer, when the leaves
Appear to sleep within a sleeping air,
They suddenly fall and the leafless sound of the wind
Is no longer a sound of summer. So great a change
Is constant. The time you call serene descends
Through a moving chaos that never ends. Mesdames,
Leaves are not always falling and the birds
Of chaos are not always sad nor lost
In melancholy distances. You held
Each other moving in a chant and danced
Beside the statue, while you sang. Your eyes
Were solemn and your gowns were blown and grief
Was under every temple-tone. You sang
A tragic lullaby, like porcelain.
But change composes, too, and chaos comes
To momentary calm, spectacular flocks
Of crimson and hoods of Venezuelan green

And the sound of z in the grass all day, though these
Are chaos and of archaic change. Shall you,
Then, fear a drastic community evolved
From the whirling, slowly and by trial; or fear
Men gathering for a mighty flight of men,
An abysmal migration into a possible blue?

VII

Dance, now, and with sharp voices cry, but cry
Like damsels daubed and let your feet be bare
To touch the grass and, as you circle, turn
Your backs upon the vivid statue. Then,
Weaving ring in radiant ring and quickly, fling
Yourselves away and at a distance join
Your hands held high and cry again, but cry,
This time, like damsels captured by the sky,
Seized by that possible blue. Be maidens formed
Of the most evasive hue of a lesser blue,
Of the least appreciable shade of green
And despicable shades of red, just seen,
And vaguely to be seen, a matinal red,
A dewy flashing blanks away from fire,
As if your gowns were woven of the light
Yet were not bright, came shining as things come
That enter day from night, came mirror-dark,
With each fold sweeping in a sweeping play.
Let your golden hands wave fastly and be gay
And your braids bear brightening of crimson bands.
Conceive that while you dance the statue falls,
The heads are severed, topple, tumble, tip
In the soil and rest. Conceive that marble men
Serenely selves, transfigured by the selves
From which they came, make real the attitudes
Appointed for them and that the pediment
Bears words that are the speech of marble men.

124

In the glassy sound of your voices, the porcelain cries,
The alto clank of the long recitation, in these
Speak, and in these repeat: *To Be Itself,*
Until the sharply-colored glass transforms
Itself into the speech of the spirit, until
The porcelain bell-borrowings become
Implicit clarities in the way you cry
And are your feelings changed to sound, without
A change, until the waterish ditherings turn
To the tense, the maudlin, true meridian
That is yourselves, when, at last, you are yourselves,
Speaking and strutting broadly, fair and bloomed,
No longer of air but of the breathing earth,
Impassioned seducers and seduced, the pale
Pitched into swelling bodies, upward, drift
In a storm blown into glittering shapes, and flames
Wind-beaten into freshest, brightest fire.

Farewell to Florida

I

Go on, high ship, since now, upon the shore,
The snake has left its skin upon the floor.
Key West sank downward under massive clouds
And silvers and greens spread over the sea. The moon
Is at the mast-head and the past is dead.
Her mind will never speak to me again.
I am free. High above the mast the moon
Rides clear of her mind and the waves make a refrain
Of this: that the snake has shed its skin upon
The floor. Go on through the darkness. The waves fly
    back.

II

Her mind had bound me round. The palms were hot
As if I lived in ashen ground, as if
The leaves in which the wind kept up its sound
From my North of cold whistled in a sepulchral South
Her South of pine and coral and coraline sea,
Her home, not mine, in the ever-freshened Keys,
Her days, her oceanic nights, calling
For music, for whisperings from the reefs.
How content I shall be in the North to which I sail
And to feel sure and to forget the bleaching sand . . .

III

I hated the weathery yawl from which the pools
Disclosed the sea floor and the wilderness
Of waving weeds. I hated the vivid blooms
Curled over the shadowless hut, the rust and bones,
The trees likes bones and the leaves half sand, half sun.
To stand here on the deck in the dark and say
Farewell and to know that that land is forever gone
And that she will not follow in any word
Or look, nor ever again in thought, except
That I loved her once . . . Farewell. Go on, high ship.

IV

My North is leafless and lies in a wintry slime
Both of men and clouds, a slime of men in crowds.
The men are moving as the water moves,
This darkened water cloven by sullen swells
Against your sides, then shoving and slithering,
The darkness shattered, turbulent with foam.
To be free again, to return to the violent mind
That is their mind, these men, and that will bind
Me round, carry me, misty deck, carry me
To the cold, go on, high ship, go on, plunge on.

A Postcard from the Volcano

Children picking up our bones
Will never know that these were once
As quick as foxes on the hill;

And that in autumn, when the grapes
Made sharp air sharper by their smell
These had a being, breathing frost;

And least will guess that with our bones
We left much more, left what still is
The look of things, left what we felt

At what we'saw. The spring clouds blow
Above the shuttered mansion-house,
Beyond our gate and the windy sky'

Cries out a literate despair.
We knew for long the mansion's look
And what we said of it became

A part of what it is . . . Children,
Still weaving budded aureoles,
Will speak our speech and never know,

Will say of the mansion that it seems
As if he that lived there left behind
A spirit storming in blank walls,

A dirty house in a gutted world,
A tatter of shadows peaked to white,
Smeared with the gold of the opulent sun.

Ghosts as Cocoons

The grass is in seed. The young birds are flying.
Yet the house is not built, not even begun.

The vetch has turned purple. But where is the bride?
It is easy to say to those bidden—But where,

Where, butcher, seducer, bloodman, reveller,
Where is sun and music and highest heaven's lust,

For which more than any words cries deeplier?
This mangled, smutted semi-world hacked out

Of dirt . . . It is not possible for the moon
To blot this with its dove-winged blendings.

She must come now. The grass is in seed and high.
Come now. Those to be born have need

Of the bride, love being a birth, have need to see
And to touch her, have need to say to her,

"The fly on the rose prevents us, O season
Excelling summer, ghost of fragrance falling

On dung." Come now, pearled and pasted, bloomy-
    leafed,
While the domes resound with chant involving chant.

The Men That Are Falling

God and all angels sing the world to sleep,
Now that the moon is rising in the heat

And crickets are loud again in the grass. The moon
Burns in the mind on lost remembrances.

He lies down and the night wind blows upon him here.
The bells grow longer. This is not sleep. This is desire.

Ah! Yes, desire . . . this leaning on his bed,
This leaning on his elbows on his bed,

Staring, at midnight, at the pillow that is black
In the catastrophic room . . . beyond despair,

Like an intenser instinct. What is it he desires?
But this he cannot know, the man that thinks,

Yet life itself, the fulfilment of desire
In the grinding ric-rac, staring steadily

At a head upon the pillow in the dark,
More than sudarium, speaking the speech

Of absolutes, bodiless, a head
Thick-lipped from riot and rebellious cries,

The head of one of the men that are falling, placed
Upon the pillow to repose and speak,

Speak and say the immaculate syllables
That he spoke only by doing what he did.

God and all angels, this was his desire,
Whose head lies blurring here, for this he died.

Taste of the blood upon his martyred lips,
O pensioners, O demagogues and pay-men!

This death was his belief though death is a stone.
This man loved earth, not heaven, enough to die.

The night wind blows upon the dreamer, bent
Over words that are life's voluble utterance.

A Thought Revolved

I

The Mechanical Optimist

A lady dying of diabetes
Listened to the radio,
Catching the lesser dithyrambs.
So heaven collects its bleating lambs.

Her useless bracelets fondly fluttered,
Paddling the melodic swirls,
The idea of god no longer sputtered
At the roots of her indifferent curls.

The idea of the Alps grew large,
Not yet, however, a thing to die in.
It seemed serener just to die,
To float off in the floweriest barge,

Accompanied by the exegesis
Of familiar things in a cheerful voice,
Like the night before Christmas and all the carols.
Dying lady, rejoice, rejoice!

II

Mystic Garden & Middling Beast

The poet striding among the cigar stores,
Ryan's lunch, hatters, insurance and medicines,
Denies that abstraction is a vice except
To the fatuous. These are his infernal walls,
A space of stone, of inexplicable base
And peaks outsoaring possible adjectives.
One man, the idea of man, that is the space,
The true abstract in which he promenades.
The era of the idea of man, the cloak
And speech of Virgil dropped, that's where he walks,
That's where his hymns come crowding, hero-hymns,
Chorals for mountain voices and the moral chant,
Happy rather than holy but happy-high,
Day hymns instead of constellated rhymes,
Hymns of the struggle of the idea of god
And the idea of man, the mystic garden and
The middling beast, the garden of paradise
And he that created the garden and peopled it.

III

Romanesque Affabulation

He sought an earthly leader who could stand
Without panache, without cockade,
Son only of man and sun of men,
The outer captain, the inner saint,

The pine, the pillar and the priest,
The voice, the book, the hidden well,

The faster's feast and heavy-fruited star,
The father, the beater of the rigid drums,

He that at midnight touches the guitar,
The solitude, the barrier, the Pole
In Paris, celui qui chante et pleure,
Winter devising summer in its breast,

Summer assaulted, thundering, illumed,
Shelter yet thrower of the summer spear,
With all his attributes no god but man
Of men whose heaven is in themselves,

Or else whose hell, foamed with their blood
And the long echo of their dying cry,
A fate intoned, a death before they die,
The race that sings and weeps and knows not why.

IV

The Leader

Behold the moralist hidalgo
Whose whore is Morning Star
Dressed in metal, silk and stone,
Syringa, cicada, his flea.

In how severe a book he read,
Until his nose grew thin and taut
And knowledge dropped upon his heart
Its pitting poison, half the night.

He liked the nobler works of man,
The gold façade round early squares,
The bronzes liquid through gay light.
He hummed to himself at such a plan.

He sat among beggars wet with dew,
Heard the dogs howl at barren bone,
Sat alone, his great toe like a horn,
The central flaw in the solar morn.

The Man with the Blue Guitar

I

The man bent over his guitar,
A shearsman of sorts. The day was green.

They said, "You have a blue guitar,
You do not play things as they are."

The man replied, "Things as they are
Are changed upon the blue guitar."

And they said then, "But play, you must,
A tune beyond us, yet ourselves,

A tune upon the blue guitar
Of things exactly as they are."

II

I cannot bring a world quite round,
Although I patch it as I can.

I sing a hero's head, large eye
And bearded bronze, but not a man,

Although I patch him as I can
And reach through him almost to man.

If to serenade almost to man
Is to miss, by that, things as they are,

Say that it is the serenade
Of a man that plays a blue guitar.

III

Ah, but to play man number one,
To drive the dagger in his heart,

To lay his brain upon the board
And pick the acrid colors out,

To nail his thought across the door,
Its wings spread wide to rain and snow,

To strike his living hi and ho,
To tick it, tock it, turn it true,

To bang it from a savage blue,
Jangling the metal of the strings . . .

IV

So that's life, then: things as they are?
It picks its way on the blue guitar.

A million people on one string?
And all their manner in the thing,

And all their manner, right and wrong,
And all their manner, weak and strong?

The feelings crazily, craftily call,
Like a buzzing of flies in autumn air,

And that's life, then: things as they are,
This buzzing of the blue guitar.

V

Do not speak to us of the greatness of poetry,
Of the torches wisping in the underground,

Of the structure of vaults upon a point of light.
There are no shadows in our sun,

Day is desire and night is sleep.
There are no shadows anywhere.

The earth, for us, is flat and bare.
There are no shadows. Poetry

Exceeding music must take the place
Of empty heaven and its hymns,

Ourselves in poetry must take their place,
Even in the chattering of your guitar.

VI

A tune beyond us as we are,
Yet nothing changed by the blue guitar;

Ourselves in the tune as if in space,
Yet nothing changed, except the place

Of things as they are and only the place
As you play them, on the blue guitar,

Placed, so, beyond the compass of change,
Perceived in a final atmosphere;

For a moment final, in the way
The thinking of art seems final when

The thinking of god is smoky dew.
The tune is space. The blue guitar

Becomes the place of things as they are,
A composing of senses of the guitar.

VII

It is the sun that shares our works.
The moon shares nothing. It is a sea.

When shall I come to say of the sun,
It is a sea; it shares nothing;

The sun no longer shares our works
And the earth is alive with creeping men,

Mechanical beetles never quite warm?
And shall I then stand in the sun, as now

I stand in the moon, and call it good,
The immaculate, the merciful good,

Detached from us, from things as they are?
Not to be part of the sun? To stand

Remote and call it merciful?
The strings are cold on the blue guitar.

VIII

The vivid, florid, turgid sky,
The drenching thunder rolling by,

The morning deluged still by night,
The clouds tumultuously bright

And the feeling heavy in cold chords
Struggling toward impassioned choirs,

Crying among the clouds, enraged
By gold antagonists in air—

I know my lazy, leaden twang
Is like the reason in a storm;

And yet it brings the storm to bear.
I twang it out and leave it there.

IX

And the color, the overcast blue
Of the air, in which the blue guitar

Is a form, described but difficult,
And I am merely a shadow hunched

Above the arrowy, still strings,
The maker of a thing yet to be made;

The color like a thought that grows
Out of a mood, the tragic robe

Of the actor, half his gesture, half
His speech, the dress of his meaning, silk

Sodden with his melancholy words,
The weather of his stage, himself.

X

Raise reddest columns. Toll a bell
And clap the hollows full of tin.

Throw papers in the streets, the wills
Of the dead, majestic in their seals.

And the beautiful trombones—behold
The approach of him whom none believes,

Whom all believe that all believe,
A pagan in a varnished car.

Roll a drum upon the blue guitar.
Lean from the steeple. Cry aloud,

"Here am I, my adversary, that
Confront you, hoo-ing the slick trombones,

Yet with a petty misery
At heart, a petty misery,

Ever the prelude to your end,
The touch that topples men and rock."

XI

Slowly the ivy on the stones
Becomes the stones. Women become

The cities, children become the fields
And men in waves become the sea.

It is the chord that falsifies.
The sea returns upon the men,

The fields entrap the children, brick
Is a weed and all the flies are caught,

Wingless and withered, but living alive.
The discord merely magnifies.

Deeper within the belly's dark
Of time, time grows upon the rock.

XII

Tom-tom, c'est moi. The blue guitar
And I are one. The orchestra

Fills the high hall with shuffling men
High as the hall. The whirling noise

Of a multitude dwindles, all said,
To his breath that lies awake at night.

I know that timid breathing. Where
Do I begin and end? And where,

As I strum the thing, do I pick up
That which momentously declares

Itself not to be I and yet
Must be. It could be nothing else.

XIII

The pale intrusions into blue
Are corrupting pallors . . . ay di mi,

Blue buds or pitchy blooms. Be content—
Expansions, diffusions—content to be

The unspotted imbecile revery,
The heraldic center of the world

Of blue, blue sleek with a hundred chins,
The amorist Adjective aflame . . .

XIV

First one beam, then another, then
A thousand are radiant in the sky.

Each is both star and orb; and day
Is the riches of their atmosphere.

The sea appends its tattery hues.
The shores are banks of muffling mist.

One says a German chandelier—
A candle is enough to light the world.

It makes it clear. Even at noon
It glistens in essential dark.

At night, it lights the fruit and wine,
The book and bread, things as they are,

In a chiaroscuro where
One sits and plays the blue guitar.

xv

Is this picture of Picasso's, this "hoard
Of destructions," a picture of ourselves,

Now, an image of our society?
Do I sit, deformed, a naked egg,

Catching at Good-bye, harvest moon,
Without seeing the harvest or the moon?

Things as they are have been destroyed.
Have I? Am I a man that is dead

At a table on which the food is cold?
Is my thought a memory, not alive?

Is the spot on the floor, there, wine or blood
And whichever it may be, is it mine?

The earth is not earth but a stone,
Not the mother that held men as they fell

But stone, but like a stone, no: not
The mother, but an oppressor, but like

An oppressor that grudges them their death,
As it grudges the living that they live.

To live in war, to live at war,
To chop the sullen psaltery,

To improve the sewers in Jerusalem,
To electrify the nimbuses—

Place honey on the altars and die,
You lovers that are bitter at heart.

XVII

The person has a mould. But not
Its animal. The angelic ones

Speak of the soul, the mind. It is
An animal. The blue guitar—

On that its claws propound, its fangs
Articulate its desert days.

The blue guitar a mould? That shell?
Well, after all, the north wind blows

A horn, on which its victory
Is a worm composing on a straw.

XVIII

A dream (to call it a dream) in which
I can believe, in face of the object,

A dream no longer a dream, a thing,
Of things as they are, as the blue guitar

After long strumming on certain nights
Gives the touch of the senses, not of the hand,

But the very senses as they touch
The wind-gloss. Or as daylight comes,

Like light in a mirroring of cliffs,
Rising upward from a sea of ex.

XIX

That I may reduce the monster to
Myself, and then may be myself

In face of the monster, be more than part
Of it, more than the monstrous player of

One of its monstrous lutes, not be
Alone, but reduce the monster and be,

Two things, the two together as one,
And play of the monster and of myself,

Or better not of myself at all,
But of that as its intelligence,

Being the lion in the lute
Before the lion locked in stone.

XX

What is there in life except one's ideas,
Good air, good friend, what is there in life?

Is it ideas that I believe?
Good air, my only friend, believe,

Believe would be a brother full
Of love, believe would be a friend,

Friendlier than my only friend,
Good air. Poor pale, poor pale guitar . . .

XXI

A substitute for all the gods:
This self, not that gold self aloft,

Alone, one's shadow magnified,
Lord of the body, looking down,

As now and called most high,
The shadow of Chocorua

In an immenser heaven, aloft,
Alone, lord of the land and lord

Of the men that live in the land, high lord.
One's self and the mountains of one's land,

Without shadows, without magnificence,
The flesh, the bone, the dirt, the stone.

XXII

Poetry is the subject of the poem,
From this the poem issues and

To this returns. Between the two,
Between issue and return, there is

An absence in reality,
Things as they are. Or so we say.

But are these separate? Is it
An absence for the poem, which acquires

Its true appearances there, sun's green,
Cloud's red, earth feeling, sky that thinks?

From these it takes. Perhaps it gives,
In the universal intercourse.

XXIII

A few final solutions, like a duet
With the undertaker: a voice in the clouds,

Another on earth, the one a voice
Of ether, the other smelling of drink,

The voice of ether prevailing, the swell
Of the undertaker's song in the snow

Apostrophizing wreaths, the voice
In the clouds serene and final, next

The grunted breath serene and final,
The imagined and the real, thought

And the truth, Dichtung und Wahrheit, all
Confusion solved, as in a refrain

One keeps on playing year by year,
Concerning the nature of things as they are.

XXIV

A poem like a missal found
In the mud, a missal for that young man,

That scholar hungriest for that book,
The very book, or, less, a page

Or, at the least, a phrase, that phrase,
A hawk of life, that latined phrase:

To know; a missal for brooding-sight.
To meet that hawk's eye and to flinch

Not at the eye but at the joy of it.
I play. But this is what I think.

XXV

He held the world upon his nose
And this-a-way he gave a fling.

His robes and symbols, ai-yi-yi—
And that-a-way he twirled the thing.

Sombre as fir-trees, liquid cats
Moved in the grass without a sound.

They did not know the grass went round.
The cats had cats and the grass turned gray

And the world had worlds, ai, this-a-way:
The grass turned green and the grass turned gray.

And the nose is eternal, that-a-way.
Things as they were, things as they are,

Things as they will be by and by . . .
A fat thumb beats out ai-yi-yi.

XXVI

The world washed in his imagination,
The world was a shore, whether sound or form

Or light, the relic of farewells,
Rock, of valedictory echoings,

To which his imagination returned,
From which it sped, a bar in space,

Sand heaped in the clouds, giant that fought
Against the murderous alphabet:

The swarm of thoughts, the swarm of dreams
Of inaccessible Utopia.

A mountainous music always seemed
To be falling and to be passing away.

XXVII

It is the sea that whitens the roof.
The sea drifts through the winter air.

It is the sea that the north wind makes.
The sea is in the falling snow.

This gloom is the darkness of the sea.
Geographers and philosophers,

Regard. But for that salty cup,
But for the icicles on the eaves—

The sea is a form of ridicule.
The iceberg settings satirize

The demon that cannot be himself,
That tours to shift the shifting scene.

XXVIII

I am a native in this world
And think in it as a native thinks,

Gesu, not native of a mind
Thinking the thoughts I call my own,

Native, a native in the world
And like a native think in it.

It could not be a mind, the wave
In which the watery grasses flow

And yet are fixed as a photograph,
The wind in which the dead leaves blow.

Here I inhale profounder strength
And as I am, I speak and move

And things are as I think they are
And say they are on the blue guitar.

XXIX

In the cathedral, I sat there, and read,
Alone, a lean Review and said,

"These degustations in the vaults
Oppose the past and the festival.

What is beyond the cathedral, outside,
Balances with nuptial song.

So it is to sit and to balance things
To and to and to the point of still,

To say of one mask it is like,
To say of another it is like,

To know that the balance does not quite rest,
That the mask is strange, however like."

The shapes are wrong and the sounds are false.
The bells are the bellowing of bulls.

Yet Franciscan don was never more
Himself than in this fertile glass.

XXX

From this I shall evolve a man.
This is his essence: the old fantoche

Hanging his shawl upon the wind,
Like something on the stage, puffed out,

His strutting studied through centuries.
At last, in spite of his manner, his eye

A-cock at the cross-piece on a pole
Supporting heavy cables, slung

Through Oxidia, banal suburb,
One-half of all its installments paid.

Dew-dapper clapper-traps, blazing
From crusty stacks above machines.

Ecce, Oxidia is the seed
Dropped out of this amber-ember pod,

Oxidia is the soot of fire,
Oxidia is Olympia.

XXXI

How long and late the pheasant sleeps . . .
The employer and employee contend,

Combat, compose their droll affair.
The bubbling sun will bubble up,

148

Spring sparkle and the cock-bird shriek.
The employer and employee will hear

And continue their affair. The shriek
Will rack the thickets. There is no place,

Here, for the lark fixed in the mind,
In the museum of the sky. The cock

Will claw sleep. Morning is not sun,
It is this posture of the nerves,

As if a blunted player clutched
The nuances of the blue guitar.

It must be this rhapsody or none,
The rhapsody of things as they are.

XXXII

Throw away the lights, the definitions,
And say of what you see in the dark

That it is this or that it is that,
But do not use the rotted names.

How should you walk in that space and know
Nothing of the madness of space,

Nothing of its jocular procreations?
Throw the lights away. Nothing must stand

Between you and the shapes you take
When the crust of shape has been destroyed.

You as you are? You are yourself.
The blue guitar surprises you.

XXXIII

That generation's dream, aviled
In the mud, in Monday's dirty light,

That's it, the only dream they knew,
Time in its final block, not time

To come, a wrangling of two dreams.
Here is the bread of time to come,

Here is its actual stone. The bread
Will be our bread, the stone will be

Our bed and we shall sleep by night.
We shall forget by day, except

The moments when we choose to play
The imagined pine, the imagined jay.

A Rabbit as King of the Ghosts

The difficulty to think at the end of day,
When the shapeless shadow covers the sun
And nothing is left except light on your fur—

There was the cat slopping its milk all day,
Fat cat, red tongue, green mind, white milk
And August the most peaceful month.

To be, in the grass, in the peacefullest time,
Without that monument of cat,
The cat forgotten in the moon;

And to feel that the light is a rabbit-light,
In which everything is meant for you
And nothing need be explained;

Then there is nothing to think of. It comes of itself;
And east rushes west and west rushes down,
No matter. The grass is full

And full of yourself. The trees around are for you,
The whole of the wideness of night is for you,
A self that touches all edges,

You become a self that fills the four corners of night.
The red cat hides away in the fur-light
And there you are humped high, humped up,

You are humped higher and higher, black as stone—
You sit with your head like a carving in space
And the little green cat is a bug in the grass.

United Dames of America

Je tâche, en restant exact, d'être poète.
—JULES RENARD

There are not leaves enough to cover the face
It wears. This is the way the orator spoke:
"The mass is nothing. The number of men in a mass
Of men is nothing. The mass is no greater than

The singular man of the mass. Masses produce
Each one its paradigm." There are not leaves
Enough to hide away the face of the man
Of this dead mass and that. The wind might fill

With faces as with leaves, be gusty with mouths,
And with mouths crying and crying day by day.
Could all these be ourselves, sounding ourselves,
Our faces circling round a central face

And then nowhere again, away and away?
Yet one face keeps returning (never the one),
The face of the man of the mass, never the face
That hermit on reef sable would have seen,

Never the naked politician taught
By the wise. There are not leaves enough to crown,
To cover, to crown, to cover—let it go—
The actor that will at last declaim our end.

The Dwarf

Now it is September and the web is woven.
The web is woven and you have to wear it.

The winter is made and you have to bear it,
The winter web, the winter woven, wind and wind,

For all the thoughts of summer that go with it
In the mind, pupa of straw, moppet of rags.

It is the mind that is woven, the mind that was jerked
And tufted in straggling thunder and shattered sun.

It is all that you are, the final dwarf of you,
That is woven and woven and waiting to be worn,

Neither as mask nor as garment but as a being,
Torn from insipid summer, for the mirror of cold,

Sitting beside your lamp, there citron to nibble
And coffee dribble . . . Frost is in the stubble.

Loneliness in Jersey City

The deer and the dachshund are one.
Well, the gods grow out of the weather.
The people grow out of the weather;
The gods grow out of the people.
Encore, encore, encore les dieux . . .

The distance between the dark steeple
And cobble ten thousand and three
Is more than a seven-foot inchworm
Could measure by moonlight in June.

Kiss, cats: for the deer and the dachshund
Are one. My window is twenty-nine three
And plenty of window for me.
The steeples are empty and so are the people,
There's nothing whatever to see
Except Polacks that pass in their motors
And play concertinas all night.
They think that things are all right,
Since the deer and the dachshund are one.

Anything Is Beautiful if You Say It Is

Under the eglantine
The fretful concubine
Said, "Phooey! Phoo!"
She whispered, "Pfui!"

The demi-monde
On the mezzanine
Said, "Phooey!" too,
And a "Hey-de-i-do!"

The bee may have all sweet
For his honey-hive-o,
From the eglantine-o.

And the chandeliers are neat . . .
But their mignon, marblish glare!
We are cold, the parrots cried,
In a place so debonair.

The Johannisberger, Hans.
I love the metal grapes,
The rusty, battered shapes
Of the pears and of the cheese

And the window's lemon light,
The very will of the nerves,
The crack across the pane,
The dirt along the sill.

A Weak Mind in the Mountains

There was the butcher's hand.
He squeezed it and the blood
Spurted from between the fingers
And fell to the floor.
And then the body fell.

So afterward, at night,
The wind of Iceland and
The wind of Ceylon,
Meeting, gripped my mind,
Gripped it and grappled my thoughts.

The black wind of the sea
And the green wind
Whirled upon me.
The blood of the mind fell
To the floor. I slept.

Yet there was a man within me
Could have risen to the clouds,
Could have touched these winds,
Bent and broken them down,
Could have stood up sharply in the sky.

Parochial Theme

Long-tailed ponies go nosing the pine-lands,
Ponies of Parisians shooting on the hill.

The wind blows. In the wind, the voices
Have shapes that are not yet fully themselves,

Are sounds blown by a blower into shapes,
The blower squeezed to the thinnest *mi* of falsetto.

The hunters run to and fro. The heavy trees,
The grunting, shuffling branches, the robust,

The nocturnal, the antique, the blue-green pines
Deepen the feelings to inhuman depths.

These are the forest. This health is holy,
This halloo, halloo, halloo heard over the cries

Of those for whom a square room is a fire,
Of those whom the statues torture and keep down.

This health is holy, this descant of a self,
This barbarous chanting of what is strong, this blare.

But salvation here? What about the rattle of sticks
On tins and boxes? What about horses eaten by wind?

When spring comes and the skeletons of the hunters
Stretch themselves to rest in their first summer's sun,

The spring will have a health of its own, with none
Of autumn's halloo in its hair. So that closely, then,

Health follows after health. Salvation there:
There's no such thing as life; or if there is,

It is faster than the weather, faster than
Any character. It is more than any scene:

Of the guillotine or of any glamorous hanging.
Piece the world together, boys, but not with your hands.

Poetry Is a Destructive Force

That's what misery is,
Nothing to have at heart.
It is to have or nothing.

It is a thing to have,
A lion, an ox in his breast.
To feel it breathing there.

Corazon, stout dog,
Young ox, bow-legged bear,
He tastes its blood, not spit.

He is like a man
In the body of a violent beast.
Its muscles are his own . . .

The lion sleeps in the sun.
Its nose is on its paws.
It can kill a man.

The Poems of Our Climate

I

Clear water in a brilliant bowl,
Pink and white carnations. The light
In the room more like a snowy air,
Reflecting snow. A newly-fallen snow
At the end of winter when afternoons return.
Pink and white carnations—one desires
So much more than that. The day itself
Is simplified: a bowl of white,
Cold, a cold porcelain, low and round,
With nothing more than the carnations there.

II

Say even that this complete simplicity
Stripped one of all one's torments, concealed
The evilly compounded, vital I
And made it fresh in a world of white,
A world of clear water, brilliant-edged,
Still one would want more, one would need more,
More than a world of white and snowy scents.

III

There would still remain the never-resting mind,
So that one would want to escape, come back
To what had been so long composed.
The imperfect is our paradise.
Note that, in this bitterness, delight,
Since the imperfect is so hot in us,
Lies in flawed words and stubborn sounds.

Study of Two Pears

I

Opusculum paedagogum.
The pears are not viols,
Nudes or bottles.
They resemble nothing else.

II

They are yellow forms
Composed of curves
Bulging toward the base.
They are touched red.

III

They are not flat surfaces
Having curved outlines.
They are round
Tapering toward the top.

IV

In the way they are modelled
There are bits of blue.
A hard dry leaf hangs
From the stem.

V

The yellow glistens.
It glistens with various yellows,
Citrons, oranges and greens
Flowering over the skin.

VI

The shadows of the pears
Are blobs on the green cloth.
The pears are not seen
As the observer wills.

159

The Glass of Water

That the glass would melt in heat,
That the water would freeze in cold,
Shows that this object is merely a state,
One of many, between two poles. So,
In the metaphysical, there are these poles.

Here in the centre stands the glass. Light
Is the lion that comes down to drink. There
And in that state, the glass is a pool.
Ruddy are his eyes and ruddy are his claws
When light comes down to wet his frothy jaws

And in the water winding weeds move round.
And there and in another state—the refractions,
The *metaphysica*, the plastic parts of poems
Crash in the mind—But, fat Jocundus, worrying
About what stands here in the centre, not the glass,

But in the centre of our lives, this time, this day,
It is a state, this spring among the politicians
Playing cards. In a village of the indigenes,
One would have still to discover. Among the dogs
    and dung,
One would continue to contend with one's ideas.

Add This to Rhetoric

It is posed and it is posed.
But in nature it merely grows.
Stones pose in the falling night;
And beggars dropping to sleep,
They pose themselves and their rags.
Shucks . . . lavender moonlight falls.
The buildings pose in the sky
And, as you paint, the clouds,
Grisaille, impearled, profound,
Pftt. . . . In the way you speak
You arrange, the thing is posed,
What in nature merely grows.

To-morrow when the sun,
For all your images,
Comes up as the sun, bull fire,
Your images will have left
No shadow of themselves.
The poses of speech, of paint,
Of music—Her body lies
Worn out, her arm falls down,
Her fingers touch the ground.
Above her, to the left,
A brush of white, the obscure,
The moon without a shape,
A fringed eye in a crypt.
The sense creates the pose.
In this it moves and speaks.
This is the figure and not
An evading metaphor.

Add this. It is to add.

Dry Loaf

It is equal to living in a tragic land
To live in a tragic time.
Regard now the sloping, mountainous rocks
And the river that batters its way over stones,
Regard the hovels of those that live in this land.

That was what I painted behind the loaf,
The rocks not even touched by snow,
The pines along the river and the dry men blown
Brown as the bread, thinking of birds
Flying from burning countries and brown sand shores,

Birds that came like dirty water in waves
Flowing above the rocks, flowing over the sky,
As if the sky was a current that bore them along,
Spreading them as waves spread flat on the shore,
One after another washing the mountains bare.

It was the battering of drums I heard
It was hunger, it was the hungry that cried
And the waves, the waves were soldiers moving,
Marching and marching in a tragic time
Below me, on the asphalt, under the trees.

It was soldiers went marching over the rocks
And still the birds came, came in watery flocks,
Because it was spring and the birds had to come.
No doubt that soldiers had to be marching
And that drums had to be rolling, rolling, rolling.

The Man on the Dump

Day creeps down. The moon is creeping up.
The sun is a corbeil of flowers the moon Blanche
Places there, a bouquet. Ho-ho . . . The dump is full
Of images. Days pass like papers from a press.
The bouquets come here in the papers. So the sun,
And so the moon, both come, and the janitor's poems
Of every day, the wrapper on the can of pears,
The cat in the paper-bag, the corset, the box
From Esthonia: the tiger chest, for tea.

The freshness of night has been fresh a long time.
The freshness of morning, the blowing of day, one says
That it puffs as Cornelius Nepos reads, it puffs
More than, less than or it puffs like this or that.
The green smacks in the eye, the dew in the green
Smacks like fresh water in a can, like the sea
On a cocoanut—how many men have copied dew
For buttons, how many women have covered themselves
With dew, dew dresses, stones and chains of dew, heads
Of the floweriest flowers dewed with the dewiest dew.
One grows to hate these things except on the dump.

Now, in the time of spring (azaleas, trilliums,
Myrtle, viburnums, daffodils, blue phlox),
Between that disgust and this, between the things
That are on the dump (azaleas and so on)
And those that will be (azaleas and so on),
One feels the purifying change. One rejects
The trash.

        That's the moment when the moon creeps up
To the bubbling of bassoons. That's the time
One looks at the elephant-colorings of tires.

Everything is shed; and the moon comes up as the moon
(All its images are in the dump) and you see
As a man (not like an image of a man),
You see the moon rise in the empty sky.

One sits and beats an old tin can, lard pail.
One beats and beats for that which one believes.
That's what one wants to get near. Could it after all
Be merely oneself, as superior as the ear
To a crow's voice? Did the nightingale torture the ear,
Pack the heart and scratch the mind? And does the ear
Solace itself in peevish birds? Is it peace,
Is it a philosopher's honeymoon, one finds
On the dump? Is it to sit among mattresses of the dead,
Bottles, pots, shoes and grass and murmur *aptest eve*:
Is it to hear the blatter of grackles and say
Invisible priest; is it to eject, to pull
The day to pieces and cry *stanza my stone*?
Where was it one first heard of the truth? The the.

On the Road Home

It was when I said,
"There is no such thing as the truth,"
That the grapes seemed fatter.
The fox ran out of his hole.

You . . . You said,
"There are many truths,
But they are not parts of a truth."
Then the tree, at night, began to change,

Smoking through green and smoking blue.
We were two figures in a wood.
We said we stood alone.

It was when I said,
"Words are not forms of a single word.
In the sum of the parts, there are only the parts.
The world must be measured by eye";

It was when you said,
"The idols have seen lots of poverty,
Snakes and gold and lice,
But not the truth";

It was at that time, that the silence was largest
And longest, the night was roundest,
The fragrance of the autumn warmest,
Closest and strongest.

The Latest Freed Man

Tired of the old descriptions of the world,
The latest freed man rose at six and sat
On the edge of his bed. He said,

                              "I suppose there is
A doctrine to this landscape. Yet, having just
Escaped from the truth, the morning is color and mist,
Which is enough: the moment's rain and sea,
The moment's sun (the strong man vaguely seen),
Overtaking the doctrine of this landscape. Of him
And of his works, I am sure. He bathes in the mist

Like a man without a doctrine. The light he gives—
It is how he gives his light. It is how he shines,
Rising upon the doctors in their beds
And on their beds. . . ."

　　　　　　　　　　　　And so the freed man said.
It was how the sun came shining into his room:
To be without a description of to be,
For a moment on rising, at the edge of the bed, to be,
To have the ant of the self changed to an ox
With its organic boomings, to be changed
From a doctor into an ox, before standing up,
To know that the change and that the ox-like struggle
Come from the strength that is the strength of the sun,
Whether it comes directly or from the sun.
It was how he was free. It was how his freedom came.
It was being without description, being an ox.
It was the importance of the trees outdoors,
The freshness of the oak-leaves, not so much
That they were oak-leaves, as the way they looked.
It was everything being more real, himself
At the centre of reality, seeing it.
It was everything bulging and blazing and big in itself,
The blue of the rug, the portrait of Vidal,
Qui fait fi des joliesses banales, the chairs.

Connoisseur of Chaos

I

A.　A violent order is disorder; and
B.　A great disorder is an order. These
Two things are one. (Pages of illustrations.)

II

If all the green of spring was blue, and it is;
If the flowers of South Africa were bright
On the tables of Connecticut, and they are;
If Englishmen lived without tea in Ceylon, and they do;
And if it all went on in an orderly way,
And it does; a law of inherent opposites,
Of essential unity, is as pleasant as port,
As pleasant as the brush-strokes of a bough,
An upper, particular bough in, say, Marchand.

III

After all the pretty contrast of life and death
Proves that these opposite things partake of one,
At least that was the theory, when bishops' books
Resolved the world. We cannot go back to that.
The squirming facts exceed the squamous mind,
If one may say so. And yet relation appears,
A small relation expanding like the shade
Of a cloud on sand, a shape on the side of a hill.

IV

A. Well, an old order is a violent one.
This proves nothing. Just one more truth, one more
Element in the immense disorder of truths.
B. It is April as I write. The wind
Is blowing after days of constant rain.
All this, of course, will come to summer soon.
But suppose the disorder of truths should ever come
To an order, most Plantagenet, most fixed . . .
A great disorder is an order. Now, A
And B are not like statuary, posed
For a vista in the Louvre. They are things chalked
On the sidewalk so that the pensive man may see.

The pensive man . . . He sees that eagle float
For which the intricate Alps are a single nest.

The Sense of the Sleight-of-Hand Man

One's grand flights, one's Sunday baths,
One's tootings at the weddings of the soul
Occur as they occur. So bluish clouds
Occurred above the empty house and the leaves
Of the rhododendrons rattled their gold,
As if someone lived there. Such floods of white
Came bursting from the clouds. So the wind
Threw its contorted strength around the sky.

Could you have said the bluejay suddenly
Would swoop to earth? It is a wheel, the rays
Around the sun. The wheel survives the myths.
The fire eye in the clouds survives the gods.
To think of a dove with an eye of grenadine
And pines that are cornets, so it occurs,
And a little island full of geese and stars:
It may be that the ignorant man, alone,
Has any chance to mate his life with life
That is the sensual, pearly spouse, the life
That is fluent in even the wintriest bronze.

Of Hartford in a Purple Light

A long time you have been making the trip
From Havre to Hartford, Master Soleil,
Bringing the lights of Norway and all that.

A long time the ocean has come with you,
Shaking the water off, like a poodle,
That splatters incessant thousands of drops,

Each drop a petty tricolor. For this,
The aunts in Pasadena, remembering,
Abhor the plaster of the western horses,

Souvenirs of museums. But, Master, there are
Lights masculine and lights feminine.
What is this purple, this parasol,

This stage-light of the Opera?
It is like a region full of intonings.
It is Hartford seen in a purple light.

A moment ago, light masculine,
Working, with big hands, on the town,
Arranged its heroic attitudes.

But now as in an amour of women
Purple sets purple round. Look, Master,
See the river, the railroad, the cathedral . . .

When male light fell on the naked back
Of the town, the river, the railroad were clear.
Now, every muscle slops away.

Hi! Whisk it, poodle, flick the spray
Of the ocean, ever-freshening,
On the irised hunks, the stone bouquet.

Variations on a Summer Day

I

Say of the gulls that they are flying
In light blue air over dark blue sea.

II

A music more than a breath, but less
Than the wind, sub-music like sub-speech,
A repetition of unconscious things,
Letters of rock and water, words
Of the visible elements and of ours.

III

The rocks of the cliffs are the heads of dogs
That turn into fishes and leap
Into the sea.

IV

Star over Monhegan, Atlantic star,
Lantern without a bearer, you drift,
You, too, are drifting, in spite of your course;
Unless in the darkness, brightly-crowned,
You are the will, if there is a will,
Or the portent of a will that was,
One of the portents of the will that was.

V

The leaves of the sea are shaken and shaken.
There was a tree that was a father,
We sat beneath it and sang our songs.

VI

It is cold to be forever young,
To come to tragic shores and flow,
In sapphire, round the sun-bleached stones,
Being, for old men, time of their time.

VII

One sparrow is worth a thousand gulls,
When it sings. The gull sits on chimney-tops.
He mocks the guinea, challenges
The crow, inciting various modes.
The sparrow requites one, without intent.

VIII

An exercise in viewing the world.
On the motive! But one looks at the sea
As one improvises, on the piano.

IX

This cloudy world, by aid of land and sea,
Night and day, wind and quiet, produces
More nights, more days, more clouds, more worlds.

X

To change nature, not merely to change ideas,
To escape from the body, so to feel
Those feelings that the body balks,
The feelings of the natures round us here:
As a boat feels when it cuts blue water.

XI

Now, the timothy at Pemaquid
That rolled in heat is silver-tipped
And cold. The moon follows the sun like a French
Translation of a Russian poet.

XII

Everywhere the spruce trees bury soldiers:
Hugh March, a sergeant, a redcoat, killed,
With his men, beyond the barbican.
Everywhere spruce trees bury spruce trees.

XIII

Cover the sea with the sand rose. Fill
The sky with the radiantiana
Of spray. Let all the salt be gone.

XIV

Words add to the senses. The words for the dazzle
Of mica, the dithering of grass,
The Arachne integument of dead trees,
Are the eye grown larger, more intense.

XV

The last island and its inhabitant,
The two alike, distinguish blues,
Until the difference between air
And sea exists by grace alone,
In objects, as white this, white that.

XVI

Round and round goes the bell of the water
And round and round goes the water itself
And that which is the pitch of its motion,
The bell of its dome, the patron of sound.

XVII

Pass through the door and through the walls,
Those bearing balsam, its field fragrance,
Pine-figures bringing sleep to sleep.

XVIII

Low tide, flat water, sultry sun.
One observes profoundest shadows rolling.
Damariscotta da da doo.

XIX

One boy swims under a tub, one sits
On top. Hurroo, the man-boat comes,
In a man-makenesse, neater than Naples.

XX

You could almost see the brass on her gleaming,
Not quite. The mist was to light what red
Is to fire. And her mainmast tapered to nothing,
Without teetering a millimeter's measure.
The beads on her rails seemed to grasp at transparence.
It was not yet the hour to be dauntlessly leaping.

Man and Bottle

The mind is the great poem of winter, the man,
Who, to find what will suffice,
Destroys romantic tenements
Of rose and ice

In the land of war. More than the man, it is
A man with the fury of a race of men,

A light at the centre of many lights,
A man at the centre of men.

It has to content the reason concerning war,
It has to persuade that war is part of itself,
A manner of thinking, a mode
Of destroying, as the mind destroys,

An aversion, as the world is averted
From an old delusion, an old affair with the sun,
An impossible aberration with the moon,
A grossness of peace.

It is not the snow that is the quill, the page.
The poem lashes more fiercely than the wind,
As the mind, to find what will suffice, destroys
Romantic tenements of rose and ice.

Of Modern Poetry

The poem of the mind in the act of finding
What will suffice. It has not always had
To find: the scene was set; it repeated what
Was in the script.
               Then the theatre was changed
To something else. Its past was a souvenir.

It has to be living, to learn the speech of the place.
It has to face the men of the time and to meet

The women of the time. It has to think about war
And it has to find what will suffice. It has
To construct a new stage. It has to be on that stage
And, like an insatiable actor, slowly and
With meditation, speak words that in the ear,
In the delicatest ear of the mind, repeat,
Exactly, that which it wants to hear, at the sound
Of which, an invisible audience listens,
Not to the play, but to itself, expressed
In an emotion as of two people, as of two
Emotions becoming one. The actor is
A metaphysician in the dark, twanging
An instrument, twanging a wiry string that gives
Sounds passing through sudden rightnesses, wholly
Containing the mind, below which it cannot descend,
Beyond which it has no will to rise.
                                        It must
Be the finding of a satisfaction, and may
Be of a man skating, a woman dancing, a woman
Combing. The poem of the act of the mind.

Arrival at the Waldorf

Home from Guatemala, back at the Waldorf.
This arrival in the wild country of the soul,
All approaches gone, being completely there,

Where the wild poem is a substitute
For the woman one loves or ought to love,
One wild rhapsody a fake for another.

You touch the hotel the way you touch moonlight
Or sunlight and you hum and the orchestra
Hums and you say "The world in a verse,

A generation sealed, men remoter than mountains,
Women invisible in music and motion and color,"
After that alien, point-blank, green and actual Guatemala.

Landscape with Boat

An anti-master-man, floribund ascetic.

He brushed away the thunder, then the clouds,
Then the colossal illusion of heaven. Yet still
The sky was blue. He wanted imperceptible air.
He wanted to see. He wanted the eye to see
And not be touched by blue. He wanted to know,
A naked man who regarded himself in the glass
Of air, who looked for the world beneath the blue,
Without blue, without any turquoise tint or phase,
Any azure under-side or after-color. Nabob
Of bones, he rejected, he denied, to arrive
At the neutral centre, the ominous element,
The single-colored, colorless, primitive.

It was not as if the truth lay where he thought,
Like a phantom, in an uncreated night.
It was easier to think it lay there. If
It was nowhere else, it was there and because
It was nowhere else, its place had to be supposed,
Itself had to be supposed, a thing supposed

In a place supposed, a thing that he reached
In a place that he reached, by rejecting what he saw
And denying what he heard. He would arrive.
He had only not to live, to walk in the dark,
To be projected by one void into
Another.

It was his nature to suppose,
To receive what others had supposed, without
Accepting. He received what he denied.
But as truth to be accepted, he supposed
A truth beyond all truths.

He never supposed
That he might be truth, himself, or part of it,
That the things that he rejected might be part
And the irregular turquoise, part, the perceptible blue
Grown denser, part, the eye so touched, so played
Upon by clouds, the ear so magnified
By thunder, parts, and all these things together,
Parts, and more things, parts. He never supposed divine
Things might not look divine, nor that if nothing
Was divine then all things were, the world itself,
And that if nothing was the truth, then all
Things were the truth, the world itself was the truth.

Had he been better able to suppose:
He might sit on a sofa on a balcony
Above the Mediterranean, emerald
Becoming emeralds. He might watch the palms
Flap green ears in the heat. He might observe
A yellow wine and follow a steamer's track
And say, "The thing I hum appears to be
The rhythm of this celestial pantomime."

Extracts from Addresses to the Academy of Fine Ideas

I

A crinkled paper makes a brilliant sound.
The wrinkled roses tinkle, the paper ones,
And the ear is glass, in which the noises pelt,
The false roses—Compare the silent rose of the sun
And rain, the blood-rose living in its smell,
With this paper, this dust. That states the point.

Messieurs,
It is an artificial world. The rose
Of paper is of the nature of its world.
The sea is so many written words; the sky
Is blue, clear, cloudy, high, dark, wide and round;
The mountains inscribe themselves upon the walls.
And, otherwise, the rainy rose belongs
To naked men, to women naked as rain.

Where is that summer warm enough to walk
Among the lascivious poisons, clean of them,
And in what covert may we, naked, be
Beyond the knowledge of nakedness, as part
Of reality, beyond the knowledge of what
Is real, part of a land beyond the mind?

Rain is an unbearable tyranny. Sun is
A monster-maker, an eye, only an eye,
A shapener of shapes for only the eye,
Of things no better than paper things, of days
That are paper days. The false and true are one.

The eye believes and its communion takes.
The spirit laughs to see the eye believe
And its communion take. And now of that.
Let the Secretary for Porcelain observe
That evil made magic, as in catastrophe,
If neatly glazed, becomes the same as the fruit
Of an emperor, the egg-plant of a prince.
The good is evil's last invention. Thus
The maker of catastrophe invents the eye
And through the eye equates ten thousand deaths
With a single well-tempered apricot, or, say,
An egg-plant of good air.

                    My beards, attend
To the laughter of evil: the fierce ricanery
With the ferocious chu-chot-chu between, the sobs
For breath to laugh the louder, the deeper gasps
Uplifting the completest rhetoric
Of sneers, the fugues commencing at the toes
And ending at the finger-tips. . . . It is death
That is ten thousand deaths and evil death.
Be tranquil in your wounds. It is good death
That puts an end to evil death and dies.
Be tranquil in your wounds. The placating star
Shall be the gentler for the death you die
And the helpless philosophers say still helpful things.
Plato, the reddened flower, the erotic bird.

III

The lean cats of the arches of the churches,
That's the old world. In the new, all men are priests.

They preach and they are preaching in a land
To be described. They are preaching in a time

To be described. Evangelists of what?
If they could gather their theses into one,
Collect their thoughts together into one,
Into a single thought, thus: into a queen,
An intercessor by innate rapport,
Or into a dark-blue king, *un roi tonnerre*,
Whose merely being was his valiance,
Panjandrum and central heart and mind of minds—
If they could! Or is it the multitude of thoughts,
Like insects in the depths of the mind, that kill
The single thought? The multitudes of men
That kill the single man, starvation's head,
One man, their bread and their remembered wine?

The lean cats of the arches of the churches
Bask in the sun in which they feel transparent,
As if designed by X, the per-noble master.
They have a sense of their design and savor
The sunlight. They bear brightly the little beyond
Themselves, the slightly unjust drawing that is
Their genius: the exquisite errors of time.

IV

On an early Sunday in April, a feeble day,
He felt curious about the winter hills
And wondered about the water in the lake.
It had been cold since December. Snow fell, first,
At New Year and, from then until April, lay
On everything. Now it had melted, leaving
The gray grass like a pallet, closely pressed;
And dirt. The wind blew in the empty place.
The winter wind blew in an empty place—
There was that difference between the and an,
The difference between himself and no man,
No man that heard a wind in an empty place.

It was time to be himself again, to see
If the place, in spite of its witheredness, was still
Within the difference. He felt curious
Whether the water was black and lashed about
Or whether the ice still covered the lake. There was still
Snow under the trees and on the northern rocks,
The dead rocks not the green rocks, the live rocks. If,
When he looked, the water ran up the air or grew white
Against the edge of the ice, the abstraction would
Be broken and winter would be broken and done,
And being would be being himself again,
Being, becoming seeing and feeling and self,
Black water breaking into reality.

v

The law of chaos is the law of ideas,
Of improvisations and seasons of belief.

Ideas are men. The mass of meaning and
The mass of men are one. Chaos is not

The mass of meaning. It is three or four
Ideas or, say, five men or, possibly, six.

In the end, these philosophic assassins pull
Revolvers and shoot each other. One remains.

The mass of meaning becomes composed again.
He that remains plays on an instrument

A good agreement between himself and night,
A chord between the mass of men and himself,

Far, far beyond the putative canzones
Of love and summer. The assassin sings

181

In chaos and his song is a consolation.
It is the music of the mass of meaning.

And yet it is a singular romance,
This warmth in the blood-world for the pure idea,

This inability to find a sound,
That clings to the mind like that right sound, that song

Of the assassin that remains and sings
In the high imagination, triumphantly.

VI

Of systematic thinking . . . Ercole,
O, skin and spine and hair of you, Ercole,
Of what do you lie thinking in your cavern?
To think it is to think the way to death . . .

That other one wanted to think his way to life,
Sure that the ultimate poem was the mind,
Or of the mind, or of the mind in these
Elysia, these days, half earth, half mind;
Half sun, half thinking of the sun; half sky,
Half desire for indifference about the sky.

He, that one, wanted to think his way to life,
To be happy because people were thinking to be.
They had to think it to be. He wanted that,
To face the weather and be unable to tell
How much of it was light and how much thought,
In these Elysia, these origins,
This single place in which we are and stay,
Except for the images we make of it,
And for it, and by which we think the way,
And, being unhappy, talk of happiness

And, talking of happiness, know that it means
That the mind is the end and must be satisfied.

It cannot be half earth, half mind; half sun,
Half thinking; until the mind has been satisfied,
Until, for him, his mind is satisfied.
Time troubles to produce the redeeming thought.
Sometimes at sleepy mid-days it succeeds,
Too vaguely that it be written in character.

VII

To have satisfied the mind and turn to see,
(That being as much belief as we may have,)
And turn to look and say there is no more
Than this, in this alone I may believe,
Whatever it may be; then one's belief
Resists each past apocalypse, rejects
Ceylon, wants nothing from the sea, *la belle*
Aux crinolines, smears out mad mountains.

What

One believes is what matters. Ecstatic identities
Between one's self and the weather and the things
Of the weather are the belief in one's element,
The casual reunions, the long-pondered
Surrenders, the repeated sayings that
There is nothing more and that it is enough
To believe in the weather and in the things and men
Of the weather and in one's self, as part of that
And nothing more. So that if one went to the moon,
Or anywhere beyond, to a different element,
One would be drowned in the air of difference,
Incapable of belief, in the difference.
And then returning from the moon, if one breathed
The cold evening, without any scent or the shade

183

Of any woman, watched the thinnest light
And the most distant, single color, about to change,
And naked of any illusion, in poverty,
In the exactest poverty, if then
One breathed the cold evening, the deepest inhalation
Would come from that return to the subtle centre.

VIII

We live in a camp . . . Stanzas of final peace
Lie in the heart's residuum . . . Amen.
But would it be amen, in choirs, if once
In total war we died and after death
Returned, unable to die again, fated
To endure thereafter every mortal wound,
Beyond a second death, as evil's end?

It is only that we are able to die, to escape
The wounds. Yet to lie buried in evil earth,
If evil never ends, is to return
To evil after death, unable to die
Again and fated to endure beyond
Any mortal end. The chants of final peace
Lie in the heart's residuum.

                          How can
We chant if we live in evil and afterward
Lie harshly buried there?

                          If earth dissolves
Its evil after death, it dissolves it while
We live. Thence come the final chants, the chants
Of the brooder seeking the acutest end
Of speech: to pierce the heart's residuum
And there to find music for a single line,

184

Equal to memory, one line in which
The vital music formulates the words.

Behold the men in helmets borne on steel,
Discolored, how they are going to defeat.

Of Bright & Blue Birds
& the Gala Sun

Some things, niño, some things are like this,
That instantly and in themselves they are gay
And you and I are such things, O most miserable . . .

For a moment they are gay and are a part
Of an element, the exactest element for us,
In which we pronounce joy like a word of our own.

It is there, being imperfect, and with these things
And erudite in happiness, with nothing learned,
That we are joyously ourselves and we think

Without the labor of thought, in that element,
And we feel, in a way apart, for a moment, as if
There was a bright *scienza* outside of ourselves,

A gaiety that is being, not merely knowing,
The will to be and to be total in belief,
Provoking a laughter, an agreement, by surprise.

Mrs. Alfred Uruguay

So what said the others and the sun went down
And, in the brown blues of evening, the lady said,
In the donkey's ear, "I fear that elegance
Must struggle like the rest." She climbed until
The moonlight in her lap, mewing her velvet,
And her dress were one and she said, "I have said no
To everything, in order to get at myself.
I have wiped away moonlight like mud. Your innocent ear
And I, if I rode naked, are what remain."

The moonlight crumbled to degenerate forms,
While she approached the real, upon her mountain,
With lofty darkness. The donkey was there to ride,
To hold by the ear, even though it wished for a bell,
Wished faithfully for a falsifying bell.
Neither the moonlight could change it. And for her,
To be, regardless of velvet, could never be more
Than to be, she could never differently be,
Her no and no made yes impossible.

Who was it passed her there on a horse all will,
What figure of capable imagination?
Whose horse clattered on the road on which she rose,
As it descended, blind to her velvet and
The moonlight? Was it a rider intent on the sun,
A youth, a lover with phosphorescent hair,
Dressed poorly, arrogant of his streaming forces,
Lost in an integration of the martyrs' bones,
Rushing from what was real; and capable?

The villages slept as the capable man went down,
Time swished on the village clocks and dreams were alive,

The enormous gongs gave edges to their sounds,
As the rider, no chevalere and poorly dressed,
Impatient of the bells and midnight forms,
Rode over the picket rocks, rode down the road,
And, capable, created in his mind,
Eventual victor, out of the martyrs' bones,
The ultimate elegance: the imagined land.

Asides on the Oboe

The prologues are over. It is a question, now,
Of final belief. So, say that final belief
Must be in a fiction. It is time to choose.

I

That obsolete fiction of the wide river in
An empty land; the gods that Boucher killed;
And the metal heroes that time granulates—
The philosophers' man alone still walks in dew,
Still by the sea-side mutters milky lines
Concerning an immaculate imagery.
If you say on the hautboy man is not enough,
Can never stand as god, is ever wrong
In the end, however naked, tall, there is still
The impossible possible philosophers' man,
The man who has had the time to think enough,
The central man, the human globe, responsive
As a mirror with a voice, the man of glass,
Who in a million diamonds sums us up.

II

He is the transparence of the place in which
He is and in his poems we find peace.

He sets this peddler's pie and cries in summer,
The glass man, cold and numbered, dewily cries,
"Thou art not August unless I make thee so."
Clandestine steps upon imagined stairs
Climb through the night, because his cuckoos call.

III

One year, death and war prevented the jasmine scent
And the jasmine islands were bloody martyrdoms.
How was it then with the central man? Did we
Find peace? We found the sum of men. We found,
If we found the central evil, the central good.
We buried the fallen without jasmine crowns.
There was nothing he did not suffer, no; nor we.

It was not as if the jasmine ever returned.
But we and the diamond globe at last were one.
We had always been partly one. It was as we came
To see him, that we were wholly one, as we heard
Him chanting for those buried in their blood,
In the jasmine haunted forests, that we knew
The glass man, without external reference.

Poem with Rhythms

The hand between the candle and the wall
Grows large on the wall.

The mind between this light or that and space,
(This man in a room with an image of the world,
That woman waiting for the man she loves,)
Grows large against space:

There the man sees the image clearly at last.
There the woman receives her lover into her heart
And weeps on his breast, though he never comes.

It must be that the hand
Has a will to grow larger on the wall,
To grow larger and heavier and stronger than
The wall; and that the mind
Turns to its own figurations and declares,
"This image, this love, I compose myself
Of these. In these, I come forth outwardly.
In these, I wear a vital cleanliness,
Not as in air, bright-blue-resembling air,
But as in the powerful mirror of my wish and will."

The Well Dressed Man with a Beard

After the final no there comes a yes
And on that yes the future world depends.
No was the night. Yes is this present sun.
If the rejected things, the things denied,
Slid over the western cataract, yet one,
One only, one thing that was firm, even
No greater than a cricket's horn, no more
Than a thought to be rehearsed all day, a speech
Of the self that must sustain itself on speech,
One thing remaining, infallible, would be
Enough. Ah! douce campagna of that thing!
Ah! douce campagna, honey in the heart,
Green in the body, out of a petty phrase,
Out of a thing believed, a thing affirmed:
The form on the pillow humming while one sleeps,
The aureole above the humming house . . .

It can never be satisfied, the mind, never.

Montrachet-le-Jardin

What more is there to love than I have loved?
And if there be nothing more, O bright, O bright,
The chick, the chidder-barn and grassy chives

And great moon, cricket-impresario,
And, hoy, the impopulous purple-plated past,
Hoy, hoy, the blue bulls kneeling down to rest.

Chome! clicks the clock, if there be nothing more.
But if, but if there be something more to love,
Something in now a senseless syllable,

A shadow in the mind, a flourisher
Of sounds resembling sounds, efflorisant,
Approaching the feelings or come down from them,

These other shadows, not in the mind, players
Of aphonies, tuned in from zero and
Beyond, futura's fuddle-fiddling lumps,

But if there be something more to love, amen,
Amen to the feelings about familiar things,
The blessed regal dropped in daggers' dew,

Amen to thought, our singular skeleton,
Salt-flicker, amen to our accustomed cell,
The moonlight in the cell, words on the wall.

To-night, night's undeciphered murmuring
Comes close to the prisoner's ear, becomes a throat
The hand can touch, neither green bronze nor marble,

The hero's throat in which the words are spoken,
From which the chant comes close upon the ear,
Out of the hero's being, the deliverer

Delivering the prisoner by his words,
So that the skeleton in the moonlight sings,
Sings of an heroic world beyond the cell,

No, not believing, but to make the cell
A hero's world in which he is the hero.
Man must become the hero of his world.

The salty skeleton must dance because
He must, in the aroma of summer nights,
Licentious violet and lascive rose,

Midsummer love and softest silences,
Weather of night creatures, whistling all day, too,
And echoing rhetorics more than our own.

He hears the earliest poems of the world
In which man is the hero. He hears the words,
Before the speaker's youngest breath is taken!

Fear never the brute clouds nor winter-stop
And let the water-belly of ocean roar
Nor feel the x malisons of other men,

Since in the hero-land to which we go,
A little nearer by each multitude,
To which we come as into bezeled plain,

The poison in the blood will have been purged,
An inner miracle and sun-sacrament,
One of the major miracles, that fall

As apples fall, without astronomy,
One of the sacraments between two breaths,
Magical only for the change they make.

The skeleton said it is a question of
The naked man, the naked man as last
And tallest hero and plus gaudiest vir.

Consider how the speechless, invisible gods
Ruled us before, from over Asia, by
Our merest apprehension of their will.

There must be mercy in Asia and divine
Shadows of scholars bent upon their books,
Divine orations from lean sacristans

Of the good, speaking of good in the voice of men.
All men can speak of it in the voice of gods.
But to speak simply of good is like to love,

To equate the root-man and the super-man,
The root-man swarming, tortured by his mass,
The super-man friseured, possessing and possessed.

A little while of Terra Paradise
I dreamed, of autumn rivers, silvas green,
Of sanctimonious mountains high in snow,

But in that dream a heavy difference
Kept waking and a mournful sense sought out,
In vain, life's season or death's element.

Bastard chateaux and smoky demoiselles,
No more. I can build towers of my own,
There to behold, there to proclaim, the grace

And free requiting of responsive fact,
To project the naked man in a state of fact,
As acutest virtue and ascetic trove.

Item: The cocks crow and the birds cry and
The sun expands, like a repetition on
One string, an absolute, not varying

Toward an inaccessible, pure sound.
Item: The wind is never rounding O
And, imageless, it is itself the most,

Mouthing its constant smatter throughout space.
Item: The green fish pensive in green reeds
Is an absolute. Item: The cataracts

As facts fall like rejuvenating rain,
Fall down through nakedness to nakedness,
To the auroral creature musing in the mind.

Item: Breathe, breathe upon the centre of
The breath life's latest, thousand senses.
But let this one sense be the single main.

And yet what good were yesterday's devotions?
I affirm and then at midnight the great cat
Leaps quickly from the fireside and is gone.

Metamorphosis

Yillow, yillow, yillow,
Old worm, my pretty quirk,
How the wind spells out
Sep - tem - ber. . . .

Summer is in bones.
Cock-robin's at Caracas.
Make o, make o, make o,
Oto - otu - bre.

And the rude leaves fall.
The rain falls. The sky
Falls and lies with the worms.
The street lamps

Are those that have been hanged,
Dangling in an illogical
To and to and fro
Fro Niz - nil - imbo.

Phosphor Reading by His Own Light

It is difficult to read. The page is dark.
Yet he knows what it is that he expects.

The page is blank or a frame without a glass
Or a glass that is empty when he looks.

The greenness of night lies on the page and goes
Down deeply in the empty glass . . .

Look, realist, not knowing what you expect.
The green falls on you as you look,

Falls on and makes and gives, even a speech.
And you think that that is what you expect,

That elemental parent, the green night,
Teaching a fusky alphabet.

Jumbo

The trees were plucked like iron bars
And jumbo, the loud general-large
Singsonged and singsonged, wildly free.

Who was the musician, fatly soft
And wildly free, whose clawing thumb
Clawed on the ear these consonants?

Who the transformer, himself transformed,
Whose single being, single form
Were their resemblances to ours?

The companion in nothingness,
Loud, general, large, fat, soft
And wild and free, the secondary man,

Cloud-clown, blue painter, sun as horn,
Hill-scholar, man that never is,
The bad-bespoken lacker,

Ancestor of Narcissus, prince
Of the secondary men. There are no rocks
And stones, only this imager.

Poem Written at Morning

A sunny day's complete Poussiniana
Divide it from itself. It is this or that
And it is not.
               By metaphor you paint
A thing. Thus, the pineapple was a leather fruit,
A fruit for pewter, thorned and palmed and blue,
To be served by men of ice.
                      The senses paint
By metaphor. The juice was fragranter
Than wettest cinnamon. It was cribled pears
Dripping a morning sap.
                   The truth must be
That you do not see, you experience, you feel,
That the buxom eye brings merely its element
To the total thing, a shapeless giant forced
Upward.
          Green were the curls upon that head.

Oak Leaves Are Hands

In Hydaspia, by Howzen,
Lived a lady, Lady Lowzen,
For whom what is was other things.

Flora she was once. She was florid
A bachelor of feen masquerie,
Evasive and metamorphorid.

197

Mac Mort she had been, ago,
Twelve-legged in her ancestral hells,
Weaving and weaving many arms.

Even now, the centre of something else,
Merely by putting hand to brow,
Brooding on centuries like shells.

As the acorn broods on former oaks
In memorials of Northern sound,
Skims the real for its unreal,

So she in Hydaspia created
Out of the movement of few words,
Flora Lowzen invigorated

Archaic and future happenings,
In glittering seven-colored changes,
By Howzen, the chromatic Lowzen.

Examination of the Hero
in a Time of War

I

Force is my lot and not pink-clustered
Roma ni Avignon ni Leyden,
And cold, my element. Death is my
Master and, without light, I dwell. There
The snow hangs heavily on the rocks, brought
By a wind that seeks out shelter from snow. Thus

Each man spoke in winter. Yet each man spoke of
The brightness of arms, said Roma wasted
In its own dirt, said Avignon was
Peace in a time of peace, said Leyden
Was always the other mind. The brightness
Of arms, the will opposed to cold, fate
In its cavern, wings subtler than any mercy,
These were the psalter of their sybils.

II

The Got whome we serve is able to deliver
Us. Good chemistry, good common man, what
Of that angelic sword? Creature of
Ten times ten times dynamite, convulsive
Angel, convulsive shatterer, gun,
Click, click, the Got whom we serve is able,
Still, still to deliver us, still magic,
Still moving yet motionless in smoke, still
One with us, in the heaved-up noise, still
Captain, the man of skill, the expert
Leader, the creator of bursting color
And rainbow sortilege, the savage weapon
Against enemies, against the prester,
Presto, whose whispers prickle the spirit.

III

They are sick of each old romance, returning,
Of each old revolving dance, the music
Like a euphony in a museum
Of euphonies, a skin from Nubia,
A helio-horn. How strange the hero
To this accurate, exacting eye. Sight
Hangs heaven with flash drapery. Sight
Is a museum of things seen. Sight,

In war, observes each man profoundly.
Yes. But these sudden sublimations
Are to combat what his exaltations
Are to the unaccountable prophet or
What any fury to its noble centre.

IV

To grasp the hero, the eccentric
On a horse, in a plane, at the piano—
At the piano, scales, arpeggios
And chords, the morning exercises,
The afternoon's reading, the night's reflection,
That's how to produce a virtuoso.
The drill of a submarine. The voyage
Beyond the oyster-beds, indigo
Shadow, up the great sea and downward
And darkly beside the vulcanic
Sea-tower, sea-pinnacles, sea-mountain.
The signal . . . The sea-tower, shaken,
Sways slightly and the pinnacles frisson.
The mountain collapses. Chopiniana.

V

The common man is the common hero.
The common hero is the hero.
Imprimatur. But then there's common fortune,
Induced by what you will: the entrails
Of a cat, twelve dollars for the devil,
A kneeling woman, a moon's farewell;
And common fortune, induced by nothing,
Unwished for, chance, the merest riding
Of the wind, rain in a dry September,
The improvisations of the cuckoos
In a clock-shop. . . . Soldier, think, in the darkness,

Repeating your appointed paces
Between two neatly measured stations,
Of less neatly measured common-places.

VI

Unless we believe in the hero, what is there
To believe? Incisive what, the fellow
Of what good. Devise. Make him of mud,
For every day. In a civiler manner,
Devise, devise, and make him of winter's
Iciest core, a north star, central
In our oblivion, of summer's
Imagination, the golden rescue:
The bread and wine of the mind, permitted
In an ascetic room, its table
Red as a red table-cloth, its windows
West Indian, the extremest power
Living and being about us and being
Ours, like a familiar companion.

VII

Gazette Guerrière. A man might happen
To prefer *L'Observateur de la Paix*, since
The hero of the *Gazette* and the hero
Of *L'Observateur*, the classic hero
And the bourgeois, are different, much.
The classic changed. There have been many.
And there are many bourgeois heroes.
There are more heroes than marbles of them.
The marbles are pinchings of an idea,
Yet there is that idea behind the marbles,
The idea of things for public gardens,
Of men suited to public ferns . . . The hero
Glides to his meeting like a lover
Mumbling a secret, passionate message.

The hero is not a person. The marbles
Of Xenophon, his epitaphs, should
Exhibit Xenophon, what he was, since
Neither his head nor horse nor knife nor
Legend were part of what he was, forms
Of a still-life, symbols, brown things to think of
In brown books. The marbles of what he was stand
Like a white abstraction only, a feeling
In a feeling mass, a blank emotion,
An anti-pathos, until we call it
Xenophon, its implement and actor.
Obscure Satanas, make a model
Of this element, this force. Transfer it
Into a barbarism as its image.

IX

If the hero is not a person, the emblem
Of him, even if Xenophon, seems
To stand taller than a person stands, has
A wider brow, large and less human
Eyes and bruted ears: the man-like body
Of a primitive. He walks with a defter
And lither stride. His arms are heavy
And his breast is greatness. All his speeches
Are prodigies in longer phrases.
His thoughts begotten at clear sources,
Apparently in air, fall from him
Like chantering from an abundant
Poet, as if he thought gladly, being
Compelled thereto by an innate music.

X

And if the phenomenon, magnified, is
Further magnified, sua voluntate,

Beyond his circumstance, projected
High, low, far, wide, against the distance,
In parades like several equipages,
Painted by mad-men, seen as magic,
Leafed out in adjectives as private
And peculiar and appropriate glory,
Even enthroned on rainbows in the sight
Of the fishes of the sea, the colored
Birds and people of this too voluminous
Air-earth—Can we live on dry descriptions,
Feel everything starving except the belly
And nourish ourselves on crumbs of whimsy?

XI

But a profane parade, the basso
Preludes a-rub, a-rub-rub, for him that
Led the emperor astray, the tom trumpets
Curling round the steeple and the people,
The elephants of sound, the tigers
In trombones roaring for the children,
Young boys resembling pastry, hip-hip,
Young men as vegetables, hip-hip,
Home and the fields give praise, hurrah, hip,
Hip, hip, hurrah. Eternal morning . . .
Flesh on the bones. The skeleton throwing
His crust away eats of this meat, drinks
Of this tabernacle, this communion,
Sleeps in the sun no thing recalling.

XII

It is not an image. It is a feeling.
There is no image of the hero.
There is a feeling as definition.
How could there be an image, an outline,

203

A design, a marble soiled by pigeons?
The hero is a feeling, a man seen
As if the eye was an emotion,
As if in seeing we saw our feeling
In the object seen and saved that mystic
Against the sight, the penetrating,
Pure eye. Instead of allegory,
We have and are the man, capable
Of his brave quickenings, the human
Accelerations that seem inhuman.

XIII

These letters of him for the little,
The imaginative, ghosts that dally
With life's salt upon their lips and savor
The taste of it, secrete within them
Too many references. The hero
Acts in reality, adds nothing
To what he does. He is the heroic
Actor and act but not divided.
It is a part of his conception,
That he be not conceived, being real.
Say that the hero is his nation,
In him made one, and in that saying
Destroy all references. This actor
Is anonymous and cannot help it.

XIV

A thousand crystals' chiming voices,
Like the shiddow-shaddow of lights revolving
To momentary ones, are blended,
In hymns, through iridescent changes,
Of the apprehending of the hero.
These hymns are like a stubborn brightness
Approaching in the dark approaches

Of time and place, becoming certain,
The organic centre of responses,
Naked of hindrance, a thousand crystals.
To meditate the highest man, not
The highest supposed in him and over,
Creates, in the blissfuller perceptions,
What unisons create in music.

XV

The highest man with nothing higher
Than himself, his self, the self that embraces
The self of the hero, the solar single,
Man-sun, man-moon, man-earth, man-ocean,
Makes poems on the syllable *fa* or
Jumps from the clouds or, from his window,
Sees the petty gildings on February . . .
The man-sun being hero rejects that
False empire . . . These are the works and pastimes
Of the highest self: he studies the paper
On the wall, the lemons on the table.
This is his day. With nothing lost, he
Arrives at the man-man as he wanted.
This is his night and meditation.

XVI

Each false thing ends. The bouquet of summer
Turns blue and on its empty table
It is stale and the water is discolored.
True autumn stands then in the doorway.
After the hero, the familiar
Man makes the hero artificial.
But was the summer false? The hero?
How did we come to think that autumn
Was the veritable season, that familiar

Man was the veritable man? So
Summer, jangling the savagest diamonds and
Dressed in its azure-doubled crimsons,
May truly bear its heroic fortunes
For the large, the solitary figure.

[Prose statement on the poetry of war]

The immense poetry of war and the poetry of a work of the imagination are two different things. In the presence of the violent reality of war, consciousness takes the place of the imagination. And consciousness of an immense war is a consciousness of fact. If that is true, it follows that the poetry of war as a consciousness of the victories and defeats of nations, is a consciousness of fact, but of heroic fact, of fact on such a scale that the mere consciousness of it affects the scale of one's thinking and constitutes a participating in the heroic.

It has been easy to say in recent times that everything tends to become real, or, rather, that everything moves in the direction of reality, that is to say, in the direction of fact. We leave fact and come back to it, come back to what we wanted fact to be, not to what it was, not to what it has too often remained. The poetry of a work of the imagination constantly illustrates the fundamental and endless struggle with fact. It goes on everywhere, even in the periods that we call peace. But in war, the desire to move in the direction of fact as we want it to be and to move quickly is overwhelming.

Nothing will ever appease this desire except a consciousness of fact as everyone is at least satisfied to have it be.

—W. S.

Notes Toward a Supreme Fiction

TO HENRY CHURCH

And for what, except for you, do I feel love?
Do I press the extremest book of the wisest man
Close to me, hidden in me day and night?
In the uncertain light of single, certain truth,
Equal in living changingness to the light
In which I meet you, in which we sit at rest,
For a moment in the central of our being,
The vivid transparence that you bring is peace.

It Must Be Abstract

I

Begin, ephebe, by perceiving the idea
Of this invention, this invented world,
The inconceivable idea of the sun.

You must become an ignorant man again
And see the sun again with an ignorant eye
And see it clearly in the idea of it.

Never suppose an inventing mind as source
Of this idea nor for that mind compose
A voluminous master folded in his fire.

How clean the sun when seen in its idea,
Washed in the remotest cleanliness of a heaven
That has expelled us and our images . . .

The death of one god is the death of all.
Let purple Phoebus lie in umber harvest,
Let Phoebus slumber and die in autumn umber,

Phoebus is dead, ephebe. But Phoebus was
A name for something that never could be named.
There was a project for the sun and is.

There is a project for the sun. The sun
Must bear no name, gold flourisher, but be
In the difficulty of what it is to be.

II

It is the celestial ennui of apartments
That sends us back to the first idea, the quick
Of this invention; and yet so poisonous

Are the ravishments of truth, so fatal to
The truth itself, the first idea becomes
The hermit in a poet's metaphors,

Who comes and goes and comes and goes all day.
May there be an ennui of the first idea?
What else, prodigious scholar, should there be?

The monastic man is an artist. The philosopher
Appoints man's place in music, say, today.
But the priest desires. The philosopher desires.

And not to have is the beginning of desire.
To have what is not is its ancient cycle.
It is desire at the end of winter, when

It observes the effortless weather turning blue
And sees the myosotis on its bush.
Being virile, it hears the calendar hymn.

It knows that what it has is what is not
And throws it away like a thing of another time,
As morning throws off stale moonlight and shabby sleep.

III

The poem refreshes life so that we share,
For a moment, the first idea . . . It satisfies
Belief in an immaculate beginning

And sends us, winged by an unconscious will,
To an immaculate end. We move between these points:
From that ever-early candor to its late plural

And the candor of them is the strong exhilaration
Of what we feel from what we think, of thought
Beating in the heart, as if blood newly came,

An elixir, an excitation, a pure power.
The poem, through candor, brings back a power again
That gives a candid kind to everything.

We say: At night an Arabian in my room,
With his damned hoobla-hoobla-hoobla-how,
Inscribes a primitive astronomy

Across the unscrawled fores the future casts
And throws his stars around the floor. By day
The wood-dove used to chant his hoobla-hoo

And still the grossest iridescence of ocean
Howls hoo and rises and howls hoo and falls.
Life's nonsense pierces us with strange relation.

IV

The first idea was not our own. Adam
In Eden was the father of Descartes
And Eve made air the mirror of herself,

Of her sons and of her daughters. They found themselves
In heaven as in a glass; a second earth;
And in the earth itself they found a green—

The inhabitants of a very varnished green.
But the first idea was not to shape the clouds
In imitation. The clouds preceded us

There was a muddy centre before we breathed.
There was a myth before the myth began,
Venerable and articulate and complete.

From this the poem springs: that we live in a place
That is not our own and, much more, not ourselves
And hard it is in spite of blazoned days.

We are the mimics. Clouds are pedagogues.
The air is not a mirror but bare board,
Coulisse bright-dark, tragic chiaroscuro

And comic color of the rose, in which
Abysmal instruments make sounds like pips
Of the sweeping meanings that we add to them.

V

The lion roars at the enraging desert,
Reddens the sand with his red-colored noise,
Defies red emptiness to evolve his match,

Master by foot and jaws and by the mane,
Most supple challenger. The elephant
Breaches the darkness of Ceylon with blares,

The glitter-goes on surfaces of tanks,
Shattering velvetest far-away. The bear,
The ponderous cinnamon, snarls in his mountain

At summer thunder and sleeps through winter snow.
But you, ephebe, look from your attic window,
Your mansard with a rented piano. You lie

In silence upon your bed. You clutch the corner
Of the pillow in your hand. You writhe and press
A bitter utterance from your writhing, dumb,

Yet voluble dumb violence. You look
Across the roofs as sigil and as ward
And in your centre mark them and are cowed . . .

These are the heroic children whom time breeds
Against the first idea—to lash the lion,
Caparison elephants, teach bears to juggle.

VI

Not to be realized because not to
Be seen, not to be loved nor hated because
Not to be realized. Weather by Franz Hals,

Brushed up by brushy winds in brushy clouds,
Wetted by blue, colder for white. Not to
Be spoken to, without a roof, without

First fruits, without the virginal of birds,
The dark-blown ceinture loosened, not relinquished.
Gay is, gay was, the gay forsythia

And yellow, yellow thins the Northern blue.
Without a name and nothing to be desired,
If only imagined but imagined well.

My house has changed a little in the sun.
The fragrance of the magnolias comes close,
False flick, false form, but falseness close to kin.

It must be visible or invisible,
Invisible or visible or both:
A seeing and unseeing in the eye.

The weather and the giant of the weather,
Say the weather, the mere weather, the mere air:
An abstraction blooded, as a man by thought.

VII

It feels good as it is without the giant,
A thinker of the first idea. Perhaps
The truth depends on a walk around a lake,

A composing as the body tires, a stop
To see hepatica, a stop to watch
A definition growing certain and

A wait within that certainty, a rest
In the swags of pine-trees bordering the lake.
Perhaps there are times of inherent excellence,

As when the cock crows on the left and all
Is well, incalculable balances,
At which a kind of Swiss perfection comes

And a familiar music of the machine
Sets up its Schwärmerei, not balances
That we achieve but balances that happen,

As a man and woman meet and love forthwith.
Perhaps there are moments of awakening,
Extreme, fortuitous, personal, in which

We more than awaken, sit on the edge of sleep,
As on an elevation, and behold
The academies like structures in a mist.

VIII

Can we compose a castle-fortress-home,
Even with the help of Viollet-le-Duc,
And set the MacCullough there as major man?

The first idea is an imagined thing.
The pensive giant prone in violet space
May be the MacCullough, an expedient,

Logos and logic, crystal hypothesis,
Incipit and a form to speak the word
And every latent double in the word,

Beau linguist. But the MacCullough is MacCullough.
It does not follow that major man is man.
If MacCullough himself lay lounging by the sea,

Drowned in its washes, reading in the sound,
About the thinker of the first idea,
He might take habit, whether from wave or phrase,

Or power of the wave, or deepened speech,
Or a leaner being, moving in on him,
Of greater aptitude and apprehension,

As if the waves at last were never broken,
As if the language suddenly, with ease,
Said things it had laboriously spoken.

IX

The romantic intoning, the declaimed clairvoyance
Are parts of apotheosis, appropriate
And of its nature, the idiom thereof.

They differ from reason's click-clack, its applied
Enflashings. But apotheosis is not
The origin of the major man. He comes,

Compact in invincible foils, from reason,
Lighted at midnight by the studious eye,
Swaddled in revery, the object of

The hum of thoughts evaded in the mind,
Hidden from other thoughts, he that reposes
On a breast forever precious for that touch,

For whom the good of April falls tenderly,
Falls down, the cock-birds calling at the time.
My dame, sing for this person accurate songs.

He is and may be but oh! he is, he is,
This foundling of the infected past, so bright,
So moving in the manner of his hand.

Yet look not at his colored eyes. Give him
No names. Dismiss him from your images.
The hot of him is purest in the heart.

The major abstraction is the idea of man
And major man is its exponent, abler
In the abstract than in his singular,

More fecund as principle than particle,
Happy fecundity, flor-abundant force,
In being more than an exception, part,

Though an heroic part, of the commonal.
The major abstraction is the commonal,
The inanimate, difficult visage. Who is it?

What rabbi, grown furious with human wish,
What chieftain, walking by himself, crying
Most miserable, most victorious,

Does not see these separate figures one by one,
And yet see only one, in his old coat,
His slouching pantaloons, beyond the town,

Looking for what was, where it used to be?
Cloudless the morning. It is he. The man
In that old coat, those sagging pantaloons,

It is of him, ephebe, to make, to confect
The final elegance, not to console
Nor sanctify, but plainly to propound.

It Must Change

I

The old seraph, parcel-gilded, among violets
Inhaled the appointed odor, while the doves
Rose up like phantoms from chronologies.

The Italian girls wore jonquils in their hair
And these the seraph saw, had seen long since,
In the bandeaux of the mothers, would see again.

The bees came booming as if they had never gone,
As if hyacinths had never gone. We say
This changes and that changes. Thus the constant

Violets, doves, girls, bees and hyacinths
Are inconstant objects of inconstant cause
In a universe of inconstancy. This means

Night-blue is an inconstant thing. The seraph
Is satyr in Saturn, according to his thoughts.
It means the distaste we feel for this withered scene

Is that it has not changed enough. It remains,
It is a repetition. The bees come booming
As if—The pigeons clatter in the air.

An erotic perfume, half of the body, half
Of an obvious acid is sure what it intends
And the booming is blunt, not broken in subtleties.

II

The President ordains the bee to be
Immortal. The President ordains. But does
The body lift its heavy wing, take up,

Again, an inexhaustible being, rise
Over the loftiest antagonist
To drone the green phrases of its juvenal?

Why should the bee recapture a lost blague,
Find a deep echo in a horn and buzz
The bottomless trophy, new hornsman after old?

The President has apples on the table
And barefoot servants round him, who adjust
The curtains to a metaphysical t

And the banners of the nation flutter, burst
On the flag-poles in a red-blue dazzle, whack
At the halyards. Why, then, when in golden fury

Spring vanishes the scraps of winter, why
Should there be a question of returning or
Of death in memory's dream? Is spring a sleep?

This warmth is for lovers at last accomplishing
Their love, this beginning, not resuming, this
Booming and booming of the new-come bee.

III

The great statue of the General Du Puy
Rested immobile, though neighboring catafalques
Bore off the residents of its noble Place.

The right, uplifted foreleg of the horse
Suggested that, at the final funeral,
The music halted and the horse stood still.

On Sundays, lawyers in their promenades
Approached this strongly-heightened effigy
To study the past, and doctors, having bathed

Themselves with care, sought out the nerveless frame
Of a suspension, a permanence, so rigid
That it made the General a bit absurd,

Changed his true flesh to an inhuman bronze.
There never had been, never could be, such
A man. The lawyers disbelieved, the doctors

Said that as keen, illustrious ornament,
As a setting for geraniums, the General,
The very Place Du Puy, in fact, belonged

Among our more vestigial states of mind.
Nothing had happened because nothing had changed.
Yet the General was rubbish in the end.

IV

Two things of opposite natures seem to depend
On one another, as a man depends
On a woman, day on night, the imagined

On the real. This is the origin of change.
Winter and spring, cold copulars, embrace
And forth the particulars of rapture come.

Music falls on the silence like a sense,
A passion that we feel, not understand.
Morning and afternoon are clasped together

And North and South are an intrinsic couple
And sun and rain a plural, like two lovers
That walk away as one in the greenest body.

In solitude the trumpets of solitude
Are not of another solitude resounding;
A little string speaks for a crowd of voices.

The partaker partakes of that which changes him.
The child that touches takes character from the thing,
The body, it touches. The captain and his men

Are one and the sailor and the sea are one.
Follow after, O my companion, my fellow, my self,
Sister and solace, brother and delight.

v

On a blue island in a sky-wide water
The wild orange trees continued to bloom and to bear,
Long after the planter's death. A few limes remained,

Where his house had fallen, three scraggy trees
     weighted
With garbled green. These were the planter's turquoise
And his orange blotches, these were his zero green,

A green baked greener in the greenest sun.
These were his beaches, his sea-myrtles in
White sand, his patter of the long sea-slushes.

There was an island beyond him on which rested,
An island to the South, on which rested like
A mountain, a pineapple pungent as Cuban summer.

And là-bas, là-bas, the cool bananas grew,
Hung heavily on the great banana tree,
Which pierces clouds and bends on half the world.

He thought often of the land from which he came,
How that whole country was a melon, pink
If seen rightly and yet a possible red.

An unaffected man in a negative light
Could not have borne his labor nor have died
Sighing that he should leave the banjo's twang.

VI

Bethou me, said sparrow, to the crackled blade, –
And you, and you, bethou me as you blow,
When in my coppice you behold me be.

Ah, ké! the bloody wren, the felon jay,
Ké-ké, the jug-throated robin pouring out,
Bethou, bethou, bethou me in my glade.

There was such idiot minstrelsy in rain,
So many clappers going without bells,
That these bethous compose a heavenly gong.

One voice repeating, one tireless chorister,
The phrases of a single phrase, ké-ké,
A single text, granite monotony,

One sole face, like a photograph of fate,
Glass-blower's destiny, bloodless episcopus,
Eye without lid, mind without any dream—

These are of minstrels lacking minstrelsy,
Of an earth in which the first leaf is the tale
Of leaves, in which the sparrow is a bird

Of stone, that never changes. Bethou him, you
And you, bethou him and bethou. It is
A sound like any other. It will end.

VII

After a lustre of the moon, we say
We have not the need of any paradise,
We have not the need of any seducing hymn.

It is true. Tonight the lilacs magnify
The easy passion, the ever-ready love
Of the lover that lies within us and we breathe

An odor evoking nothing, absolute.
We encounter in the dead middle of the night
The purple odor, the abundant bloom.

The lover sighs as for accessible bliss,
Which he can take within him on his breath,
Possess in his heart, conceal and nothing known.

For easy passion and ever-ready love
Are of our earthy birth and here and now
And where we live and everywhere we live,

As in the top-cloud of a May night-evening,
As in the courage of the ignorant man,
Who chants by book, in the heat of the scholar, who
    writes

The book, hot for another accessible bliss:
The fluctuations of certainty, the change
Of degrees of perception in the scholar's dark.

221

On her trip around the world, Nanzia Nunzio
Confronted Ozymandias. She went
Alone and like a vestal long-prepared.

I am the spouse. She took her necklace off
And laid it in the sand. As I am, I am
The spouse. She opened her stone-studded belt.

I am the spouse, divested of bright gold,
The spouse beyond emerald or amethyst,
Beyond the burning body that I bear.

I am the woman stripped more nakedly
Than nakedness, standing before an inflexible
Order, saying I am the contemplated spouse.

Speak to me that, which spoken, will array me
In its own only precious ornament.
Set on me the spirit's diamond coronal.

Clothe me entire in the final filament,
So that I tremble with such love so known
And myself am precious for your perfecting.

Then Ozymandias said the spouse, the bride
Is never naked. A fictive covering
Weaves always glistening from the heart and mind.

IX

The poem goes from the poet's gibberish to
The gibberish of the vulgate and back again.
Does it move to and fro or is it of both

At once? Is it a luminous flittering
Or the concentration of a cloudy day?
Is there a poem that never reaches words

And one that chaffers the time away?
Is the poem both peculiar and general?
There's a meditation there, in which there seems

To be an evasion, a thing not apprehended or
Not apprehended well. Does the poet
Evade us, as in a senseless element?

Evade, this hot, dependent orator,
The spokesman at our bluntest barriers,
Exponent by a form of speech, the speaker

Of a speech only a little of the tongue?
It is the gibberish of the vulgate that he seeks.
He tries by a peculiar speech to speak

The peculiar potency of the general,
To compound the imagination's Latin with
The lingua franca et jocundissima.

                    x
A bench was his catalepsy, Theatre
Of Trope. He sat in the park. The water of
The lake was full of artificial things,

Like a page of music, like an upper air,
Like a momentary color, in which swans
Were seraphs, were saints, were changing essences.

The west wind was the music, the motion, the force
To which the swans curveted, a will to change,
A will to make iris frettings on the blank.

There was a will to change, a necessitous
And present way, a presentation, a kind
Of volatile world, too constant to be denied,

The eye of a vagabond in metaphor
Thát catches our own. The casual is not
Enough. The freshness of transformation is

The freshness of a world. It is our own,
It is ourselves, the freshness of ourselves,
And that necessity and that presentation

Are rubbings of a glass in which we peer.
Of these beginnings, gay and green, propose
The suitable amours. Time will write them down.

It Must Give Pleasure

I

To sing jubilas at exact, accustomed times,
To be crested and wear the mane of a multitude
And so, as part, to exult with its great throat,

To speak of joy and to sing of it, borne on
The shoulders of joyous men, to feel the heart
That is the common, the bravest fundament,

This is a facile exercise. Jerome
Begat the tubas and the fire-wind strings,
The golden fingers picking dark-blue air:

For companies of voices moving there,
To find of sound the bleakest ancestor,
To find of light a music issuing

Whereon it falls in more than sensual mode.
But the difficultest rigor is forthwith,
On the image of what we see, to catch from that

Irrational moment its unreasoning,
As when the sun comes rising, when the sea
Clears deeply, when the moon hangs on the wall

Of heaven-haven. These are not things transformed.
Yet we are shaken by them as if they were.
We reason about them with a later reason.

II

The blue woman, linked and lacquered, at her window
Did not desire that feathery argentines
Should be cold silver, neither that frothy clouds

Should foam, be foamy waves, should move like them,
Nor that the sexual blossoms should repose
Without their fierce addictions, nor that the heat

Of summer, growing fragrant in the night,
Should strengthen her abortive dreams and take
In sleep its natural form. It was enough

For her that she remembered: the argentines
Of spring come to their places in the grape leaves
To cool their ruddy pulses; the frothy clouds

Are nothing but frothy clouds; the frothy blooms
Waste without puberty; and afterward,
When the harmonious heat of August pines

Enters the room, it drowses and is the night.
It was enough for her that she remembered.
The blue woman looked and from her window named

The corals of the dogwood, cold and clear,
Cold, coldly delineating, being real,
Clear and, except for the eye, without intrusion.

III

A lasting visage in a lasting bush,
A face of stone in an unending red,
Red-emerald, red-slitted-blue, a face of slate,

An ancient forehead hung with heavy hair,
The channel slots of rain, the red-rose-red
And weathered and the ruby-water-worn,

The vines around the throat, the shapeless lips,
The frown like serpents basking on the brow,
The spent feeling leaving nothing of itself,

Red-in-red repetitions never going
Away, a little rusty, a little rouged,
A little roughened and ruder, a crown

The eye could not escape, a red renown
Blowing itself upon the tedious ear.
An effulgence faded, dull cornelian

Too venerably used. That might have been.
It might and might have been. But as it was,
A dead shepherd brought tremendous chords from hell

And bade the sheep carouse. Or so they said.
Children in love with them brought early flowers
And scattered them about, no two alike.

<h3 style="text-align:center">IV</h3>

We reason of these things with later reason
And we make of what we see, what we see clearly
And have seen, a place dependent on ourselves.

There was a mystic marriage in Catawba,
At noon it was on the mid-day of the year
Between a great captain and the maiden Bawda.

This was their ceremonial hymn: Anon
We loved but would no marriage make. Anon
The one refused the other one to take,

Foreswore the sipping of the marriage wine.
Each must the other take not for his high,
His puissant front nor for her subtle sound,

The shoo-shoo-shoo of secret cymbals round.
Each must the other take as sign, short sign
To stop the whirlwind, balk the elements.

The great captain loved the ever-hill Catawba
And therefore married Bawda, whom he found there,
And Bawda loved the captain as she loved the sun.

They married well because the marriage-place
Was what they loved. It was neither heaven nor hell.
They were love's characters come face to face.

v

We drank Meursault, ate lobster Bombay with mango
Chutney. Then the Canon Aspirin declaimed
Of his sister, in what a sensible ecstasy

She lived in her house. She had two daughters, one
Of four, and one of seven, whom she dressed
The way a painter of pauvred color paints.

But still she painted them, appropriate to
Their poverty, a gray-blue yellowed out
With ribbon, a rigid statement of them, white,

With Sunday pearls, her widow's gayety.
She hid them under simple names. She held
Them closelier to her by rejecting dreams.

The words they spoke were voices that she heard.
She looked at them and saw them as they were
And what she felt fought off the barest phrase.

The Canon Aspirin, having said these things,
Reflected, humming an outline of a fugue
Of praise, a conjugation done by choirs.

Yet when her children slept, his sister herself
Demanded of sleep, in the excitements of silence
Only the unmuddled self of sleep, for them.

228

VI

When at long midnight the Canon came to sleep
And normal things had yawned themselves away,
The nothingness was a nakedness, a point,

Beyond which fact could not progress as fact.
Thereon the learning of the man conceived
Once more night's pale illuminations, gold

Beneath, far underneath, the surface of
His eye and audible in the mountain of
His ear, the very material of his mind.

So that he was the ascending wings he saw
And moved on them in orbits' outer stars
Descending to the children's bed, on which

They lay. Forth then with huge pathetic force
Straight to the utmost crown of night he flew.
The nothingness was a nakedness, a point

Beyond which thought could not progress as thought.
He had to choose. But it was not a choice
Between excluding things. It was not a choice

Between, but of. He chose to include the things
That in each other are included, the whole,
The complicate, the amassing harmony.

VII

He imposes orders as he thinks of them,
As the fox and snake do. It is a brave affair.
Next he builds capitols and in their corridors,

Whiter than wax, sonorous, fame as it is,
He establishes statues of reasonable men,
Who surpassed the most literate owl, the most erudite

Of elephants. But to impose is not
To discover. To discover an order as of
A season, to discover summer and know it,

To discover winter and know it well, to find,
Not to impose, not to have reasoned at all,
Out of nothing to have come on major weather,

It is possible, possible, possible. It must
Be possible. It must be that in time
The real will from its crude compoundings come,

Seeming, at first, a beast disgorged, unlike,
Warmed by a desperate milk. To find the real,
To be stripped of every fiction except one,

The fiction of an absolute—Angel,
Be silent in your luminous cloud and hear
The luminous melody of proper sound.

VIII

What am I to believe? If the angel in his cloud,
Serenely gazing at the violent abyss,
Plucks on his strings to pluck abysmal glory,

Leaps downward through evening's revelations, and
On his spredden wings, needs nothing but deep space,
Forgets the gold centre, the golden destiny,

Grows warm in the motionless motion of his flight,
Am I that imagine this angel less satisfied?
Are the wings his, the lapis-haunted air?

Is it he or is it I that experience this?
Is it I then that keep saying there is an hour
Filled with expressible bliss, in which I have

No need, am happy, forget need's golden hand,
Am satisfied without solacing majesty,
And if there is an hour there is a day,

There is a month, a year, there is a time
In which majesty is a mirror of the self:
I have not but I am and as I am, I am.

These external regions, what do we fill them with
Except reflections, the escapades of death,
Cinderella fulfilling herself beneath the roof?

IX

Whistle aloud, too weedy wren. I can
Do all that angels can. I enjoy like them,
Like men besides, like men in light secluded,

Enjoying angels. Whistle, forced bugler,
That bugles for the mate, nearby the nest,
Cock bugler, whistle and bugle and stop just short,

Red robin, stop in your preludes, practicing
Mere repetitions. These things at least comprise
An occupation, an exercise, a work,

231

A thing final in itself and, therefore, good:
One of the vast repetitions final in
Themselves and, therefore, good, the going round

And round and round, the merely going round,
Until merely going round is a final good,
The way wine comes at a table in a wood.

And we enjoy like men, the way a leaf
Above the table spins its constant spin,
So that we look at it with pleasure, look

At it spinning its eccentric measure. Perhaps,
The man-hero is not the exceptional monster,
But he that of repetition is most master.

x

Fat girl, terrestrial, my summer, my night,
How is it I find you in difference, see you there
In a moving contour, a change not quite completed?

You are familiar yet an aberration.
Civil, madam, I am, but underneath
A tree, this unprovoked sensation requires

That I should name you flatly, waste no words,
Check your evasions, hold you to yourself.
Even so when I think of you as strong or tired,

Bent over work, anxious, content, alone,
You remain the more than natural figure. You
Become the soft-footed phantom, the irrational

Distortion, however fragrant, however dear.
That's it: the more than rational distortion,
The fiction that results from feeling. Yes, that.

They will get it straight one day at the Sorbonne.
We shall return at twilight from the lecture
Pleased that the irrational is rational,

Until flicked by feeling, in a gildered street,
I call you by name, my green, my fluent mundo.
You will have stopped revolving except in crystal.

———————

Soldier, there is a war between the mind
And sky, between thought and day and night. It is
For that the poet is always in the sun,

Patches the moon together in his room
To his Virgilian cadences, up down,
Up down. It is a war that never ends.

Yet it depends on yours. The two are one.
They are a plural, a right and left, a pair,
Two parallels that meet if only in

The meeting of their shadows or that meet
In a book in a barrack, a letter from Malay.
But your war ends. And after it you return

With six meats and twelve wines or else without
To walk another room . . . Monsieur and comrade,
The soldier is poor without the poet's lines,

His petty syllabi, the sounds that stick,
Inevitably modulating, in the blood.
And war for war, each has its gallant kind.

How simply the fictive hero becomes the real;
How gladly with proper words the soldier dies,
If he must, or lives on the bread of faithful speech.

God Is Good. It Is a Beautiful Night

Look round, brown moon, brown bird, as you rise to fly,
Look round at the head and zither
On the ground.

Look round you as you start to rise, brown moon,
At the book and shoe, the rotted rose
At the door.

This was the place to which you came last night,
Flew close to, flew to without rising away.
Now, again,

In your light, the head is speaking. It reads the book.
It becomes the scholar again, seeking celestial
Rendezvous,

Picking thin music on the rustiest string,
Squeezing the reddest fragrance from the stump
Of summer.

The venerable song falls from your fiery wings.
The song of the great space of your age pierces
The fresh night.

Certain Phenomena of Sound

The cricket in the telephone is still.
A geranium withers on the window-sill.

Cat's milk is dry in the saucer. Sunday song
Comes from the beating of the locust's wings,

That do not beat by pain, but calendar,
Nor meditate the world as it goes round.

Someone has left for a ride in a balloon
Or in a bubble examines the bubble of air.

The room is emptier than nothingness.
Yet a spider spins in the left shoe under the bed—

And old John Rocket dozes on his pillow.
It is safe to sleep to a sound that time brings back.

So you're home again, Redwood Roamer, and ready
To feast . . . Slice the mango, Naaman, and dress it

With white wine, sugar and lime juice. Then bring it,
After we've drunk the Moselle, to the thickest shade

Of the garden. We must prepare to hear the Roamer's
Story . . . The sound of that slick sonata,

Finding its way from the house, makes music seem
To be a nature, a place in which itself

Is that which produces everything else, in which
The Roamer is a voice taller than the redwoods,

Engaged in the most prolific narrative,
A sound producing the things that are spoken.

III

Eulalia, I lounged on the hospital porch,
On the east, sister and nun, and opened wide
A parasol, which I had found, against
The sun. The interior of a parasol,
It is a kind of blank in which one sees.
So seeing, I beheld you walking, white,
Gold-shined by sun, perceiving as I saw
That of that light Eulalia was the name.
Then I, Semiramide, dark-syllabled,
Contrasting our two names, considered speech.
You were created of your name, the word
Is that of which you were the personage.
There is no life except in the word of it.
I write *Semiramide* and in the script
I am and have a being and play a part.
You are that white Eulalia of the name.

Dutch Graves in Bucks County

Angry men and furious machines
Swarm from the little blue of the horizon
To the great blue of the middle height.
Men scatter throughout clouds.
The wheels are too large for any noise.

And you, my semblables, in sooty residence
Tap skeleton drums inaudibly.

There are shouts and voices.
There are men shuffling on foot in air.
Men are moving and marching
And shuffling lightly, with the heavy lightness
Of those that are marching, many together.

And you, my semblables—the old flag of Holland
Flutters in tiny darkness.

There are circles of weapons in the sun.
The air attends the brightened guns,
As if sounds were forming
Out of themselves, a saying,
An expressive on-dit, a profession.

And you, my semblables, are doubly killed
To be buried in desert and deserted earth.

The flags are natures newly found.
Rifles grow sharper on the sight.
There is a rumble of autumnal marching,
From which no soft sleeve relieves us.
Fate is the present desperado.

And you, my semblables, are crusts that lie
In the shrivellings of your time and place.

There is a battering of the drums. The bugles
Cry loudly, cry out in the powerful heart.
A force gathers that will cry loudlier
Than the most metal music, loudlier,
Like an instinctive incantation.

And you, my semblables, in the total
Of remembrance share nothing of ourselves.

An end must come in a merciless triumph,
An end of evil in a profounder logic,
In a peace that is more than a refuge,
In the will of what is common to all men,
Spelled from spent living and spent dying.

And you, my semblables, in gaffer-green,
Know that the past is not part of the present.

There were other soldiers, other people,
Men came as the sun comes, early children
And late wanderers creeping under the barb of night,
Year, year and year, defeated at last and lost
In an ignorance of sleep with nothing won.

And you, my semblables, know that this time
Is not an early time that has grown late.

But these are not those rusted armies.
There are the lewdest and the lustiest,
The hullaballoo of health and have,
The much too many disinherited
In a storm of torn-up testaments.

And you, my semblables, know that your children
Are not your children, not your selves.

Who are the mossy cronies muttering,
Monsters antique and haggard with past thought?
What is this crackling of voices in the mind,
This pitter-patter of archaic freedom,
Of the thousands of freedoms except our own?

And you, my semblables, whose ecstasy
Was the glory of heaven in the wilderness—

Freedom is like a man who kills himself
Each night, an incessant butcher, whose knife
Grows sharp in blood. The armies kill themselves,
And in their blood an ancient evil dies—
The action of incorrigible tragedy.

And you, my semblables, behold in blindness
That a new glory of new men assembles.

This is the pit of torment that placid end
Should be illusion, that the mobs of birth
Avoid our stale perfections, seeking out
Their own, waiting until we go
To picnic in the ruins that we leave.

So that the stars, my semblables, chimeres,
Shine on the very living of those alive.

These violent marchers of the present,
Rumbling along the autumnal horizon,
Under the arches, over the arches, in arcs
Of a chaos composed in more than order,
March toward a generation's centre.

Time was not wasted in your subtle temples.
No: nor divergence made too steep to follow down.

The Motive for Metaphor

You like it under the trees in autumn,
Because everything is half dead.
The wind moves like a cripple among the leaves
And repeats words without meaning.

In the same way, you were happy in spring,
With the half colors of quarter-things,
The slightly brighter sky, the melting clouds,
The single bird, the obscure moon—

The obscure moon lighting an obscure world
Of things that would never be quite expressed,
Where you yourself were never quite yourself
And did not want nor have to be,

Desiring the exhilarations of changes:
The motive for metaphor, shrinking from
The weight of primary noon,
The A B C of being,

The ruddy temper, the hammer
Of red and blue, the hard sound—
Steel against intimation—the sharp flash,
The vital, arrogant, fatal, dominant X.

Chocorua to its Neighbor

I

To speak quietly at such a distance, to speak
And to be heard is to be large in space,
That, like your own, is large, hence, to be part
Of sky, of sea, large earth, large air. It is
To perceive men without reference to their form.

II

The armies are forms in number, as cities are.
The armies are cities in movement. But a war
Between cities is a gesticulation of forms,
A swarming of number over number, not
One foot approaching, one uplifted arm.

III

At the end of night last night a crystal star,
The crystal-pointed star of morning, rose
And lit the snow to a light congenial
To this prodigious shadow, who then came
In an elemental freedom, sharp and cold.

IV

The feeling of him was the feel of day,
And of a day as yet unseen, in which
To see was to be. He was the figure in
A poem for Liadoff, the self of selves:
To think of him destroyed the body's form.

V

He was a shell of dark blue glass, or ice,
Or air collected in a deep essay,
Or light embodied, or almost, a flash
On more than muscular shoulders, arms and chest,
Blue's last transparence as it turned to black,

VI

The glitter of a being, which the eye
Accepted yet which nothing understood,
A fusion of night, its blue of the pole of blue
And of the brooding mind, fixed but for a slight
Illumination of movement as he breathed.

VII

He was as tall as a tree in the middle of
The night. The substance of his body seemed
Both substance and non-substance, luminous flesh
Or shapely fire: fire from an underworld,
Of less degree than flame and lesser shine.

VIII

Upon my top he breathed the pointed dark.
He was not man yet he was nothing else.
If in the mind, he vanished, taking there
The mind's own limits, like a tragic thing
Without existence, existing everywhere.

IX

He breathed in crystal-pointed change the whole
Experience of night, as if he breathed
A consciousness from solitude, inhaled
A freedom out of silver-shaping size,
Against the whole experience of day.

X

The silver-shapeless, gold-encrusted size
Of daylight came while he sat thinking. He said,
"The moments of enlargement overlook
The enlarging of the simplest soldier's cry
In what I am, as he falls. Of what I am,

XI

The cry is part. My solitaria
Are the meditations of a central mind.
I hear the motions of the spirit and the sound
Of what is secret becomes, for me, a voice
That is my own voice speaking in my ear.

XII

There lies the misery, the coldest coil
That grips the centre, the actual bite, that life
Itself is like a poverty in the space of life,
So that the flapping of wind around me here
Is something in tatters that I cannot hold."

XIII

In spite of this, the gigantic bulk of him
Grew strong, as if doubt never touched his heart.
Of what was this the force? From what desire
And from what thinking did his radiance come?
In what new spirit had his body birth?

XIV

He was more than an external majesty,
Beyond the sleep of those that did not know,
More than a spokesman of the night to say
Now, time stands still. He came from out of sleep.
He rose because men wanted him to be.

XV

They wanted him by day to be, image,
But not the person, of their power, thought,
But not the thinker, large in their largeness, beyond
Their form, beyond their life, yet of themselves,
Excluding by his largeness their defaults.

Last night at the end of night his starry head,
Like the head of fate, looked out in darkness, part
Thereof and part desire and part the sense
Of what men are. The collective being knew
There were others like him safely under roof:

The captain squalid on his pillow, the great
Cardinal, saying the prayers of earliest day;
The stone, the categorical effigy;
And the mother, the music, the name; the scholar,
Whose green mind bulges with complicated hues:

True transfigurers fetched out of the human mountain,
True genii for the diminished, spheres,
Gigantic embryos of populations,
Blue friends in shadows, rich conspirators,
Confiders and comforters and lofty kin.

To say more than human things with human voice,
That cannot be; to say human things with more
Than human voice, that, also, cannot be;
To speak humanly from the height or from the depth
Of human things, that is acutest speech.

Now, I, Chocorua, speak of this shadow as
A human thing. It is an eminence,
But of nothing, trash of sleep that will disappear
With the special things of night, little by little,
In day's constellation, and yet remain, yet be,

Not father, but bare brother, megalfrere,
Or by whatever boorish name a man
Might call the common self, interior fons
And fond, the total man of glubbal glub,
Political tramp with an heraldic air,

Cloud-casual, metaphysical metaphor,
But resting on me, thinking in my snow,
Physical if the eye is quick enough,
So that, where he was, there is an enkindling, where
He is, the air changes and grows fresh to breathe.

The air changes, creates and re-creates, like strength,
And to breathe is a fulfilling of desire,
A clearing, a detecting, a completing,
A largeness lived and not conceived, a space
That is an instant nature, brilliantly.

Integration for integration, the great arms
Of the armies, the solid men, make big the fable.
This is their captain and philosopher,
He that is fortelleze, though he be
Hard to perceive and harder still to touch.

Last night at the end of night and in the sky,
The lesser night, the less than morning light,
Fell on him, high and cold, searching for what
Was native to him in that height, searching
The pleasure of his spirit in the cold.

How singular he was as man, how large,
If nothing more than that, for the moment, large
In my presence, the companion of presences
Greater than mine, of his demanding, head
And, of human realizings, rugged roy . . .

So-And-So Reclining on Her Couch

On her side, reclining on her elbow.
This mechanism, this apparition,
Suppose we call it Projection A.

She floats in air at the level of
The eye, completely anonymous,
Born, as she was, at twenty-one,

Without lineage or language, only
The curving of her hip, as motionless gesture,
Eyes dripping blue, so much to learn.

If just above her head there hung,
Suspended in air, the slightest crown
Of Gothic prong and practick bright,

The suspension, as in solid space,
The suspending hand withdrawn, would be
An invisible gesture. Let this be called

Projection B. To get at the thing
Without gestures is to get at it as
Idea. She floats in the contention, the flux

Between the thing as idea and
The idea as thing. She is half who made her.
This is the final Projection, C.

The arrangement contains the desire of
The artist. But one confides in what has no
Concealed creator. One walks easily

The unpainted shore, accepts the world
As anything but sculpture. Good-bye,
Mrs. Pappadopoulos, and thanks.

No Possum, No Sop, No Taters

He is not here, the old sun,
As absent as if we were asleep.

The field is frozen. The leaves are dry.
Bad is final in this light.

In this bleak air the broken stalks
Have arms without hands. They have trunks

Without legs or, for that, without heads.
They have heads in which a captive cry

Is merely the moving of a tongue.
Snow sparkles like eyesight falling to earth,

Like seeing fallen brightly away.
The leaves hop, scraping on the ground.

It is deep January. The sky is hard.
The stalks are firmly rooted in ice.

It is in this solitude, a syllable,
Out of these gawky flitterings,

Intones its single emptiness,
The savagest hollow of winter-sound.

It is here, in this bad, that we reach
The last purity of the knowledge of good.

The crow looks rusty as he rises up.
Bright is the malice in his eye . . .

One joins him there for company.
But at a distance, in another tree.

The Lack of Repose

A young man seated at his table
Holds in his hand a book you have never written
Staring at the secretions of the words as
They reveal themselves.

It is not midnight. It is mid-day,
The young man is well-disclosed, one of the gang,
Andrew Jackson Something. But this book
Is a cloud in which a voice mumbles.

It is a ghost that inhabits a cloud,
But a ghost for Andrew, not lean, catarrhal
And pallid. It is the grandfather he liked,
With an understanding compounded by death

And the associations beyond death, even if only
Time. What a thing it is to believe that
One understands, in the intense disclosures
Of a parent in the French sense.

And not yet to have written a book in which
One is already a grandfather and to have put there
A few sounds of meaning, a momentary end
To the complication, is good, is a good.

Somnambulisma

On an old shore, the vulgar ocean rolls
Noiselessly, noiselessly, resembling a thin bird,
That thinks of settling, yet never settles, on a nest.

The wings keep spreading and yet are never wings.
The claws keep scratching on the shale, the shallow shale,
The sounding shallow, until by water washed away.

The generations of the bird are all
By water washed away. They follow after.
They follow, follow, follow, in water washed away.

Without this bird that never settles, without
Its generations that follow in their universe,
The ocean, falling and falling on the hollow shore,

Would be a geography of the dead: not of that land
To which they may have gone, but of the place in which
They lived, in which they lacked a pervasive being,

In which no scholar, separately dwelling,
Poured forth the fine fins, the gawky beaks, the personalia,
Which, as a man feeling everything, were his.

The Creations of Sound

If the poetry of X was music,
So that it came to him of its own,
Without understanding, out of the wall

Or in the ceiling, in sounds not chosen,
Or chosen quickly, in a freedom
That was their element, we should not know

That X is an obstruction, a man
Too exactly himself, and that there are words
Better without an author, without a poet,

Or having a separate author, a different poet,
An accretion from ourselves, intelligent
Beyond intelligence, an artificial man

At a distance, a secondary expositor,
A being of sound, whom one does not approach
Through any exaggeration. From him, we collect.

Tell X that speech is not dirty silence
Clarified. It is silence made still dirtier.
It is more than an imitation for the ear.

He lacks this venerable complication.
His poems are not of the second part of life.
They do not make the visible a little hard

To see nor, reverberating, eke out the mind
On peculiar horns, themselves eked out
By the spontaneous particulars of sound.

We do not say ourselves like that in poems.
We say ourselves in syllables that rise
From the floor, rising in speech we do not speak.

Esthétique du Mal

I

He was at Naples writing letters home
And, between his letters, reading paragraphs
On the sublime. Vesuvius had groaned
For a month. It was pleasant to be sitting there,
While the sultriest fulgurations, flickering,
Cast corners in the glass. He could describe
The terror of the sound because the sound
Was ancient. He tried to remember the phrases: pain
Audible at noon, pain torturing itself,
Pain killing pain on the very point of pain.
The volcano trembled in another ether,
As the body trembles at the end of life.

It was almost time for lunch. Pain is human.
There were roses in the cool café. His book
Made sure of the most correct catastrophe.
Except for us, Vesuvius might consume
In solid fire the utmost earth and know
No pain (ignoring the cocks that crow us up
To die). This is a part of the sublime
From which we shrink. And yet, except for us,
The total past felt nothing when destroyed.

II

At a town in which acacias grew, he lay
On his balcony at night. Warblings became
Too dark, too far, too much the accents of
Afflicted sleep, too much the syllables
That would form themselves, in time, and communicate
The intelligence of his despair, express
What meditation never quite achieved.

The moon rose up as if it had escaped
His meditation. It evaded his mind.
It was part of a supremacy always
Above him. The moon was always free from him,
As night was free from him. The shadow touched
Or merely seemed to touch him as he spoke
A kind of elegy he found in space:

It is pain that is indifferent to the sky
In spite of the yellow of the acacias, the scent
Of them in the air still hanging heavily
In the hoary-hanging night. It does not regard
This freedom, this supremacy, and in
Its own hallucination never sees
How that which rejects it saves it in the end.

III

His firm stanzas hang like hives in hell
Or what hell was, since now both heaven and hell
Are one, and here, O terra infidel.

The fault lies with an over-human god,
Who by sympathy has made himself a man
And is not to be distinguished, when we cry

Because we suffer, our oldest parent, peer
Of the populace of the heart, the reddest lord,
Who has gone before us in experience.

If only he would not pity us so much,
Weaken our fate, relieve us of woe both great
And small, a constant fellow of destiny,

A too, too human god, self-pity's kin
And uncourageous genesis . . . It seems
As if the health of the world might be enough.

It seems as if the honey of common summer
Might be enough, as if the golden combs
Were part of a sustenance itself enough,

As if hell, so modified, had disappeared,
As if pain, no longer satanic mimicry,
Could be borne, as if we were sure to find our way.

IV

Livre de Toutes Sortes de Fleurs D'Après Nature.
All sorts of flowers. That's the sentimentalist.
When B. sat down at the piano and made
A transparence in which we heard music, made music
In which we heard transparent sounds, did he play
All sorts of notes? Or did he play only one
In an ecstasy of its associates,
Variations in the tones of a single sound,
The last, or sounds so single they seemed one?
And then that Spaniard of the rose, itself
Hot-hooded and dark-blooded, rescued the rose
From nature, each time he saw it, making it,
As he saw it, exist in his own especial eye.
Can we conceive of him as rescuing less,
As muffing the mistress for her several maids,
As foregoing the nakedest passion for barefoot
Philandering? . . . The genius of misfortune
Is not a sentimentalist. He is
That evil, that evil in the self, from which
In desperate hallow, rugged gesture, fault
Falls out on everything: the genius of
The mind, which is our being, wrong and wrong,
The genius of the body, which is our world,
Spent in the false engagements of the mind.

254

V

Softly let all true sympathizers come,
Without the inventions of sorrow or the sob
Beyond invention. Within what we permit,
Within the actual, the warm, the near,
So great a unity, that it is bliss,
Ties us to those we love. For this familiar,
This brother even in the father's eye,
This brother half-spoken in the mother's throat
And these regalia, these things disclosed,
These nebulous brilliancies in the smallest look
Of the being's deepest darling, we forego
Lament, willingly forfeit the ai-ai
Of parades in the obscurer selvages.
Be near me, come closer, touch my hand, phrases
Compounded of dear relation, spoken twice,
Once by the lips, once by the services
Of central sense, these minutiae mean more
Than clouds, benevolences, distant heads.
These are within what we permit, in-bar
Exquisite in poverty against the suns
Of ex-bar, in-bar retaining attributes
With which we vested, once, the golden forms
And the damasked memory of the golden forms
And ex-bar's flower and fire of the festivals
Of the damasked memory of the golden forms,
Before we were wholly human and knew ourselves.

VI

The sun, in clownish yellow, but not a clown,
Brings the day to perfection and then fails. He dwells
In a consummate prime, yet still desires
A further consummation. For the lunar month
He makes the tenderest research, intent
On a transmutation which, when seen, appears

255

To be askew. And space is filled with his
Rejected years. A big bird pecks at him
For food. The big bird's boney appetite
Is as insatiable as the sun's. The bird
Rose from an imperfection of its own
To feed on the yellow bloom of the yellow fruit
Dropped down from turquoise leaves. In the land-
    scape of
The sun, its grossest appetite becomes less gross,
Yet, when corrected, has its curious lapses,
Its glitters, its divinations of serene
Indulgence out of all celestial sight.

The sun is the country wherever he is. The bird
In the brightest landscape downwardly revolves
Disdaining each astringent ripening,
Evading the point of redness, not content
To repose in an hour or season or long era
Of the country colors crowding against it, since
The yellow grassman's mind is still immense,
Still promises perfections cast away.

VII

How red the rose that is the soldier's wound,
The wounds of many soldiers, the wounds of all
The soldiers that have fallen, red in blood,
The soldier of time grown deathless in great size.

A mountain in which no ease is ever found,
Unless indifference to deeper death
Is ease, stands in the dark, a shadows' hill,
And there the soldier of time has deathless rest.

Concentric circles of shadows, motionless
Of their own part, yet moving on the wind,

Form mystical convolutions in the sleep
Of time's red soldier deathless on his bed.

The shadows of his fellows ring him round
In the high night, the summer breathes for them
Its fragrance, a heavy somnolence, and for him,
For the soldier of time, it breathes a summer sleep,

In which his wound is good because life was.
No part of him was ever part of death.
A woman smoothes her forehead with her hand
And the soldier of time lies calm beneath that stroke.

VIII

The death of Satan was a tragedy
For the imagination. A capital
Negation destroyed him in his tenement
And, with him, many blue phenomena.
It was not the end he had foreseen. He knew
That his revenge created filial
Revenges. And negation was eccentric.
It had nothing of the Julian thunder-cloud:
The assassin flash and rumble . . . He was denied.

Phantoms, what have you left? What underground?
What place in which to be is not enough
To be? You go, poor phantoms, without place
Like silver in the sheathing of the sight,
As the eye closes . . . How cold the vacancy
When the phantoms are gone and the shaken realist
First sees reality. The mortal no
Has its emptiness and tragic expirations.
The tragedy, however, may have begun,
Again, in the imagination's new beginning,
In the yes of the realist spoken because he must

Say yes, spoken because under every no
Lay a passion for yes that had never been broken.

IX

Panic in the face of the moon—round effendi
Or the phosphored sleep in which he walks abroad
Or the majolica dish heaped up with phosphored fruit
That he sends ahead, out of the goodness of his heart,
To anyone that comes—panic, because
The moon is no longer these nor anything
And nothing is left but comic ugliness
Or a lustred nothingness. Effendi, he
That has lost the folly of the moon becomes
The prince of the proverbs of pure poverty.
To lose sensibility, to see what one sees,
As if sight had not its own miraculous thrift,
To hear only what one hears, one meaning alone,
As if the paradise of meaning ceased
To be paradise, it is this to be destitute.
This is the sky divested of its fountains.
Here in the west indifferent crickets chant
Through our indifferent crises. Yet we require
Another chant, an incantation, as in
Another and later genesis, music
That buffets the shapes of its possible halcyon
Against the haggardie . . . A loud, large water
Bubbles up in the night and drowns the crickets' sound.
It is a declaration, a primitive ecstasy,
Truth's favors sonorously exhibited.

X

He had studied the nostalgias. In these
He sought the most grossly maternal, the creature

258

Who most fecundly assuaged him, the softest
Woman with a vague moustache and not the mauve
Maman. His anima liked its animal
And liked it unsubjugated, so that home
Was a return to birth, a being born
Again in the savagest severity,
Desiring fiercely, the child of a mother fierce
In his body, fiercer in his mind, merciless
To accomplish the truth in his intelligence.
It is true there were other mothers, singular
In form, lovers of heaven and earth, she-wolves
And forest tigresses and women mixed
With the sea. These were fantastic. There were homes
Like things submerged with their englutted sounds
That were never wholly still. The softest woman,
Because she is as she was, reality,
The gross, the fecund, proved him against the touch
Of impersonal pain. Reality explained.
It was the last nostalgia: that he
Should understand. That he might suffer or that
He might die was the innocence of living, if life
Itself was innocent. To say that it was
Disentangled him from sleek ensolacings.

XI

Life is a bitter aspic. We are not
At the centre of a diamond. At dawn,
The paratroopers fall and as they fall
They mow the lawn. A vessel sinks in waves
Of people, as big bell-billows from its bell
Bell-bellow in the village steeple. Violets,
Great tufts, spring up from buried houses
Of poor, dishonest people, for whom the steeple,
Long since, rang out farewell, farewell, farewell.

Natives of poverty, children of malheur,
The gaiety of language is our seigneur.

A man of bitter appetite despises
A well-made scene in which paratroopers
Select adieux; and he despises this:
A ship that rolls on a confected ocean,
The weather pink, the wind in motion; and this:
A steeple that tip-tops the classic sun's
Arrangements; and the violets' exhumo.

The tongue caresses these exacerbations.
They press it as epicure, distinguishing
Themselves from its essential savor,
Like hunger that feeds on its own hungriness.

XII

He disposes the world in categories, thus:
The peopled and the unpeopled. In both, he is
Alone. But in the peopled world, there is,
Besides the people, his knowledge of them. In
The unpeopled, there is his knowledge of himself.
Which is more desperate in the moments when
The will demands that what he thinks be true?

Is it himself in them that he knows or they
In him? If it is himself in them, they have
No secret from him. If it is they in him,
He has no secret from them. This knowledge
Of them and of himself destroys both worlds,
Except when he escapes from it. To be
Alone is not to know them or himself.

This creates a third world without knowledge,
In which no one peers, in which the will makes no
Demands. It accepts whatever is as true,
Including pain, which, otherwise, is false.
In the third world, then, there is no pain. Yes, but
What lover has one in such rocks, what woman,
However known, at the centre of the heart?

XIII

It may be that one life is a punishment
For another, as the son's life for the father's.
But that concerns the secondary characters.
It is a fragmentary tragedy
Within the universal whole. The son
And the father alike and equally are spent,
Each one, by the necessity of being
Himself, the unalterable necessity
Of being this unalterable animal.
This force of nature in action is the major
Tragedy. This is destiny unperplexed,
The happiest enemy. And it may be
That in his Mediterranean cloister a man,
Reclining, eased of desire, establishes
The visible, a zone of blue and orange
Versicolorings, establishes a time
To watch the fire-feinting sea and calls it good,
The ultimate good, sure of a reality
Of the longest meditation, the maximum,
The assassin's scene. Evil in evil is
Comparative. The assassin discloses himself,
The force that destroys us is disclosed, within
This maximum, an adventure to be endured
With the politest helplessness. Ay-mi!
One feels its action moving in the blood.

XIV

Victor Serge said, "I followed his argument
With the blank uneasiness which one might feel
In the presence of a logical lunatic."
He said it of Konstantinov. Revolution
Is the affair of logical lunatics.
The politics of emotion must appear
To be an intellectual structure. The cause
Creates a logic not to be distinguished
From lunacy . . . One wants to be able to walk
By the lake at Geneva and consider logic:
To think of the logicians in their graves
And of the worlds of logic in their great tombs.
Lakes are more reasonable than oceans. Hence,
A promenade amid the grandeurs of the mind,
By a lake, with clouds like lights among great tombs,
Gives one a blank uneasiness, as if
One might meet Konstantinov, who would interrupt
With his lunacy. He would not be aware of the lake.
He would be the lunatic of one idea
In a world of ideas, who would have all the people
Live, work, suffer and die in that idea
In a world of ideas. He would not be aware of the clouds,
Lighting the martyrs of logic with white fire.
His extreme of logic would be illogical.

XV

The greatest poverty is not to live
In a physical world, to feel that one's desire
Is too difficult to tell from despair. Perhaps,
After death, the non-physical people, in paradise,
Itself non-physical, may, by chance, observe
The green corn gleaming and experience
The minor of what we feel. The adventurer

In humanity has not conceived of a race
Completely physical in a physical world.
The green corn gleams and the metaphysicals
Lie sprawling in majors of the August heat,
The rotund emotions, paradise unknown.

This is the thesis scrivened in delight,
The reverberating psalm, the right chorale.

One might have thought of sight, but who could think
Of what it sees, for all the ill it sees?
Speech found the ear, for all the evil sound,
But the dark italics it could not propound.
And out of what one sees and hears and out
Of what one feels, who could have thought to make
So many selves, so many sensuous worlds,
As if the air, the mid-day air, was swarming
With the metaphysical changes that occur,
Merely in living as and where we live.

The Bed of Old John Zeller

This structure of ideas, these ghostly sequences
Of the mind, result only in disaster. It follows,
Casual poet, that to add your own disorder to disaster

Makes more of it. It is easy to wish for another structure
Of ideas and to say as usual that there must be
Other ghostly sequences and, it would be, luminous

Sequences, thought of among spheres in the old peak of night:
This is the habit of wishing, as if one's grandfather lay
In one's heart and wished as he had always wished, unable

To sleep in that bed for its disorder, talking of ghostly
Sequences that would be sleep and ting-tang tossing, so that
He might slowly forget. It is more difficult to evade

That habit of wishing and to accept the structure
Of things as the structure of ideas. It was the structure
Of things at least that was thought of in the old peak of night.

Less and Less Human, O Savage Spirit

If there must be a god in the house, must be,
Saying things in the rooms and on the stair,

Let him move as the sunlight moves on the floor,
Or moonlight, silently, as Plato's ghost

Or Aristotle's skeleton. Let him hang out
His stars on the wall. He must dwell quietly.

He must be incapable of speaking, closed,
As those are: as light, for all its motion, is;

As color, even the closest to us, is;
As shapes, though they portend us, are.

It is the human that is the alien,
The human that has no cousin in the moon.

It is the human that demands his speech
From beasts or from the incommunicable mass.

If there must be a god in the house, let him be one
That will not hear us when we speak: a coolness,

A vermilioned nothingness, any stick of the mass
Of which we are too distantly a part.

The Pure Good of Theory

I

All the Preludes to Felicity

It is time that beats in the breast and it is time
That batters against the mind, silent and proud,
The mind that knows it is destroyed by time.

Time is a horse that runs in the heart, a horse
Without a rider on a road at night.
The mind sits listening and hears it pass.

It is someone walking rapidly in the street.
The reader by the window has finished his book
And tells the hour by the lateness of the sounds.

Even breathing is the beating of time, in kind:
A retardation of its battering,
A horse grotesquely taut, a walker like

A shadow in mid-earth . . . If we propose
A large-sculptured, platonic person, free from time,
And imagine for him the speech he cannot speak,

A form, then, protected from the battering, may
Mature: A capable being may replace
Dark horse and walker walking rapidly.

Felicity, ah! Time is the hooded enemy,
The inimical music, the enchantered space
In which the enchanted preludes have their place.

II
Description of a Platonic Person

Then came Brazil to nourish the emaciated
Romantic with dreams of her avoirdupois, green glade
Of serpents like z rivers simmering,

Green glade and holiday hotel and world
Of the future, in which the memory had gone
From everything, flying the flag of the nude,

The flag of the nude above the holiday hotel.
But there was one invalid in that green glade
And beneath that handkerchief drapeau, severe,

Signal, a character out of solitude,
Who was what people had been and still were,
Who lay in bed on the west wall of the sea,

Ill of a question like a malady,
Ill of a constant question in his thought,
Unhappy about the sense of happiness.

Was it that—a sense and beyond intelligence?
Could the future rest on a sense and be beyond
Intelligence? On what does the present rest?

This platonic person discovered a soul in the world
And studied it in his holiday hotel.
He was a Jew from Europe or might have been.

III
Fire-Monsters in the Milky Brain

Man, that is not born of woman but of air,
That comes here in the solar chariot,
Like rhetoric in a narration of the eye—

We knew one parent must have been divine,
Adam of beau regard, from fat Elysia,
Whose mind malformed this morning metaphor,

While all the leaves leaked gold. His mind made
    morning,
As he slept. He woke in a metaphor: this was
A metamorphosis of paradise,

Malformed, the world was paradise malformed . . .
Now, closely the ear attends the varying
Of this precarious music, the change of key

Not quite detected at the moment of change
And, now, it attends the difficult difference.
To say the solar chariot is junk

Is not a variation but an end.
Yet to speak of the whole world as metaphor
Is still to stick to the contents of the mind

And the desire to believe in a metaphor.
It is to stick to the nicer knowledge of
Belief, that what it believes in is not true.

IV

Dry Birds Are Fluttering in Blue Leaves—

It is never the thing but the version of the thing:
The fragrance of the woman not her self,
Her self in her manner not the solid block,

The day in its color not perpending time,
Time in its weather, our most sovereign lord,
The weather in words and words in sounds of sound.

These devastations are the divertissements
Of a destroying spiritual that digs-a-dog,
Whines in its hole for puppies to come see,

Springs outward, being large, and, in the dust,
Being small, inscribes ferocious alphabets,
Flies like a bat expanding as it flies,

Until its wings bear off night's middle witch;
And yet remains the same, the beast of light,
Groaning in half-exploited gutturals

The need of its element, the final need
Of final access to its element—
Of access like the page of a wiggy book,

Touched suddenly by the universal flare
For a moment, a moment in which we read and repeat
The eloquences of light's faculties.

Paisant Chronicle

What are the major men? All men are brave.
All men endure. The great captain is the choice
Of chance. Finally, the most solemn burial
Is a paisant chronicle.

              Men live to be
Admired by men and all men, therefore, live
To be admired by all men. Nations live
To be admired by nations. The race is brave.
The race endures. The funeral pomps of the race
Are a multitude of individual pomps
And the chronicle of humanity is the sum
Of paisant chronicles.

              The major men—
That is different. They are characters beyond
Reality, composed thereof. They are
The fictive man created out of men.
They are men but artificial men. They are
Nothing in which it is not possible
To believe, more than the casual hero, more
Than Tartuffe as myth, the most Molière,
The easy projection long prohibited.

The baroque poet may see him as still a man
As Virgil, abstract. But see him for yourself,
The fictive man. He may be seated in
A café. There may be a dish of country cheese
And a pineapple on the table. It must be so.

Flyer's Fall

This man escaped the dirty fates,
Knowing that he died nobly, as he died.

Darkness, nothingness of human after-death,
Receive and keep him in the deepnesses of space—

Profundum, physical thunder, dimension in which
We believe without belief, beyond belief.

Description without Place

I

It is possible that to seem—it is to be,
As the sun is something seeming and it is.

The sun is an example. What it seems
It is and in such seeming all things are.

Thus things are like a seeming of the sun
Or like a seeming of the moon or night

Or sleep. It was a queen that made it seem
By the illustrious nothing of her name.

Her green mind made the world around her green.
The queen is an example . . . This green queen

In the seeming of the summer of her sun
By her own seeming made the summer change.

In the golden vacancy she came, and comes,
And seems to be on the saying of her name.

Her time becomes again, as it became,
The crown and week-day coronal of her fame.

II

Such seemings are the actual ones: the way
Things look each day, each morning, or the style

Peculiar to the queen, this queen or that,
The lesser seeming original in the blind

Forward of the eye that, in its backward, sees
The greater seeming of the major mind.

An age is a manner collected from a queen.
An age is green or red. An age believes

Or it denies. An age is solitude
Or a barricade against the singular man

By the incalculably plural. Hence
Its identity is merely a thing that seems,

In the seeming of an original in the eye,
In the major manner of a queen, the green

The red, the blue, the argent queen. If not,
What subtlety would apparition have?

In flat appearance we should be and be,
Except for delicate clinkings not explained.

These are the actual seemings that we see,
Hear, feel and know. We feel and know them so.

III

There are potential seemings, arrogant
To be, as on the youngest poet's page,

Or in the dark musician, listening
To hear more brightly the contriving chords.

There are potential seemings turbulent
In the death of a soldier, like the utmost will,

The more than human commonplace of blood,
The breath that gushes upward and is gone,

And another breath emerging out of death,
That speaks for him such seemings as death gives.

There might be, too, a change immenser than
A poet's metaphors in which being would

Come true, a point in the fire of music where
Dazzle yields to a clarity and we observe,

And observing is completing and we are content,
In a world that shrinks to an immediate whole,

That we do not need to understand, complete
Without secret arrangements of it in the mind.

There might be in the curling-out of spring
A purple-leaping element that forth

Would froth the whole heaven with its seeming-so,
The intentions of a mind as yet unknown,

The spirit of one dwelling in a seed,
Itself that seed's ripe, unpredictable fruit.

Things are as they seemed to Calvin or to **Anne**
Of England, to Pablo Neruda in Ceylon,

To Nietzsche in Basel, to Lenin by a lake.
But the integrations of the past are like

A *Museo Olimpico*, so much
So little, our affair, which is the affair

Of the possible: seemings that are to be,
Seemings that it is possible may be.

IV

Nietzsche in Basel studied the deep pool
Of these discolorations, mastering

The moving and the moving of their forms
In the much-mottled motion of blank time.

His revery was the deepness of the pool,
The very pool, his thoughts the colored forms,

The eccentric souvenirs of human shapes,
Wrapped in their seemings, crowd on curious crowd,

In a kind of total affluence, all first,
All final, colors subjected in revery

To an innate grandiose, an innate light,
The sun of Nietzsche gildering the pool,

Yes: gildering the swarm-like manias
In perpetual revolution, round and round . . .

Lenin on a bench beside a lake disturbed
The swans. He was not the man for swans.

The slouch of his body and his look were not
In suavest keeping. The shoes, the clothes, the hat

Suited the decadence of those silences,
In which he sat. All chariots were drowned. The swans

Moved on the buried water where they lay.
Lenin took bread from his pocket, scattered it—

The swans fled outward to remoter reaches,
As if they knew of distant beaches; and were

Dissolved. The distances of space and time
Were one and swans far off were swans to come.

The eye of Lenin kept the far-off shapes.
His mind raised up, down-drowned, the chariots.

And reaches, beaches, tomorrow's regions became
One thinking of apocalyptic legions.

v

If seeming is description without place,
The spirit's universe, then a summer's day,

Even the seeming of a summer's day,
Is description without place. It is a sense

274

To which we refer experience, a knowledge
Incognito, the column in the desert,

On which the dove alights. Description is
Composed of a sight indifferent to the eye.

It is an expectation, a desire,
A palm that rises up beyond the sea,

A little different from reality:
The difference that we make in what we see

And our memorials of that difference,
Sprinklings of bright particulars from the sky.

The future is description without place,
The categorical predicate, the arc.

It is a wizened starlight growing young,
In which old stars are planets of morning, fresh

In the brilliantest descriptions of new day,
Before it comes, the just anticipation

Of the appropriate creatures, jubilant,
The forms that are attentive in thin air.

VI

Description is revelation. It is not
The thing described, nor false facsimile.

It is an artificial thing that exists,
In its own seeming, plainly visible,

Yet not too closely the double of our lives,
Intenser than any actual life could be,

A text we should be born that we might read,
More explicit than the experience of sun

And moon, the book of reconciliation,
Book of a concept only possible

In description, canon central in itself,
The thesis of the plentifullest John.

VII

Thus the theory of description matters most.
It is the theory of the word for those

For whom the word is the making of the world,
The buzzing world and lisping firmament.

It is a world of words to the end of it,
In which nothing solid is its solid self.

As, men make themselves their speech: the hard hidalgo
Lives in the mountainous character of his speech;

And in that mountainous mirror Spain acquires
The knowledge of Spain and of the hidalgo's hat—

A seeming of the Spaniard, a style of life,
The invention of a nation in a phrase,

In a description hollowed out of hollow-bright,
The artificer of subjects still half night.

It matters, because everything we say
Of the past is description without place, a cast

Of the imagination, made in sound;
And because what we say of the future must portend,

Be alive with its own seemings, seeming to be
Like rubies reddened by rubies reddening.

Thinking of a Relation between the Images of Metaphors

The wood-doves are singing along the Perkiomen.
The bass lie deep, still afraid of the Indians.

In the one ear of the fisherman, who is all
One ear, the wood-doves are singing a single song.

The bass keep looking ahead, upstream, in one
Direction, shrinking from the spit and splash

Of waterish spears. The fisherman is all
One eye, in which the dove resembles the dove.

There is one dove, one bass, one fisherman.
Yet coo becomes rou-coo, rou-coo. How close

To the unstated theme each variation comes . . .
In that one ear it might strike perfectly:

State the disclosure. In that one eye the dove
Might spring to sight and yet remain a dove.

The fisherman might be the single man
In whose breast, the dove, alighting, would grow still.

Chaos in Motion and Not in Motion

Oh, that this lashing wind was something more
Than the spirit of Ludwig Richter . . .

The rain is pouring down. It is July.
There is lightning and the thickest thunder.

It is a spectacle. Scene 10 becomes 11,
In Series X, Act IV, et cetera.

People fall out of windows, trees tumble down,
Summer is changed to winter, the young grow old,

The air is full of children, statues, roofs
And snow. The theatre is spinning round,

Colliding with deaf-mute churches and optical trains.
The most massive sopranos are singing songs of scales.

And Ludwig Richter, turbulent Schlemihl,
Has lost the whole in which he was contained,

Knows desire without an object of desire,
All mind and violence and nothing felt.

He knows he has nothing more to think about,
Like the wind that lashes everything at once.

The House Was Quiet and the World Was Calm

The house was quiet and the world was calm.
The reader became the book; and summer night

Was like the conscious being of the book.
The house was quiet and the world was calm.

The words were spoken as if there was no book,
Except that the reader leaned above the page,

Wanted to lean, wanted much most to be
The scholar to whom his book is true, to whom

The summer night is like a perfection of thought.
The house was quiet because it had to be.

The quiet was part of the meaning, part of the mind:
The access of perfection to the page.

And the world was calm. The truth in a calm world,
In which there is no other meaning, itself

Is calm, itself is summer and night, itself
Is the reader leaning late and reading there.

Late Hymn from the Myrrh-Mountain

Unsnack your snood, madanna, for the stars
Are shining on all brows of Neversink.

Already the green bird of summer has flown
Away. The night-flies acknowledge these planets,

Predestined to this night, this noise and the place
Of summer. Tomorrow will look like today,

Will appear like it. But it will be an appearance,
A shape left behind, with like wings spreading out,

Brightly empowered with like colors, swarmingly,
But not quite molten, not quite the fluid thing,

A little changed by tips of artifice, changed
By the glints of sound from the grass. These are not

The early constellations, from which came the first
Illustrious intimations—uncertain love,

The knowledge of being, sense without sense of time.
Take the diamonds from your hair and lay them down.

The deer-grass is thin. The timothy is brown.
The shadow of an external world comes near.

Man Carrying Thing

The poem must resist the intelligence
Almost successfully. Illustration:

A brune figure in winter evening resists
Identity. The thing he carries resists

The most necessitous sense. Accept them, then,
As secondary (parts not quite perceived

Of the obvious whole, uncertain particles
Of the certain solid, the primary free from doubt,

Things floating like the first hundred flakes of snow
Out of a storm we must endure all night,

Out of a storm of secondary things),
A horror of thoughts that suddenly are real.

We must endure our thoughts all night, until
The bright obvious stands motionless in cold.

Men Made out of Words

What should we be without the sexual myth,
The human revery or poem of death?

Castratos of moon-mash—Life consists
Of propositions about life. The human

Revery is a solitude in which
We compose these propositions, torn by dreams,

By the terrible incantations of defeats
And by the fear that defeats and dreams are one.

The whole race is a poet that writes down
The eccentric propositions of its fate.

A Woman Sings a Song for a Soldier Come Home

The wound kills that does not bleed.
It has no nurse nor kin to know
Nor kin to care.

And the man dies that does not fall.
He walks and dies. Nothing survives
Except what was,

Under the white clouds piled and piled
Like gathered-up forgetfulness,
In sleeping air.

The clouds are over the village, the town,
To which the walker speaks
And tells of his wound,

Without a word to the people, unless
One person should come by chance,
This man or that,

So much a part of the place, so little
A person he knows, with whom he might
Talk of the weather—

And let it go, with nothing lost,
Just out of the village, at its edge,
In the quiet there.

The Good Man Has No Shape

Through centuries he lived in poverty.
God only was his only elegance.

Then generation by generation he grew
Stronger and freer, a little better off.

He lived each life because, if it was bad,
He said a good life would be possible.

At last the good life came, good sleep, bright fruit,
And Lazarus betrayed him to the rest,

Who killed him, sticking feathers in his flesh
To mock him. They placed with him in his grave

Sour wine to warn him, an empty book to read;
And over it they set a jagged sign,

Epitaphium to his death, which read,
The Good Man Has No Shape, as if they knew.

From the Packet of Anacharsis

In his packet Anacharsis found the lines:
"The farm was fat and the land in which it lay
Seemed in the morning like a holiday."

He had written them near Athens. The farm was white.
The buildings were of marble and stood in marble light.
It was his clarity that made the vista bright.

A subject for Puvis. He would compose
The scene in his gray-rose with violet rocks.
And Bloom would see what Puvis did, protest

And speak of the floridest reality . . .
In the punctual centre of all circles white
Stands truly. The circles nearest to it share

Its color, but less as they recede, impinged
By difference and then by definition
As a tone defines itself and separates

And the circles quicken and crystal colors come
And flare and Bloom with his vast accumulation
Stands and regards and repeats the primitive lines.

The Dove in the Belly

The whole of appearance is a toy. For this,
The dove in the belly builds his nest and coos,

Selah, tempestuous bird. How is it that
The rivers shine and hold their mirrors up,

Like excellence collecting excellence?
How is it that the wooden trees stand up

And live and heap their panniers of green
And hold them round the sultry day? Why should

These mountains being high be, also, bright,
Fetched up with snow that never falls to earth?

And this great esplanade of corn, miles wide,
Is something wished for made effectual

And something more. And the people in costumes,
Though poor, though raggeder than ruin, have that

Within them right for terraces—oh, brave salut!
Deep dove, placate you in your hiddenness.

Mountains Covered with Cats

The sea full of fishes in shoals, the woods that let
One seed alone grow wild, the railway-stops
In Russia at which the same statue of Stalin greets
The same railway passenger, the ancient tree
In the centre of its cones, the resplendent flights
Of red facsimiles through related trees,
White houses in villages, black communicants—
The catalogue is too commodious.

Regard the invalid personality
Instead, outcast, without the will to power
And impotent, like the imagination seeking
To propagate the imagination or like
War's miracle begetting that of peace.

Freud's eye was the microscope of potency.
By fortune, his gray ghost may meditate
The spirits of all the impotent dead, seen clear,
And quickly understand, without their flesh,
How truly they had not been what they were.

The Prejudice Against the Past

Day is the children's friend.
It is Marianna's Swedish cart.
It is that and a very big hat.

Confined by what they see,
Aquiline pedants treat the cart,
As one of the relics of the heart.

They treat the philosopher's hat,
Left thoughtlessly behind,
As one of the relics of the mind . . .

Of day, then, children make
What aquiline pedants take
For souvenirs of time, lost time,

Adieux, shapes, images—
No, not of day, but of themselves,
Not of perpetual time.

And, therefore, aquiline pedants find
The philosopher's hat to be part of the mind,
The Swedish cart to be part of the heart.

Credences of Summer

I

Now in midsummer come and all fools slaughtered
And spring's infuriations over and a long way
To the first autumnal inhalations, young broods
Are in the grass, the roses are heavy with a weight
Of fragrance and the mind lays by its trouble.

Now the mind lays by its trouble and considers.
The fidgets of remembrance come to this.
This is the last day of a certain year
Beyond which there is nothing left of time.
It comes to this and the imagination's life.

There is nothing more inscribed nor thought nor felt
And this must comfort the heart's core against
Its false disasters—these fathers standing round,
These mothers touching, speaking, being near,
These lovers waiting in the soft dry grass.

II

Postpone the anatomy of summer, as
The physical pine, the metaphysical pine.
Let's see the very thing and nothing else.
Let's see it with the hottest fire of sight.
Burn everything not part of it to ash.

Trace the gold sun about the whitened sky
Without evasion by a single metaphor.
Look at it in its essential barrenness
And say this, this is the centre that I seek.
Fix it in an eternal foliage

And fill the foliage with arrested peace,
Joy of such permanence, right ignorance
Of change still possible. Exile desire
For what is not. This is the barrenness
Of the fertile thing that can attain no more.

III

It is the natural tower of all the world,
The point of survey, green's green apogee,
But a tower more precious than the view beyond,
A point of survey squatting like a throne,
Axis of everything, green's apogee

And happiest folk-land, mostly marriage-hymns.
It is the mountain on which the tower stands,

It is the final mountain. Here the sun,
Sleepless, inhales his proper air, and rests.
This is the refuge that the end creates.

It is the old man standing on the tower,
Who reads no book. His ruddy ancientness
Absorbs the ruddy summer and is appeased,
By an understanding that fulfils his age,
By a feeling capable of nothing more.

IV

One of the limits of reality
Presents itself in Oley when the hay,
Baked through long days, is piled in mows. It is
A land too ripe for enigmas, too serene.
There the distant fails the clairvoyant eye

And the secondary senses of the ear
Swarm, not with secondary sounds, but choirs,
Not evocations but last choirs, last sounds
With nothing else compounded, carried full,
Pure rhetoric of a language without words.

Things stop in that direction and since they stop
The direction stops and we accept what is
As good. The utmost must be good and is
And is our fortune and honey hived in the trees
And mingling of colors at a festival.

V

One day enriches a year. One woman makes
The rest look down. One man becomes a race,
Lofty like him, like him perpetual.
Or do the other days enrich the one?
And is the queen humble as she seems to be,

The charitable majesty of her whole kin?
The bristling soldier, weather-foxed, who looms
In the sunshine is a filial form and one
Of the land's children, easily born, its flesh,
Not fustian. The more than casual blue

Contains the year and other years and hymns
And people, without souvenir. The day
Enriches the year, not as embellishment.
Stripped of remembrance, it displays its strength—
The youth, the vital son, the heroic power.

VI

The rock cannot be broken. It is the truth.
It rises from land and sea and covers them.
It is a mountain half way green and then,
The other immeasurable half, such rock
As placid air becomes. But it is not

A hermit's truth nor symbol in hermitage.
It is the visible rock, the audible,
The brilliant mercy of a sure repose,
On this present ground, the vividest repose,
Things certain sustaining us in certainty.

It is the rock of summer, the extreme,
A mountain luminous half way in bloom
And then half way in the extremest light
Of sapphires flashing from the central sky,
As if twelve princes sat before a king.

VII

Far in the woods they sang their unreal songs,
Secure. It was difficult to sing in face

Of the object. The singers had to avert themselves
Or else avert the object. Deep in the woods
They sang of summer in the common fields.

They sang desiring an object that was near,
In face of which desire no longer moved,
Nor made of itself that which it could not find . . .
Three times the concentred self takes hold, three times
The thrice concentred self, having possessed

The object, grips it in savage scrutiny,
Once to make captive, once to subjugate
Or yield to subjugation, once to proclaim
The meaning of the capture, this hard prize,
Fully made, fully apparent, fully found.

VIII

The trumpet of morning blows in the clouds and through
The sky. It is the visible announced,
It is the more than visible, the more
Than sharp, illustrious scene. The trumpet cries
This is the successor of the invisible.

This is its substitute in stratagems
Of the spirit. This, in sight and memory,
Must take its place, as what is possible
Replaces what is not. The resounding cry
Is like ten thousand tumblers tumbling down

To share the day. The trumpet supposes that
A mind exists, aware of division, aware
Of its cry as clarion, its diction's way
As that of a personage in a multitude:
Man's mind grown venerable in the unreal.

Fly low, cock bright, and stop on a bean pole. Let
Your brown breast redden, while you wait for warmth.
With one eye watch the willow, motionless.
The gardener's cat is dead, the gardener gone
And last year's garden grows salacious weeds.

A complex of emotions falls apart,
In an abandoned spot. Soft, civil bird,
The decay that you regard: of the arranged
And of the spirit of the arranged, *douceurs*,
Tristesses, the fund of life and death, suave bush

And polished beast, this complex falls apart.
And on your bean pole, it may be, you detect
Another complex of other emotions, not
So soft, so civil, and you make a sound,
Which is not part of the listener's own sense.

X

The personae of summer play the characters
Of an inhuman author, who meditates
With the gold bugs, in blue meadows, late at night.
He does not hear his characters talk. He sees
Them mottled, in the moodiest costumes,

Of blue and yellow, sky and sun, belted
And knotted, sashed and seamed, half pales of red,
Half pales of green, appropriate habit for
The huge decorum, the manner of the time,
Part of the mottled mood of summer's whole,

In which the characters speak because they want
To speak, the fat, the roseate characters,
Free, for a moment, from malice and sudden cry,
Complete in a completed scene, speaking
Their parts as in a youthful happiness.

A Pastoral Nun

Finally, in the last year of her age,
Having attained a present blessedness,
She said poetry and apotheosis are one.

This is the illustration that she used:
If I live according to this law I live
In an immense activity, in which

Everything becomes morning, summer, the hero,
The enraptured woman, the sequestered night,
The man that suffered, lying there at ease,

Without his envious pain in body, in mind,
The favorable transformations of the wind
As of a general being or human universe.

There was another illustration, in which
The two things compared their tight resemblances:
Each matters only in that which it conceives.

Two Versions of the Same Poem

That Which Cannot Be Fixed

I

Once more he turned to that which could not be fixed,
By the sea, insolid rock, stentor, and said:

Lascar, is there a body, turbulent
With time, in wavering water lies, swollen

With thought, through which it cannot see? Does it
Lie lengthwise like the cloud of sleep, not quite

Reposed? And does it have a puissant heart
To toll its pulses, vigors of its self?

Lascar, and water-carcass never-named,
These vigors make, thrice-triple-syllabled,

The difficult images of possible shapes,
That cannot now be fixed. Only there is

A beating and a beating in the centre of
The sea, a strength that tumbles everywhere,

Like more and more becoming less and less,
Like space dividing its blue and by division

Being changed from space to the sailor's metier,
Or say from that which was conceived to that

Which was realized, like reason's constant ruin.
Sleep deep, good eel, in your perverse marine.

II

The human ocean beats against this rock
Of earth, rises against it, tide by tide,

Continually. And old John Zeller stands
On his hill, watching the rising and falling, and says:

Of what are these the creatures, what element
Or—yes: what elements, unreconciled

Because there is no golden solvent here?
If they were creatures of the sea alone,

But singular, they would, like water, scale
The uptopping top and tip of things, borne up

By the·cadaver of these caverns, half-asleep.
But if they are of sea, earth, sky—water

And fire and air and things not discomposed
From ignorance, not an undivided whole,

It is an ocean of watery images
And shapes of fire, and wind that bears them down.

Perhaps these forms are seeking to escape
Cadaverous undulations. Rest, old mould . . .

Someone Puts a Pineapple Together

I

O juventes, O filii, he contemplates
A wholly artificial nature, in which
The profusion of metaphor has been increased.

It is something on a table that he sees,
The root of a form, as of this fruit, a fund,
The angel at the centre of this rind,

This husk of Cuba, tufted emerald,
Himself, may be, the irreducible X
At the bottom of imagined artifice,

Its inhabitant and elect expositor.
It is as if there were three planets: the sun,
The moon and the imagination, or, say,

Day, night and man and his endless effigies.
If he sees an object on a table, much like
A jar of the shoots of an infant country, green

And bright, or like a venerable urn,
Which, from the ash within it, fortifies
A green that is the ash of what green is,

He sees it in this tangent of himself.
And in this tangent it becomes a thing
Of weight, on which the weightless rests: from which

The ephemeras of the tangent swarm, the chance
Concourse of planetary originals,
Yet, as it seems, of human residence.

II

He must say nothing of the fruit that is
Not true, nor think it, less. He must defy
The metaphor that murders metaphor.

He seeks as image a second of the self,
Made subtle by truth's most jealous subtlety,
Like the true light of the truest sun, the true

Power in the waving of the wand of the moon,
Whose shining is the intelligence of our sleep.
He seeks an image certain as meaning is

To sound, sound's substance and executant,
The particular tingle in a proclamation
That makes it say the little thing it says,

Below the prerogative jumble. The fruit so seen
As a part of the nature that he contemplates
Is fertile with more than changes of the light

On the table or in the colors of the room.
Its propagations are more erudite,
Like precious scholia jotted down in the dark.

Did not the age that bore him bear him among
Its infiltrations? There had been an age
When a pineapple on the table was enough,

Without the forfeit scholar coming in,
Without his enlargings and pale arrondissements,
Without the furious roar in his capital.

Green had, those days, its own implacable sting.
But now a habit of the truth had formed
To protect him in a privacy, in which

The scholar, captious, told him what he could
Of there, where the truth was not the respect of one,
But always of many things. He had not to be told

Of the incredible subjects of poetry.
He was willing they should remain incredible,
Because the incredible, also, had its truth,

Its tuft of emerald that is real, for all
Its invitation to false metaphor.
The incredible gave him a purpose to believe.

How thick this gobbet is with overlays,
The double fruit of boisterous epicures,
Like the same orange repeating on one tree

A single self. Divest reality
Of its propriety. Admit the shaft
Of that third planet to the table and then:

1. The hut stands by itself beneath the palms.
2. Out of their bottle the green genii come.
3. A vine has climbed the other side of the wall.

4. The sea is spouting upward out of rocks.
5. The symbol of feasts and of oblivion . . .
6. White sky, pink sun, trees on a distant peak.

7. These lozenges are nailed-up lattices.
8. The owl sits humped. It has a hundred eyes.
9. The cocoanut and cockerel in one.

10. This is how yesterday's volcano looks.
11. There is an island Palahude by name —
12. An uncivil shape like a gigantic haw.

These casual exfoliations are
Of the tropic of resemblances, sprigs
Of Capricorn or as the sign demands,

Apposites, to the slightest edge, of the whole
Undescribed composition of the sugar-cone,
Shiftings of an inchoate crystal tableau,

The momentary footings of a climb
Up the pineapple, a table Alp and yet
An Alp, a purple Southern mountain bisqued

With the molten mixings of related things,
Cat's taste possibly or possibly Danish lore,
The small luxuriations that portend

Universal delusions of universal grandeurs,
The slight incipiencies, of which the form,
At last, is the pineapple on the table or else

An object the sum of its complications, seen
And unseen. This is everybody's world.
Here the total artifice reveals itself

As the total reality. Therefore it is
One says even of the odor of this fruit,
That steeps the room, quickly, then not at all,

It is more than the odor of this core of earth
And water. It is that which is distilled
In the prolific ellipses that we know,

In the planes that tilt hard revelations on
The eye, a geometric glitter, tiltings
As of sections collecting toward the greenest cone.

Of Ideal Time and Choice

Since thirty mornings are required to make
A day of which we say, this is the day
That we desired, a day of blank, blue wheels,

Involving the four corners of the sky,
Lapised and lacqued and freely emeraldine
In the space it fills, the silent motioner

There, of clear, revolving crystalline;
Since thirty summers are needed for a year
And thirty years, in the galaxies of birth,

Are time for counting and remembering,
And fill the earth with young men centuries old
And old men, who have chosen, and are cold

Because what they have chosen is their choice
No more and because they lack the will to tell
A matin gold from gold of Hesperus

The dot, the pale pole of resemblances
Experienced yet not well seen; of how
Much choosing is the final choice made up,

And who shall speak it, what child or wanderer
Or woman weeping in a room or man,
The last man given for epitome,

Upon whose lips the dissertation sounds,
And in what place, what exultant terminal,
And at what time both of the year and day;

And what heroic nature of what text
Shall be the celebration in the words
Of that oration, the happiest sense in which

A world agrees, thought's compromise, resolved
At last, the centre of resemblance, found
Under the bones of time's philosophers?

The orator will say that we ourselves
Stand at the centre of ideal time,
The inhuman making choice of a human self.

The Ultimate Poem Is Abstract

This day writhes with what? The lecturer
On This Beautiful World Of Ours composes himself
And hems the planet rose and haws it ripe,

And red, and right. The particular question—here
The particular answer to the particular question
Is not in point—the question is in point.

If the day writhes, it is not with revelations.
One goes on asking questions. That, then, is one
Of the categories. So said, this placid space

Is changed. It is not so blue as we thought. To be blue,
There must be no questions. It is an intellect
Of windings round and dodges to and fro,

Writhings in wrong obliques and distances,
Not an intellect in which we are fleet: present
Everywhere in space at once, cloud-pole

Of communication. It would be enough
If we were ever, just once, at the middle, fixed
In This Beautiful World Of Ours and not as now,

Helplessly at the edge, enough to be
Complete, because at the middle, if only in sense,
And in that enormous sense, merely enjoy.

The Owl in the Sarcophagus

I

Two forms move among the dead, high sleep
Who by his highness quiets them, high peace
Upon whose shoulders even the heavens rest,

Two brothers. And a third form, she that says
Good-by in the darkness, speaking quietly there,
To those that cannot say good-by themselves.

These forms are visible to the eye that needs,
Needs out of the whole necessity of sight.
The third form speaks, because the ear repeats,

Without a voice, inventions of farewell.
These forms are not abortive figures, rocks,
Impenetrable symbols, motionless. They move

About the night. They live without our light,
In an element not the heaviness of time,
In which reality is prodigy.

There sleep the brother is the father, too,
And peace is cousin by a hundred names
And she that in the syllable between life

And death cries quickly, in a flash of voice,
Keep you, keep you, I am gone, oh keep you as
My memory, is the mother of us all,

The earthly mother and the mother of
The dead. Only the thought of those dark three
Is dark, thought of the forms of dark desire.

II

There came a day, there was a day—one day
A man walked living among the forms of thought
To see their lustre truly as it is

And in harmonious prodigy to be,
A while, conceiving his passage as into a time
That of itself stood still, perennial,

Less time than place, less place than thought of place
And, if of substance, a likeness of the earth,
That by resemblance twanged him through and through,

Releasing an abysmal melody,
A meeting, an emerging in the light,
A dazzle of remembrance and of sight.

There he saw well the foldings in the height
Of sleep, the whiteness folded into less,
Like many robings, as moving masses are,

As a moving mountain is, moving through day
And night, colored from distances, central
Where luminous agitations come to rest,

In an ever-changing, calmest unity,
The unique composure, harshest streakings joined
In a vanishing-vanished violet that wraps round

The giant body the meanings of its folds,
The weaving and the crinkling and the vex,
As on water of an afternoon in the wind

After the wind has passed. Sleep realized
Was the whiteness that is the ultimate intellect,
A diamond jubilance beyond the fire,

That gives its power to the wild-ringed eye.
Then he breathed deeply the deep atmosphere
Of sleep, the accomplished, the fulfilling air.

IV

There peace, the godolphin and fellow, estranged,
    estranged,
Hewn in their middle as the beam of leaves,
The prince of shither-shade and tinsel lights,

Stood flourishing the world. The brilliant height
And hollow of him by its brilliance calmed,
Its brightness burned the way good solace seethes.

This was peace after death, the brother of sleep,
The inhuman brother so much like, so near,
Yet vested in a foreign absolute,

Adorned with cryptic stones and sliding shines,
An immaculate personage in nothingness,
With the whole spirit sparkling in its cloth,

Generations of the imagination piled
In the manner of its stitchings, of its thread,
In the weaving round the wonder of its need,

And the first flowers upon it, an alphabet
By which to spell out holy doom and end,
A bee for the remembering of happiness.

Peace stood with our last blood adorned, last mind,
Damasked in the originals of green,
A thousand begettings of the broken bold.

This is that figure stationed at our end,
Always, in brilliance, fatal, final, formed
Out of our lives to keep us in our death,

To watch us in the summer of Cyclops
Underground, a king as candle by our beds
In a robe that is our glory as he guards.

v

But she that says good-by losing in self
The sense of self, rosed out of prestiges
Of rose, stood tall in self not symbol, quick

And potent, an influence felt instead of seen.
She spoke with backward gestures of her hand.
She held men closely with discovery,

Almost as speed discovers, in the way
Invisible change discovers what is changed,
In the way what was has ceased to be what is.

It was not her look but a knowledge that she had.
She was a self that knew, an inner thing,
Subtler than look's declaiming, although she moved

With a sad splendor, beyond artifice,
Impassioned by the knowledge that she had,
There on the edges of oblivion.

O exhalation, O fling without a sleeve
And motion outward, reddened and resolved
From sight, in the silence that follows her last word—

VI

This is the mythology of modern death
And these, in their mufflings, monsters of elegy,
Of their own marvel made, of pity made,

Compounded and compounded, life by life,
These are death's own supremest images,
The pure perfections of parental space,

The children of a desire that is the will,
Even of death, the beings of the mind
In the light-bound space of the mind, the floreate flare. . .

It is a child that sings itself to sleep,
The mind, among the creatures that it makes,
The people, those by which it lives and dies.

The Auroras of Autumn

This is where the serpent lives, the bodiless.
His head is air. Beneath his tip at night
Eyes open and fix on us in every sky.

Or is this another wriggling out of the egg,
Another image at the end of the cave,
Another bodiless for the body's slough?

This is where the serpent lives. This is his nest,
These fields, these hills, these tinted distances,
And the pines above and along and beside the sea.

This is form gulping after formlessness,
Skin flashing to wished-for disappearances
And the serpent body flashing without the skin.

This is the height emerging and its base . . .
These lights may finally attain a pole
In the midmost midnight and find the serpent there,

In another nest, the master of the maze
Of body and air and forms and images,
Relentlessly in possession of happiness.

This is his poison: that we should disbelieve
Even that. His meditations in the ferns,
When he moved so slightly to make sure of sun,

Made us no less as sure. We saw in his head,
Black beaded on the rock, the flecked animal,
The moving grass, the Indian in his glade.

Farewell to an idea . . . A cabin stands,
Deserted, on a beach. It is white,
As by a custom or according to

An ancestral theme or as a consequence
Of an infinite course. The flowers against the wall
Are white, a little dried, a kind of mark

Reminding, trying to remind, of a white
That was different, something else, last year
Or before, not the white of an aging afternoon,

Whether fresher or duller, whether of winter cloud
Or of winter sky, from horizon to horizon.
The wind is blowing the sand across the floor.

Here, being visible is being white,
Is being of the solid of white, the accomplishment
Of an extremist in an exercise . . .

The season changes. A cold wind chills the beach.
The long lines of it grow longer, emptier,
A darkness gathers though it does not fall

And the whiteness grows less vivid on the wall.
The man who is walking turns blankly on the sand.
He observes how the north is always enlarging the change,

With its frigid brilliances, its blue-red sweeps
And gusts of great enkindlings, its polar green,
The color of ice and fire and solitude.

Farewell to an idea . . . The mother's face,
The purpose of the poem, fills the room.
They are together, here, and it is warm,

With none of the prescience of oncoming dreams.
It is evening. The house is evening, half dissolved.
Only the half they can never possess remains,

Still-starred. It is the mother they possess,
Who gives transparence to their present peace.
She makes that gentler that can gentle be.

And yet she too is dissolved, she is destroyed.
She gives transparence. But she has grown old.
The necklace is a carving not a kiss.

The soft hands are a motion not a touch.
The house will crumble and the books will burn.
They are at ease in a shelter of the mind

And the house is of the mind and they and time,
Together, all together. Boreal night
Will look like frost as it approaches them

And to the mother as she falls asleep
And as they say good-night, good-night. Upstairs
The windows will be lighted, not the rooms.

A wind will spread its windy grandeurs round
And knock like a rifle-butt against the door.
The wind will command them with invincible sound.

Farewell to an idea . . . The cancellings,
The negations are never final: The father sits
In space, wherever he sits, of bleak regard,

As one that is strong in the bushes of his eyes.
He says no to no and yes to yes. He says yes
To no; and in saying yes he says farewell.

He measures the velocities of change.
He leaps from heaven to heaven more rapidly
Than bad angels leap from heaven to hell in flames.

But now he sits in quiet and green-a-day.
He assumes the great speeds of space and flutters them
From cloud to cloudless, cloudless to keen clear

In flights of eye and ear, the highest eye
And the lowest ear, the deep ear that discerns,
At evening, things that attend it until it hears

The supernatural preludes of its own,
At the moment when the angelic eye defines
Its actors approaching, in company, in their masks.

Master O master seated by the fire
And yet in space and motionless and yet
Of motion the ever-brightening origin,

Profound, and yet the king and yet the crown,
Look at this present throne. What company,
In masks, can choir it with the naked wind?

The mother invites humanity to her house
And table. The father fetches tellers of tales
And musicians who mute much, muse much, on the tales.

The father fetches negresses to dance,
Among the children, like curious ripenesses
Of pattern in the dance's ripening.

For these the musicians make insidious tones,
Clawing the sing-song of their instruments.
The children laugh and jangle a tinny time.

The father fetches pageants out of air,
Scenes of the theatre, vistas and blocks of woods
And curtains like a naive pretence of sleep.

Among these the musicians strike the instinctive poem.
The father fetches his unherded herds,
Of barbarous tongue, slavered and panting halves

Of breath, obedient to his trumpet's touch.
This then is Chatillon or as you please.
We stand in the tumult of a festival.

What festival? This loud, disordered mooch?
These hospitaliers? These brute-like guests?
These musicians dubbing at a tragedy,

A-dub, a-dub, which is made up of this:
That there are no lines to speak? There is no play.
Or, the persons act one merely by being here.

It is a theatre floating through the clouds,
Itself a cloud, although of misted rock
And mountains running like water, wave on wave,

Through waves of light. It is of cloud transformed
To cloud transformed again, idly, the way
A season changes color to no end,

Except the lavishing of itself in change,
As light changes yellow into gold and gold
To its opal elements and fire's delight,

Splashed wide-wise because it likes magnificence
And the solemn pleasures of magnificent space.
The cloud drifts idly through half-thought-of forms.

The theatre is filled with flying birds,
Wild wedges, as of a volcano's smoke, palm-eyed
And vanishing, a web in a corridor

Or massive portico. A capitol,
It may be, is emerging or has just
Collapsed. The denouement has to be postponed . . .

This is nothing until in a single man contained,
Nothing until this named thing nameless is
And is destroyed. He opens the door of his house

On flames. The scholar of one candle sees
An Arctic effulgence flaring on the frame
Of everything he is. And he feels afraid.

Is there an imagination that sits enthroned
As grim as it is benevolent, the just
And the unjust, which in the midst of summer stops

To imagine winter? When the leaves are dead,
Does it take its place in the north and enfold itself,
Goat-leaper, crystalled and luminous, sitting

In highest night? And do these heavens adorn
And proclaim it, the white creator of black, jetted
By extinguishings, even of planets as may be,

Even of earth, even of sight, in snow,
Except as needed by way of majesty,
In the sky, as crown and diamond cabala?

It leaps through us, through all our heavens leaps,
Extinguishing our planets, one by one,
Leaving, of where we were and looked, of where

We knew each other and of each other thought,
A shivering residue, chilled and foregone,
Except for that crown and mystical cabala.

But it dare not leap by chance in its own dark.
It must change from destiny to slight caprice.
And thus its jetted tragedy, its stele

And shape and mournful making move to find
What must unmake it and, at last, what can,
Say, a flippant communication under the moon.

There may be always a time of innocence.
There is never a place. Or if there is no time,
If it is not a thing of time, nor of place,

Existing in the idea of it, alone,
In the sense against calamity, it is not
Less real. For the oldest and coldest philosopher,

There is or may be a time of innocence
As pure principle. Its nature is its end,
That it should be, and yet not be, a thing

That pinches the pity of the pitiful man,
Like a book at evening beautiful but untrue,
Like a book on rising beautiful and true.

It is like a thing of ether that exists
Almost as predicate. But it exists,
It exists, it is visible, it is, it is.

So, then, these lights are not a spell of light,
A saying out of a cloud, but innocence.
An innocence of the earth and no false sign

Or symbol of malice. That we partake thereof,
Lie down like children in this holiness,
As if, awake, we lay in the quiet of sleep,

As if the innocent mother sang in the dark
Of the room and on an accordion, half-heard,
Created the time and place in which we breathed . . .

And of each other thought—in the idiom
Of the work, in the idiom of an innocent earth,
Not of the enigma of the guilty dream.

We were as Danes in Denmark all day long
And knew each other well, hale-hearted landsmen,
For whom the outlandish was another day

Of the week, queerer than Sunday. We thought alike
And that made brothers of us in a home
In which we fed on being brothers, fed

And fattened as on a decorous honeycomb.
This drama that we live—We lay sticky with sleep.
This sense of the activity of fate—

The rendezvous, when she came alone,
By her coming became a freedom of the two,
An isolation which only the two could share.

Shall we be found hanging in the trees next spring?
Of what disaster is this the imminence:
Bare limbs, bare trees and a wind as sharp as salt?

The stars are putting on their glittering belts.
They throw around their shoulders cloaks that flash
Like a great shadow's last embellishment.

It may come tomorrow in the simplest word,
Almost as part of innocence, almost,
Almost as the tenderest and the truest part.

An unhappy people in a happy world—
Read, rabbi, the phases of this difference.
An unhappy people in an unhappy world—

Here are too many mirrors for misery.
A happy people in an unhappy world—
It cannot be. There's nothing there to roll

On the expressive tongue, the finding fang.
A happy people in a happy world—
Buffo! A ball, an opera, a bar.

Turn back to where we were when we began:
An unhappy people in a happy world.
Now, solemnize the secretive syllables.

Read to the congregation, for today
And for tomorrow, this extremity,
This contrivance of the spectre of the spheres,

Contriving balance to contrive a whole,
The vital, the never-failing genius,
Fulfilling his meditations, great and small.

In these unhappy he meditates a whole,
The full of fortune and the full of fate,
As if he lived all lives, that he might know,

In hall harridan, not hushful paradise,
To a haggling of wind and weather, by these lights
Like a blaze of summer straw, in winter's nick.

A Primitive Like an Orb

I

The essential poem at the centre of things,
The arias that spiritual fiddlings make,
Have gorged the cast-iron of our lives with good
And the cast-iron of our works. But it is, dear sirs,
A difficult apperception, this gorging good,
Fetched by such slick-eyed nymphs, this essential gold,
This fortune's finding, disposed and re-disposed
By such slight genii in such pale air.

We do not prove the existence of the poem.
It is something seen and known in lesser poems.
It is the huge, high harmony that sounds
A little and a little, suddenly,
By means of a separate sense. It is and it
Is not and, therefore, is. In the instant of speech,
The breadth of an accelerando moves,
Captives the being, widens—and was there.

What milk there is in such captivity,
What wheaten bread and oaten cake and kind,
Green guests and table in the woods and songs
At heart, within an instant's motion, within
A space grown wide, the inevitable blue
Of secluded thunder, an illusion, as it was,
Oh as, always too heavy for the sense
To seize, the obscurest as, the distant was . . .

One poem proves another and the whole,
For the clairvoyant men that need no proof:
The lover, the believer and the poet.
Their words are chosen out of their desire,
The joy of language, when it is themselves.
With these they celebrate the central poem,
The fulfillment of fulfillments, in opulent,
Last terms, the largest, bulging still with more,

V

Until the used-to earth and sky, and the tree
And cloud, the used-to tree and used-to cloud,
Lose the old uses that they made of them,
And they: these men, and earth and sky, inform
Each other by sharp informations, sharp,
Free knowledges, secreted until then,
Breaches of that which held them fast. It is
As if the central poem became the world,

And the world the central poem, each one the mate
Of the other, as if summer was a spouse,
Espoused each morning, each long afternoon,
And the mate of summer: her mirror and her look,
Her only place and person, a self of her
That speaks, denouncing separate selves, both one.
The essential poem begets the others. The light
Of it is not a light apart, up-hill.

VII

The central poem is the poem of the whole,
The poem of the composition of the whole,
The composition of blue sea and of green,
Of blue light and of green, as lesser poems,

And the miraculous multiplex of lesser poems,
Not merely into a whole, but a poem of
The whole, the essential compact of the parts,
The roundness that pulls tight the final ring

VIII

And that which in an altitude would soar,
A vis, a principle or, it may be,
The meditation of a principle,
Or else an inherent order active to be
Itself, a nature to its natives all
Beneficence, a repose, utmost repose,
The muscles of a magnet aptly felt,
A giant, on the horizon, glistening,

IX

And in bright excellence adorned, crested
With every prodigal, familiar fire,
And unfamiliar escapades: whirroos
And scintillant sizzlings such as children like,
Vested in the serious folds of majesty,
Moving around and behind, a following,
A source of trumpeting seraphs in the eye,
A source of pleasant outbursts on the ear.

X

It is a giant, always, that is evolved,
To be in scale, unless virtue cuts him, snips
Both size and solitude or thinks it does,
As in a signed photograph on a mantelpiece.
But the virtuoso never leaves his shape,
Still on the horizon elongates his cuts,
And still angelic and still plenteous,
Imposes power by the power of his form.

XI

Here, then, is an abstraction given head,
A giant on the horizon, given arms,
A massive body and long legs, stretched out,
A definition with an illustration, not
Too exactly labelled, a large among the smalls
Of it, a close, parental magnitude,
At the centre on the horizon, concentrum, grave
And prodigious person, patron of origins.

That's it. The lover writes, the believer hears,
The poet mumbles and the painter sees,
Each one, his fated eccentricity,
As a part, but part, but tenacious particle,
Of the skeleton of the ether, the total
Of letters, prophecies, perceptions, clods
Of color, the giant of nothingness, each one
And the giant ever changing, living in change.

Large Red Man Reading

There were ghosts that returned to earth to hear his phrases,
As he sat there reading, aloud, the great blue tabulae.
They were those from the wilderness of stars that had expected
    more.

There were those that returned to hear him read from the poem
    of life,
Of the pans above the stove, the pots on the table, the tulips
    among them.
They were those that would have wept to step barefoot into
    reality,

That would have wept and been happy, have shivered in the
    frost
And cried out to feel it again, have run fingers over leaves
And against the most coiled thorn, have seized on what was ugly

And laughed, as he sat there reading, from out of the purple
    tabulae,
The outlines of being and its expressings, the syllables of its
    law:
Poesis, poesis, the literal characters, the vatic lines,

Which in those ears and in those thin, those spended hearts,
Took on color, took on shape and the size of things as they are
And spoke the feeling for them, which was what they had
    lacked.

This Solitude of Cataracts

He never felt twice the same about the flecked river,
Which kept flowing and never the same way twice, flowing

Through many places, as if it stood still in one,
Fixed like a lake on which the wild ducks fluttered,

Ruffling its common reflections, thought-like Monadnocks.
There seemed to be an apostrophe that was not spoken.

There was so much that was real that was not real at all.
He wanted to feel the same way over and over.

He wanted the river to go on flowing the same way,
To keep on flowing. He wanted to walk beside it,

Under the buttonwoods, beneath a moon nailed fast.
He wanted his heart to stop beating and his mind to rest

In a permanent realization, without any wild ducks
Or mountains that were not mountains, just to know how it
    would be,

Just to know how it would feel, released from destruction,
To be a bronze man breathing under archaic lapis,

Without the oscillations of planetary pass-pass,
Breathing his bronzen breath at the azury centre of time.

In a Bad Time

How mad would he have to be to say, "He beheld
An order and thereafter he belonged
To it"? He beheld the order of the northern sky.

But the beggar gazes on calamity
And thereafter he belongs to it, to bread
Hard found, and water tasting of misery.

For him cold's glacial beauty is his fate.
Without understanding, he belongs to it
And the night, and midnight, and after, where it is.

What has he? What he has he has. But what?
It is not a question of captious repartee.
What has he that becomes his heart's strong core?

He has his poverty and nothing more.
His poverty becomes his heart's strong core—
A forgetfulness of summer at the pole.

Sordid Melpomene, why strut bare boards,
Without scenery or lights, in the theatre's bricks,
Dressed high in heliotrope's inconstant hue,

The muse of misery? Speak loftier lines.
Cry out, "I am the purple muse." Make sure
The audience beholds you, not your gown.

Metaphor as Degeneration

If there is a man white as marble
Sits in a wood, in the greenest part,
Brooding sounds of the images of death,

So there is a man in black space
Sits in nothing that we know,
Brooding sounds of river noises;

And these images, these reverberations,
And others, make certain how being
Includes death and the imagination.

The marble man remains himself in space.
The man in the black wood descends unchanged.
It is certain that the river

Is not Swatara. The swarthy water
That flows round the earth and through the skies,
Twisting among the universal spaces,

Is not Swatara. It is being.
That is the flock-flecked river, the water,
The blown sheen—or is it air?

How, then, is metaphor degeneration,
When Swatara becomes this undulant river
And the river becomes the landless, waterless ocean?

Here the black violets grow down to its banks
And the memorial mosses hang their green
Upon it, as it flows ahead.

Our Stars Come from Ireland

I

Tom McGreevy, in America, Thinks of Himself as a Boy

Out of him that I loved,
Mal Bay I made,
I made Mal Bay
And him in that water.

Over the top of the Bank of Ireland,
The wind blows quaintly
Its thin-stringed music,
As he heard it in Tarbert.

These things were made of him
And out of myself.
He stayed in Kerry, died there.
I live in Pennsylvania.

Out of him I made Mal Bay
And not a bald and tasselled saint.
What would the water have been,
Without that that he makes of it?

The stars are washing up from Ireland
And through and over the puddles of Swatara
And Schuylkill. The sound of him
Comes from a great distance and is heard.

II

The Westwardness of Everything

These are the ashes of fiery weather,
Of nights full of the green stars from Ireland,
Wet out of the sea, and luminously wet,
Like beautiful and abandoned refugees.

The whole habit of the mind is changed by them,
These Gaeled and fitful-fangled darknesses
Made suddenly luminous, themselves a change,
An east in their compelling westwardness,

Themselves an issue as at an end, as if
There was an end at which in a final change,
When the whole habit of the mind was changed,
The ocean breathed out morning in one breath.

World Without Peculiarity

The day is great and strong—
But his father was strong, that lies now
In the poverty of dirt.

Nothing could be more hushed than the way
The moon moves toward the night.
But what his mother was returns and cries on his breast.

The red ripeness of round leaves is thick
With the spices of red summer.
But she that he loved turns cold at his light touch.

What good is it that the earth is justified,
That it is complete, that it is an end,
That in itself it is enough?

It is the earth itself that is humanity . . .
He is the inhuman son and she,
She is the fateful mother, whom he does not know.

She is the day, the walk of the moon
Among the breathless spices and, sometimes,
He, too, is human and difference disappears

And the poverty of dirt, the thing upon his breast,
The hating woman, the meaningless place,
Become a single being, sure and true.

The Woman in Sunshine

It is only that this warmth and movement are like
The warmth and movement of a woman.

It is not that there is any image in the air
Nor the beginning nor end of a form:

It is empty. But a woman in threadless gold
Burns us with brushings of her dress

And a dissociated abundance of being,
More definite for what she is—

Because she is disembodied,
Bearing the odors of the summer fields,

Confessing the taciturn and yet indifferent,
Invisibly clear, the only love.

Imago

Who can pick up the weight of Britain,
Who can move the German load
Or say to the French here is France again?
Imago. Imago. Imago.

It is nothing, no great thing, nor man
Of ten brilliancies of battered gold
And fortunate stone. It moves its parade
Of motions in the mind and heart,

A gorgeous fortitude. Medium man
In February hears the imagination's hymns
And sees its images, its motions
And multitude of motions

And feels the imagination's mercies,
In a season more than sun and south wind,
Something returning from a deeper quarter,
A glacier running through delirium,

Making this heavy rock a place,
Which is not of our lives composed . . .
Lightly and lightly, O my land,
Move lightly through the air again.

Saint John and the Back-Ache

The Back-Ache
    The mind is the terriblest force in the world, father,
    Because, in chief, it, only, can defend
    Against itself. At its mercy, we depend
        Upon it.
Saint John
            The world is presence and not force.
    Presence is not mind.
The Back-Ache
                Presence is *Kinder-Scenen.*
Saint John
    It fills the being before the mind can think.
    The effect of the object is beyond the mind's

Extremest pinch and, easily, as in
A sudden color on the sea. But it is not
That big-brushed green. Or in a tragic mode,
As at the moment of the year when, tick,
Autumn howls upon half-naked summer. But
It is not the unravelling of her yellow shift.
Presence is not the woman, come upon,
Not yet accustomed, yet, at sight, humane
To most incredible depths. I speak below
The tension of the lyre. My point is that
These illustrations are neither angels, no,
Nor brilliant blows thereof, ti-rill-a-roo,
Nor all one's luck at once in a play of strings.
They help us face the dumbfoundering abyss
Between us and the object, external cause,
The little ignorance that is everything,
The possible nest in the invisible tree,
Which in a composite season, now unknown,
Denied, dismissed, may hold a serpent, loud
In our captious hymns, erect and sinuous,
Whose venom and whose wisdom will be one.
Then the stale turtle will grow limp from age.
We shall be heavy with the knowledge of that day.

The Back-Ache

It may be, may be. It is possible.
Presence lies far too deep, for me to know
Its irrational reaction, as from pain.

Puella Parvula

Every thread of summer is at last unwoven.
By one caterpillar is great Africa devoured
And Gibraltar is dissolved like spit in the wind.

But over the wind, over the legends of its roaring,
The elephant on the roof and its elephantine blaring,
The bloody lion in the yard at night or ready to spring

From the clouds in the midst of trembling trees
Making a great gnashing, over the water wallows
Of a vacant sea declaiming with wide throat,

Over all these the mighty imagination triumphs
Like a trumpet and says, in this season of memory,
When the leaves fall like things mournful of the past,

Keep quiet in the heart, O wild bitch. O mind
Gone wild, be what he tells you to be: *Puella.*
Write *pax* across the window pane. And then

Be still. The *summarium in excelsis* begins . . .
Flame, sound, fury composed . . . Hear what he says,
The dauntless master, as he starts the human tale.

An Ordinary Evening in New Haven

The eye's plain version is a thing apart,
The vulgate of experience. Of this,
A few words, an and yet, and yet, and yet—

As part of the never-ending meditation,
Part of the question that is a giant himself:
Of what is this house composed if not of the sun,

These houses, these difficult objects, dilapidate
Appearances of what appearances,
Words, lines, not meanings, not communications,

Dark things without a double, after all,
Unless a second giant kills the first—
A recent imagining of reality,

Much like a new resemblance of the sun,
Down-pouring, up-springing and inevitable,
A larger poem for a larger audience,

As if the crude collops came together as one,
A mythological form, a festival sphere,
A great bosom, beard and being, alive with age.

II

Suppose these houses are composed of ourselves,
So that they become an impalpable town, full of
Impalpable bells, transparencies of sound,

Sounding in transparent dwellings of the self,
Impalpable habitations that seem to move
In the movement of the colors of the mind,

The far-fire flowing and the dim-coned bells
Coming together in a sense in which we are poised,
Without regard to time or where we are,

In the perpetual reference, object
Of the perpetual meditation, point
Of the enduring, visionary love,

Obscure, in colors whether of the sun
Or mind, uncertain in the clearest bells,
The spirit's speeches, the indefinite,

Confused illuminations and sonorities,
So much ourselves, we cannot tell apart
The idea and the bearer-being of the idea.

III

The point of vision and desire are the same.
It is to the hero of midnight that we pray
On a hill of stones to make beau mont thereof.

If it is misery that infuriates our love,
If the black of night stands glistening on beau mont,
Then, ancientest saint ablaze with ancientest truth,

Say next to holiness is the will thereto,
And next to love is the desire for love,
The desire for its celestial ease in the heart,

Which nothing can frustrate, that most secure,
Unlike love in possession of that which was
To be possessed and is. But this cannot

Possess. It is desire, set deep in the eye,
Behind all actual seeing, in the actual scene,
In the street, in a room, on a carpet or a wall,

Always in emptiness that would be filled,
In denial that cannot contain its blood,
A porcelain, as yet in the bats thereof.

IV

The plainness of plain things is savagery,
As: the last plainness of a man who has fought
Against illusion and was, in a great grinding

Of growling teeth, and falls at night, snuffed out
By the obese opiates of sleep. Plain men in plain towns
Are not precise about the appeasement they need.

They only know a savage assuagement cries
With a savage voice; and in that cry they hear
Themselves transposed, muted and comforted

In a savage and subtle and simple harmony,
A matching and mating of surprised accords,
A responding to a diviner opposite.

So lewd spring comes from winter's chastity.
So, after summer, in the autumn air,
Comes the cold volume of forgotten ghosts,

But soothingly, with pleasant instruments,
So that this cold, a children's tale of ice,
Seems like a sheen of heat romanticized.

V

Inescapable romance, inescapable choice
Of dreams, disillusion as the last illusion,
Reality as a thing seen by the mind,

Not that which is but that which is apprehended,
A mirror, a lake of reflections in a room,
A glassy ocean lying at the door,

A great town hanging pendent in a shade,
An enormous nation happy in a style,
Everything as unreal as real can be,

In the inexquisite eye. Why, then, inquire
Who has divided the world, what entrepreneur?
No man. The self, the chrysalis of all men

Became divided in the leisure of blue day
And more, in branchings after day. One part
Held fast tenaciously in common earth

And one from central earth to central sky
And in moonlit extensions of them in the mind
Searched out such majesty as it could find.

VI

Reality is the beginning not the end,
Naked Alpha, not the hierophant Omega,
Of dense investiture, with luminous vassals.

It is the infant A standing on infant legs,
Not twisted, stooping, polymathic Z,
He that kneels always on the edge of space

In the pallid perceptions of its distances.
Alpha fears men or else Omega's men
Or else his prolongations of the human.

These characters are around us in the scene.
For one it is enough; for one it is not;
For neither is it profound absentia,

Since both alike appoint themselves the choice
Custodians of the glory of the scene,
The immaculate interpreters of life.

But that's the difference: in the end and the way
To the end. Alpha continues to begin.
Omega is refreshed at every end.

VII

In the presence of such chapels and such schools,
The impoverished architects appear to be
Much richer, more fecund, sportive and alive.

The objects tingle and the spectator moves
With the objects. But the spectator also moves
With lesser things, with things exteriorized

Out of rigid realists. It is as if
Men turning into things, as comedy,
Stood, dressed in antic symbols, to display

The truth about themselves, having lost, as things,
That power to conceal they had as men,
Not merely as to depth but as to height

As well, not merely as to the commonplace
But, also, as to their miraculous,
Conceptions of new mornings of new worlds,

The tips of cock-cry pinked out pastily,
As that which was incredible becomes,
In misted contours, credible day again.

VIII

We fling ourselves, constantly longing, on this form.
We descend to the street and inhale a health of air
To our sepulchral hollows. Love of the real

Is soft in three-four cornered fragrances
From five-six cornered leaves, and green, the signal
To the lover, and blue, as of a secret place

In the anonymous color of the universe.
Our breath is like a desperate element
That we must calm, the origin of a mother tongue

With which to speak to her, the capable
In the midst of foreignness, the syllable
Of recognition, avowal, impassioned cry,

The cry that contains its converse in itself,
In which looks and feelings mingle and are part
As a quick answer modifies a question,

Not wholly spoken in a conversation between
Two bodies disembodied in their talk,
Too fragile, too immediate for any speech.

IX

We keep coming back and coming back
To the real: to the hotel instead of the hymns
That fall upon it out of the wind. We seek

The poem of pure reality, untouched
By trope or deviation, straight to the word,
Straight to the transfixing object, to the object

At the exactest point at which it is itself,
Transfixing by being purely what it is,
A view of New Haven, say, through the certain eye,

The eye made clear of uncertainty, with the sight
Of simple seeing, without reflection. We seek
Nothing beyond reality. Within it,

Everything, the spirit's alchemicana
Included, the spirit that goes roundabout
And through included, not merely the visible,

The solid, but the movable, the moment,
The coming on of feasts and the habits of saints,
The pattern of the heavens and high, night air.

X

It is fatal in the moon and empty there.
But, here, allons. The enigmatical
Beauty of each beautiful enigma

Becomes amassed in a total double-thing.
We do not know what is real and what is not.
We say of the moon, it is haunted by the man

Of bronze whose mind was made up and who, there-
        fore, died.
We are not men of bronze and we are not dead.
His spirit is imprisoned in constant change.

But ours is not imprisoned. It resides
In a permanence composed of impermanence,
In a faithfulness as against the lunar light,

So that morning and evening are like promises kept,
So that the approaching sun and its arrival,
Its evening feast and the following festival,

This faithfulness of reality, this mode,
This tendance and venerable holding-in
Make gay the hallucinations in surfaces.

XI

In the metaphysical streets of the physical town
We remember the lion of Juda and we save
The phrase . . . Say of each lion of the spirit

It is a cat of a sleek transparency
That shines with a nocturnal shine alone.
The great cat must stand potent in the sun.

The phrase grows weak. The fact takes up the strength
Of the phrase. It contrives the self-same evocations
And Juda becomes New Haven or else must.

In the metaphysical streets, the profoundest forms
Go with the walker subtly walking there.
These he destroys with wafts of wakening,

Free from their majesty and yet in need
Of majesty, of an invincible clou,
A minimum of making in the mind,

A verity of the most veracious men,
The propounding of four seasons and twelve months,
The brilliancy at the central of the earth.

XII

The poem is the cry of its occasion,
Part of the res itself and not about it.
The poet speaks the poem as it is,

Not as it was: part of the reverberation
Of a windy night as it is, when the marble statues
Are like newspapers blown by the wind. He speaks

By sight and insight as they are. There is no
Tomorrow for him. The wind will have passed by,
The statues will have gone back to be things about.

The mobile and the immobile flickering
In the area between is and was are leaves,
Leaves burnished in autumnal burnished trees

And leaves in whirlings in the gutters, whirlings
Around and away, resembling the presence of thought,
Resembling the presences of thoughts, as if,

In the end, in the whole psychology, the self,
The town, the weather, in a casual litter,
Together, said words of the world are the life of the
    world.

XIII

The ephebe is solitary in his walk.
He skips the journalism of subjects, seeks out
The perquisites of sanctity, enjoys

A strong mind in a weak neighborhood and is
A serious man without the serious,
Inactive in his singular respect.

He is neither priest nor proctor at low eve,
Under the birds, among the perilous owls,
In the big X of the returning primitive.

It is a fresh spiritual that he defines,
A coldness in a long, too-constant warmth,
A thing on the side of a house, not deep in a cloud,

A difficulty that we predicate:
The difficulty of the visible
To the nations of the clear invisible,

The actual landscape with its actual horns
Of baker and butcher blowing, as if to hear,
Hear hard, gets at an essential integrity.

XIV

The dry eucalyptus seeks god in the rainy cloud.
Professor Eucalyptus of New Haven seeks him
In New Haven with an eye that does not look

Beyond the object. He sits in his room, beside
The window, close to the ramshackle spout in which
The rain falls with a ramshackle sound. He seeks

339

God in the object itself, without much choice.
It is a choice of the commodious adjective
For what he sees, it comes in the end to that:

The description that makes it divinity, still speech
As it touches the point of reverberation—not grim
Reality but reality grimly seen

And spoken in paradisal parlance new
And in any case never grim, the human grim
That is part of the indifference of the eye

Indifferent to what it sees. The tink-tonk
Of the rain in the spout is not a substitute.
It is of the essence not yet well perceived.

xv

He preserves himself against the repugnant rain
By an instinct for a rainless land, the self
Of his self, come at upon wide delvings of wings.

The instinct for heaven had its counterpart:
The instinct for earth, for New Haven, for his room,
The gay tournamonde as of a single world

In which he is and as and is are one.
For its counterpart a kind of counterpoint
Irked the wet wallows of the water-spout.

The rain kept falling loudly in the trees
And on the ground. The hibernal dark that hung
In primavera, the shadow of bare rock,

Becomes the rock of autumn, glittering,
Ponderable source of each imponderable,
The weight we lift with the finger of a dream,

340

The heaviness we lighten by light will,
By the hand of desire, faint, sensitive, the soft
Touch and trouble of the touch of the actual hand.

XVI

Among time's images, there is not one
Of this present, the venerable mask above
The dilapidation of dilapidations.

The oldest-newest day is the newest alone.
The oldest-newest night does not creak by,
With lanterns, like a celestial ancientness.

Silently it heaves its youthful sleep from the sea—
The Oklahoman—the Italian blue
Beyond the horizon with its masculine,

Their eyes closed, in a young palaver of lips.
And yet the wind whimpers oldly of old age
In the western night. The venerable mask,

In this perfection, occasionally speaks
And something of death's poverty is heard.
This should be tragedy's most moving face.

It is a bough in the electric light
And exhalations in the eaves, so little
To indicate the total leaflessness.

XVII

The color is almost the color of comedy,
Not quite. It comes to the point and at the point,
It fails. The strength at the centre is serious.

Perhaps instead of failing it rejects
As a serious strength rejects pin-idleness.
A blank underlies the trials of device,

The dominant blank, the unapproachable.
This is the mirror of the high serious:
Blue verdured into a damask's lofty symbol,

Gold easings and ouncings and fluctuations of thread
And beetling of belts and lights of general stones,
Like blessed beams from out a blessed bush

Or the wasted figurations of the wastes
Of night, time and the imagination,
Saved and beholden, in a robe of rays.

These fitful sayings are, also, of tragedy:
The serious reflection is composed
Neither of comic nor tragic but of commonplace.

XVIII

It is the window that makes it difficult
To say good-by to the past and to live and to be
In the present state of things as, say, to paint

In the present state of painting and not the state
Of thirty years ago. It is looking out
Of the window and walking in the street and seeing,

As if the eyes were the present or part of it,
As if the ears heard any shocking sound,
As if life and death were ever physical.

The life and death of this carpenter depend
On a fuchsia in a can—and iridescences
Of petals that will never be realized,

Things not yet true which he perceives through truth,
Or thinks he does, as he perceives the present,
Or thinks he does, a carpenter's iridescences,

342

Wooden, the model for astral apprentices,
A city slapped up like a chest of tools,
The eccentric exterior of which the clocks talk.

XIX

The moon rose in the mind and each thing there
Picked up its radial aspect in the night,
Prostrate below the singleness of its will.

That which was public green turned private gray.
At another time, the radial aspect came
From a different source. But there was always one:

A century in which everything was part
Of that century and of its aspect, a personage,
A man who was the axis of his time,

An image that begot its infantines,
Imaginary poles whose intelligence
Streamed over chaos their civilities.

What is the radial aspect of this place,
This present colony of a colony
Of colonies, a sense in the changing sense

Of things? A figure like Ecclesiast,
Rugged and luminous, chants in the dark
A text that is an answer, although obscure.

XX

The imaginative transcripts were like clouds,
Today; and the transcripts of feeling, impossible
To distinguish. The town was a residuum,

A neuter shedding shapes in an absolute.
Yet the transcripts of it when it was blue remain;
And the shapes that it took in feeling, the persons that

It became, the nameless, flitting characters—
These actors still walk in a twilight muttering lines.
It may be that they mingle, clouds and men, in the air

Or street or about the corners of a man,
Who sits thinking in the corners of a room.
In this chamber the pure sphere escapes the impure,

Because the thinker himself escapes. And yet
To have evaded clouds and men leaves him
A naked being with a naked will

And everything to make. He may evade
Even his own will and in his nakedness
Inhabit the hypnosis of that sphere.

XXI

But he may not. He may not evade his will,
Nor the wills of other men; and he cannot evade
The will of necessity, the will of wills—

Romanza out of the black shepherd's isle,
Like the constant sound of the water of the sea
In the hearing of the shepherd and his black forms;

Out of the isle, but not of any isle.
Close to the senses there lies another isle
And there the senses give and nothing take,

The opposite of Cythère, an isolation
At the centre, the object of the will, this place,
The things around—the alternate romanza

Out of the surfaces, the windows, the walls,
The bricks grown brittle in time's poverty,
The clear. A celestial mode is paramount,

If only in the branches sweeping in the rain:
The two romanzas, the distant and the near,
Are a single voice in the boo-ha of the wind.

XXII

Professor Eucalyptus said, "The search
For reality is as momentous as
The search for god." It is the philosopher's search

For an interior made exterior
And the poet's search for the same exterior made
Interior: breathless things broodingly abreath

With the inhalations of original cold
And of original earliness. Yet the sense
Of cold and earliness is a daily sense,

Not the predicate of bright origin.
Creation is not renewed by images
Of lone wanderers. To re-create, to use

The cold and earliness and bright origin
Is to search. Likewise to say of the evening star,
The most ancient light in the most ancient sky,

That it is wholly an inner light, that it shines
From the sleepy bosom of the real, re-creates,
Searches a possible for its possibleness.

XXIII

The sun is half the world, half everything,
The bodiless half. There is always this bodiless half,
This illumination, this elevation, this future

Or, say, the late going colors of that past,
Effete green, the woman in black cassimere.
If, then, New Haven is half sun, what remains,

345

At evening, after dark, is the other half,
Lighted by space, big over those that sleep,
Of the single future of night, the single sleep,

As of a long, inevitable sound,
A kind of cozening and coaxing sound,
And the goodness of lying in a maternal sound,

Unfretted by day's separate, several selves,
Being part of everything come together as one.
In this identity, disembodiments

Still keep occurring. What is, uncertainly,
Desire prolongs its adventure to create
Forms of farewell, furtive among green ferns.

XXIV

The consolations of space are nameless things.
It was after the neurosis of winter. It was
In the genius of summer that they blew up

The statue of Jove among the boomy clouds.
It took all day to quieten the sky
And then to refill its emptiness again,

So that at the edge of afternoon, not over,
Before the thought of evening had occurred
Or the sound of Incomincia had been set,

There was a clearing, a readiness for first bells,
An opening for outpouring, the hand was raised:
There was a willingness not yet composed,

A knowing that something certain had been proposed,
Which, without the statue, would be new,
An escape from repetition, a happening

In space and the self, that touched them both at once
And alike, a point of the sky or of the earth
Or of a town poised at the horizon's dip.

XXV

Life fixed him, wandering on the stair of glass,
With its attentive eyes. And, as he stood,
On his balcony, outsensing distances,

There were looks that caught him out of empty air.
C'est toujours la vie qui me regarde . . . This was
Who watched him, always, for unfaithful thought.

This sat beside his bed, with its guitar,
To keep him from forgetting, without a word,
A note or two disclosing who it was.

Nothing about him ever stayed the same,
Except this hidalgo and his eye and tune,
The shawl across one shoulder and the hat.

The commonplace became a rumpling of blazons.
What was real turned into something most unreal,
Bare beggar-tree, hung low for fruited red

In isolated moments—isolations
Were false. The hidalgo was permanent, abstract,
A hatching that stared and demanded an answering look.

XXVI

How facilely the purple blotches fell
On the walk, purple and blue, and red and gold,
Blooming and beaming and voluming colors out.

Away from them, capes, along the afternoon Sound,
Shook off their dark marine in lapis light.
The sea shivered in transcendent change, rose up

347

As rain and booming, gleaming, blowing, swept
The wateriness of green wet in the sky.
Mountains appeared with greater eloquence

Than that of their clouds. These lineaments were the
earth,
Seen as inamorata, of loving fame
Added and added out of a fame-full heart . . .

But, here, the inamorata, without distance
And thereby lost, and naked or in rags,
Shrunk in the poverty of being close,

Touches, as one hand touches another hand,
Or as a voice that, speaking without form,
Gritting the ear, whispers humane repose.

XXVII

A scholar, in his Segmenta, left a note,
As follows, "The Ruler of Reality,
If more unreal than New Haven, is not

A real ruler, but rules what is unreal."
In addition, there were draftings of him, thus:
"He is the consort of the Queen of Fact.

Sunrise is his garment's hem, sunset is hers.
He is the theorist of life, not death,
The total excellence of its total book."

Again, "The sibilance of phrases is his
Or partly his. His voice is audible,
As the fore-meaning in music is." Again,

"This man abolishes by being himself
That which is not ourselves: the regalia,
The attributions, the plume and helmet-ho."

Again, "He has thought it out, he thinks it out,
As he has been and is and, with the Queen
Of Fact, lies at his ease beside the sea."

XXVIII

If it should be true that reality exists
In the mind: the tin plate, the loaf of bread on it,
The long-bladed knife, the little to drink and her

Misericordia, it follows that
Real and unreal are two in one: New Haven
Before and after one arrives or, say,

Bergamo on a postcard, Rome after dark,
Sweden described, Salzburg with shaded eyes
Or Paris in conversation at a café.

This endlessly elaborating poem
Displays the theory of poetry,
As the life of poetry. A more severe,

More harassing master would extemporize
Subtler, more urgent proof that the theory
Of poetry is the theory of life,

As it is, in the intricate evasions of as,
In things seen and unseen, created from nothingness,
The heavens, the hells, the worlds, the longed-for lands.

XXIX

In the land of the lemon trees, yellow and yellow were
Yellow-blue, yellow-green, pungent with citron-sap,
Dangling and spangling, the mic-mac of mocking birds.

In the land of the elm trees, wandering mariners
Looked on big women, whose ruddy-ripe images
Wreathed round and round the round wreath of autumn.

They rolled their r's, there, in the land of the citrons.
In the land of big mariners, the words they spoke
Were mere brown clods, mere catching weeds of talk.

When the mariners came to the land of the lemon trees,
At last, in that blond atmosphere, bronzed hard,
They said, "We are back once more in the land of the
    elm trees,

But folded over, turned round." It was the same,
Except for the adjectives, an alteration
Of words that was a change of nature, more

Than the difference that clouds make over a town.
The countrymen were changed and each constant thing.
Their dark-colored words had redescribed the citrons.

XXX

The last leaf that is going to fall has fallen.
The robins are là-bas, the squirrels, in tree-caves,
Huddle together in the knowledge of squirrels.

The wind has blown the silence of summer away.
It buzzes beyond the horizon or in the ground:
In mud under ponds, where the sky used to be reflected.

The barrenness that appears is an exposing.
It is not part of what is absent, a halt
For farewells, a sad hanging on for remembrances.

It is a coming on and a coming forth.
The pines that were fans and fragrances emerge,
Staked solidly in a gusty grappling with rocks.

The glass of the air becomes an element—
It was something imagined that has been washed away.
A clearness has returned. It stands restored.

It is not an empty clearness, a bottomless sight.
It is a visibility of thought,
In which hundreds of eyes, in one mind, see at once.

XXXI

The less legible meanings of sounds, the little reds
Not often realized, the lighter words
In the heavy drum of speech, the inner men

Behind the outer shields, the sheets of music
In the strokes of thunder, dead candles at the window
When day comes, fire-foams in the motions of the sea,

Flickings from finikin to fine finikin
And the general fidget from busts of Constantine
To photographs of the late president, Mr. Blank,

These are the edgings and inchings of final form,
The swarming activities of the formulae
Of statement, directly and indirectly getting at,

Like an evening evoking the spectrum of violet,
A philosopher practicing scales on his piano,
A woman writing a note and tearing it up.

It is not in the premise that reality
Is a solid. It may be a shade that traverses
A dust, a force that traverses a shade.

The Old Lutheran Bells at Home

These are the voices of the pastors calling
In the names of St. Paul and of the halo-John
And of other holy and learned men, among them

Great choristers, propounders of hymns, trumpeters,
Jerome and the scrupulous Francis and Sunday women,
The nurses of the spirit's innocence.

These are the voices of the pastors calling
Much rough-end being to smooth Paradise,
Spreading out fortress walls like fortress wings.

Deep in their sound the stentor Martin sings.
Dark Juan looks outward through his mystic brow . . .
Each sexton has his sect. The bells have none.

These are the voices of the pastors calling
And calling like the long echoes in long sleep,
Generations of shepherds to generations of sheep.

Each truth is a sect though no bells ring for it.
And the bells belong to the sextons, after all,
As they jangle and dangle and kick their feet.

Questions Are Remarks

In the weed of summer comes this green sprout why.
The sun aches and ails and then returns halloo
Upon the horizon amid adult enfantillages.

Its fire fails to pierce the vision that beholds it,
Fails to destroy the antique acceptances,
Except that the grandson sees it as it is,

Peter the voyant, who says "Mother, what is that"—
The object that rises with so much rhetoric,
But not for him. His question is complete.

It is the question of what he is capable.
It is the extreme, the expert aetat. 2.
He will never ride the red horse she describes.

His question is complete because it contains
His utmost statement. It is his own array,
His own pageant and procession and display,

As far as nothingness permits . . . Hear him.
He does not say, "Mother, my mother, who are you,"
The way the drowsy, infant, old men do.

Angel Surrounded by Paysans

One of the countrymen:

                                                    There is
A welcome at the door to which no one comes?
The angel:
I am the angel of reality,
Seen for a moment standing in the door.

I have neither ashen wing nor wear of ore
And live without a tepid aureole,

Or stars that follow me, not to attend,
But, of my being and its knowing, part.

I am one of you and being one of you
Is being and knowing what I am and know.

Yet I am the necessary angel of earth,
Since, in my sight, you see the earth again,

Cleared of its stiff and stubborn, man-locked set,
And, in my hearing, you hear its tragic drone

Rise liquidly in liquid lingerings,
Like watery words awash; like meanings said

By repetitions of half-meanings. Am I not,
Myself, only half of a figure of a sort,

A figure half seen, or seen for a moment, a man
Of the mind, an apparition apparelled in

Apparels of such lightest look that a turn
Of my shoulder and quickly, too quickly, I am gone?

Things of August

I

These locusts by day, these crickets by night
Are the instruments on which to play
Of an old and disused ambit of the soul
Or of a new aspect, bright in discovery—

A disused ambit of the spirit's way,
The sort of thing that August crooners sing,
By a pure fountain, that was a ghost, and is,
Under the sun-slides of a sloping mountain;

Or else a new aspect, say the spirit's sex,
Its attitudes, its answers to attitudes
And the sex of its voices, as the voice of one
Meets nakedly another's naked voice.

Nothing is lost, loud locusts. No note fails.
These sounds are long in the living of the ear.
The honky-tonk out of the somnolent grasses
Is a memorizing, a trying out, to keep.

II

We make, although inside an egg,
Variations on the words spread sail.

The morning-glories grow in the egg.
It is full of the myrrh and camphor of summer

And Adirondack glittering. The cat hawks it
And the hawk cats it and we say spread sail,

Spread sail, we say spread white, spread way.
The shell is a shore. The egg of the sea

And the egg of the sky are in shells, in walls, in skins
And the egg of the earth lies deep within an egg.

Spread outward. Crack the round dome. Break
    through.
Have liberty not as the air within a grave

Or down a well. Breathe freedom, oh, my native,
In the space of horizons that neither love nor hate.

III

High poetry and low:
Experience in perihelion
Or in the penumbra of summer night—

The solemn sentences,
Like interior intonations,
The speech of truth in its true solitude,
A nature that is created in what it says,
The peace of the last intelligence;

Or the same thing without desire,
He that in this intelligence
Mistakes it for a world of objects,
Which, being green and blue, appease him,
By chance, or happy chance, or happiness,
According to his thought, in the Mediterranean
Of the quiet of the middle of the night,
With the broken statues standing on the shore.

IV

The sad smell of the lilacs—one remembered it,
Not as the fragrance of Persephone,
Nor of a widow Dooley,
But as of an exhumation returned to earth,

The rich earth, of its own self made rich,
Fertile of its own leaves and days and wars,
Of its brown wheat rapturous in the wind,
The nature of its women in the air,

The stern voices of its necessitous men,
This chorus as of those that wanted to live.
The sentiment of the fatal is a part
Of filial love. Or is it the element,

An approximation of an element,
A little thing to think of on Sunday walks,
Something not to be mentioned to Mrs. Dooley,
An arrogant dagger darting its arrogance,

In the parent's hand, perhaps parental love?
One wished that there had been a season,
Longer and later, in which the lilacs opened
And spread about them a warmer, rosier odor.

v

We'll give the week-end to wisdom, to Weisheit, the
    rabbi,
Lucidity of his city, joy of his nation,
The state of circumstance.

The thinker as reader reads what has been written.
He wears the words he reads to look upon
Within his being,

A crown within him of crispest diamonds,
A reddened garment falling to his feet,
A hand of light to turn the page,

A finger with a ring to guide his eye
From line to line, as we lie on the grass and listen
To that which has no speech,

357

The voluble intentions of the symbols,
The ghostly celebrations of the picnic,
The secretions of insight.

VI

The world imagines for the beholder.
He is born the blank mechanic of the mountains,

The blank frere of fields, their matin laborer.
He is the possessed of sense not the possessor.

He does not change the sea from crumpled tinfoil
To chromatic crawler. But it is changed.

He does not raise the rousing of fresh light
On the still, black-slatted eastward shutters.

The woman is chosen but not by him,
Among the endlessly emerging accords.

The world? The inhuman as human? That which
    thinks not,
Feels not, resembling thought, resembling feeling?

It habituates him to the invisible,
By its faculty of the exceptional,

The faculty of ellipses and deviations,
In which he exists but never as himself.

VII

He turned from the tower to the house,
From the spun sky and the high and deadly view,
To the novels on the table,
The geraniums on the sill.

358

He could understand the things at home.
And being up high had helped him when up high,
As if on a taller tower
He would be certain to see

That, in the shadowless atmosphere,
The knowledge of things lay round but unperceived:
The height was not quite proper;
The position was wrong.

It was curious to have to descend
And, seated in the nature of his chair,
To feel the satisfactions
Of that transparent air.

VIII

When was it that the particles became
The whole man, that tempers and beliefs became
Temper and belief and that differences lost
Difference and were one? It had to be
In the presence of a solitude of the self,
An expanse and the abstraction of an expanse,
A zone of time without the ticking of clocks,
A color that moved us with forgetfulness.
When was it that we heard the voice of union?

Was it as we sat in the park and the archaic form
Of a woman with a cloud on her shoulder rose
Against the trees and then against the sky
And the sense of the archaic touched us at once
In a movement of the outlines of similarity?

We resembled one another at the sight.
The forgetful color of the autumn day
Was full of these archaic forms, giants

Of sense, evoking one thing in many men,
Evoking an archaic space, vanishing
In the space, leaving an outline of the size
Of the impersonal person, the wanderer,
The father, the ancestor, the bearded peer,
The total of human shadows bright as glass.

IX

A new text of the world,
A scribble of fret and fear and fate,
From a bravura of the mind,
A courage of the eye,

In which, for all the breathings
From the edge of night,
And for all the white voices
That were rosen once,

The meanings are our own—
It is a text that we shall be needing,
To be the footing of noon,
The pillar of midnight,

That comes from ourselves, neither from knowing
Nor not knowing, yet free from question,
Because we wanted it so
And it had to be,

A text of intelligent men
At the centre of the unintelligible,
As in a hermitage, for us to think,
Writing and reading the rigid inscription.

X

The mornings grow silent, the never-tiring wonder.
The trees are reappearing in poverty.

Without rain, there is the sadness of rain
And an air of lateness. The moon is a tricorn

Waved in pale adieu. The rex Impolitor
Will come stamping here, the ruler of less than men,

In less than nature. He is not here yet.
Here the adult one is still banded with fulgor,

Is still warm with the love with which she came,
Still touches solemnly with what she was

And willed. She has given too much, but not enough.
She is exhausted and a little old.

As at a Theatre

Another sunlight might make another world,
Green, more or less, in green and blue in blue,
Like taste distasting the first fruit of a vine,
Like an eye too young to grapple its primitive,
Like the artifice of a new reality,
Like the chromatic calendar of time to come.

It might be the candle of another being,
Ragged in unkempt perceptions, that stands
And meditates an image of itself,
Studies and shapes a tallowy image, swarmed
With slight, prismatic reeks not recollected,
A bubble without a wall on which to hang.

The curtains, when pulled, might show another whole,
An azure outre-terre, oranged and rosed,
At the elbow of Copernicus, a sphere,
A universe without life's limp and lack,
Philosophers' end . . . What difference would it make,
So long as the mind, for once, fulfilled itself?

The Rock

Seventy Years Later

It is an illusion that we were ever alive,
Lived in the houses of mothers, arranged ourselves
By our own motions in a freedom of air.

Regard the freedom of seventy years ago.
It is no longer air. The houses still stand,
Though they are rigid in rigid emptiness.

Even our shadows, their shadows, no longer remain.
The lives these lived in the mind are at an end.
They never were . . . The sounds of the guitar

Were not and are not. Absurd. The words spoken
Were not and are not. It is not to be believed.
The meeting at noon at the edge of the field seems like

An invention, an embrace between one desperate clod
And another in a fantastic consciousness,
In a queer assertion of humanity:

A theorem proposed between the two—
Two figures in a nature of the sun,
In the sun's design of its own happiness,

As if nothingness contained a métier,
A vital assumption, an impermanence
In its permanent cold, an illusion so desired

That the green leaves came and covered the high rock,
That the lilacs came and bloomed, like a blindness cleaned,
Exclaiming bright sight, as it was satisfied,

In a birth of sight. The blooming and the musk
Were being alive, an incessant being alive,
A particular of being, that gross universe.

II

The Poem as Icon

It is not enough to cover the rock with leaves.
We must be cured of it by a cure of the ground
Or a cure of ourselves, that is equal to a cure

Of the ground, a cure beyond forgetfulness.
And yet the leaves, if they broke into bud,
If they broke into bloom, if they bore fruit,

And if we ate the incipient colorings
Of their fresh culls might be a cure of the ground.
The fiction of the leaves is the icon

Of the poem, the figuration of blessedness,
And the icon is the man. The pearled chaplet of spring,
The magnum wreath of summer, time's autumn snood,

Its copy of the sun, these cover the rock.
These leaves are the poem, the icon and the man.
These are a cure of the ground and of ourselves,

In the predicate that there is nothing else.
They bud and bloom and bear their fruit without change.
They are more than leaves that cover the barren rock.

They bud the whitest eye, the pallidest sprout,
New senses in the engenderings of sense,
The desire to be at the end of distances,

The body quickened and the mind in root.
They bloom as a man loves, as he lives in love.
They bear their fruit so that the year is known,

As if its understanding was brown skin,
The honey in its pulp, the final found,
The plenty of the year and of the world.

In this plenty, the poem makes meanings of the rock,
Of such mixed motion and such imagery
That its barrenness becomes a thousand things

And so exists no more. This is the cure
Of leaves and of the ground and of ourselves.
His words are both the icon and the man.

III
Forms of the Rock in a Night-Hymn

The rock is the gray particular of man's life,
The stone from which he rises, up—and—ho,
The step to the bleaker depths of his descents . . .

The rock is the stern particular of the air,
The mirror of the planets, one by one,
But through man's eye, their silent rhapsodist,

Turquoise the rock, at odious evening bright
With redness that sticks fast to evil dreams;
The difficult rightness of half-risen day.

The rock is the habitation of the whole,
Its strength and measure, that which is near, point A
In a perspective that begins again

At B: the origin of the mango's rind.
It is the rock where tranquil must adduce
Its tranquil self, the main of things, the mind,

The starting point of the human and the end,
That in which space itself is contained, the gate
To the enclosure, day, the things illumined

By day, night and that which night illumines,
Night and its midnight-minting fragrances,
Night's hymn of the rock, as in a vivid sleep.

A Discovery of Thought

At the antipodes of poetry, dark winter,
When the trees glitter with that which despoils them,
Daylight evaporates, like a sound one hears in sickness.

One is a child again. The gold beards of waterfalls
Are dissolved as in an infancy of blue snow.
It is an arbor against the wind, a pit in the mist,

A trinkling in the parentage of the north,
The cricket of summer forming itself out of ice.
And always at this antipodes, of leaden loaves

Held in the hands of blue men that are lead within,
One thinks that it could be that the first word spoken,
The desire for speech and meaning gallantly fulfilled,

The gathering of the imbecile against his motes
And the wry antipodes whirled round the world away—
One thinks, when the houses of New England catch the first
    sun,

The first word would be of the susceptible being arrived,
The immaculate disclosure of the secret no more obscured.
The sprawling of winter might suddenly stand erect,

Pronouncing its new life and ours, not autumn's prodigal re-
    turned,
But an antipodal, far-fetched creature, worthy of birth,
The true tone of the metal of winter in what it says:

The accent of deviation in the living thing
That is its life preserved, the effort to be born
Surviving being born, the event of life.

The Course of a Particular

Today the leaves cry, hanging on branches swept by wind,
Yet the nothingness of winter becomes a little less.
It is still full of icy shades and shapen snow.

The leaves cry . . . One holds off and merely hears the cry.
It is a busy cry, concerning someone else.
And though one says that one is part of everything,

There is a conflict, there is a resistance involved;
And being part is an exertion that declines:
One feels the life of that which gives life as it is.

The leaves cry. It is not a cry of divine attention,
Nor the smoke-drift of puffed-out heroes, nor human cry.
It is the cry of leaves that do not transcend themselves,

In the absence of fantasia, without meaning more
Than they are in the final finding of the ear, in the thing
Itself, until, at last, the cry concerns no one at all.

Final Soliloquy of the Interior Paramour

Light the first light of evening, as in a room
In which we rest and, for small reason, think
The world imagined is the ultimate good.

This is, therefore, the intensest rendezvous.
It is in that thought that we collect ourselves,
Out of all the indifferences, into one thing:

367

Within a single thing, a single shawl
Wrapped tightly round us, since we are poor, a warmth,
A light, a power, the miraculous influence.

Here, now, we forget each other and ourselves.
We feel the obscurity of an order, a whole,
A knowledge, that which arranged the rendezvous,

Within its vital boundary, in the mind.
We say God and the imagination are one . . .
How high that highest candle lights the dark.

Out of this same light, out of the central mind,
We make a dwelling in the evening air,
In which being there together is enough.

Madame La Fleurie

Weight him down, O side-stars, with the great weightings of
　　the end.
Seal him there. He looked in a glass of the earth and thought he
　　lived in it.
Now, he brings all that he saw into the earth, to the waiting
　　parent.
His crisp knowledge is devoured by her, beneath a dew.

Weight him, weight, weight him with the sleepiness of the
　　moon.
It was only a glass because he looked in it. It was nothing he
　　could be told.
It was a language he spoke, because he must, yet did not know.
It was a page he had found in the handbook of heartbreak.

The black fugatos are strumming the blacknesses of black . . .
The thick strings stutter the finial gutturals.
He does not lie there remembering the blue-jay, say the jay.
His grief is that his mother should feed on him, himself and
    what he saw,
In that distant chamber, a bearded queen, wicked in her dead
    light.

A Quiet Normal Life

His place, as he sat and as he thought, was not
In anything that he constructed, so frail,
So barely lit, so shadowed over and naught,

As, for example, a world in which, like snow,
He became an inhabitant, obedient
To gallant notions on the part of cold.

It was here. This was the setting and the time
Of year. Here in his house and in his room,
In his chair, the most tranquil thought grew peaked

And the oldest and the warmest heart was cut
By gallant notions on the part of night—
Both late and alone, above the crickets' chords,

Babbling, each one, the uniqueness of its sound.
There was no fury in transcendent forms.
But his actual candle blazed with artifice.

Long and Sluggish Lines

It makes so little difference, at so much more
Than seventy,   here one looks, one has been there before.

Wood-smoke rises through trees, is caught in an upper flow
Of air and whirled away. But it has been often so.

The trees have a look as if they bore sad names
And kept saying over and over one same, same thing,

In a kind of uproar, because an opposite, a contradiction,
Has enraged them and made them want to talk it down.

What opposite? Could it be that yellow patch, the side
Of a house, that makes one think the house is laughing;

Or these—escent—issant pre-personae: first fly,
A comic infanta among the tragic drapings,

Babyishness of forsythia, a snatch of belief,
The spook and makings of the nude magnolia?

. . . Wanderer, this is the pre-history of February.
The life of the poem in the mind has not yet begun.

You were not born yet when the trees were crystal
Nor are you now, in this wakefulness inside a sleep.

To an Old Philosopher in Rome

On the threshold of heaven, the figures in the street
Become the figures of heaven, the majestic movement
Of men growing small in the distances of space,
Singing, with smaller and still smaller sound,
Unintelligible absolution and an end—

The threshold, Rome, and that more merciful Rome
Beyond, the two alike in the make of the mind.
It is as if in a human dignity
Two parallels become one, a perspective, of which
Men are part both in the inch and in the mile.

How easily the blown banners change to wings . . .
Things dark on the horizons of perception
Become accompaniments of fortune, but
Of the fortune of the spirit, beyond the eye,
Not of its sphere, and yet not far beyond,

The human end in the spirit's greatest reach,
The extreme of the known in the presence of the extreme
Of the unknown. The newsboys' muttering
Becomes another murmuring; the smell
Of medicine, a fragrantness not to be spoiled . . .

The bed, the books, the chair, the moving nuns,
The candle as it evades the sight, these are
The sources of happiness in the shape of Rome,
A shape within the ancient circles of shapes,
And these beneath the shadow of a shape

In a confusion on bed and books, a portent
On the chair, a moving transparence on the nuns,
A light on the candle tearing against the wick
To join a hovering excellence, to escape
From fire and be part only of that of which

Fire is the symbol: the celestial possible.
Speak to your pillow as if it was yourself.
Be orator but with an accurate tongue
And without eloquence, O, half-asleep,
Of the pity that is the memorial of this room,

So that we feel, in this illumined large,
The veritable small, so that each of us
Beholds himself in you, and hears his voice
In yours, master and commiserable man,
Intent on your particles of nether-do,

Your dozing in the depths of wakefulness,
In the warmth of your bed, at the edge of your chair, alive
Yet living in two worlds, impenitent
As to one, and, as to one, most penitent,
Impatient for the grandeur that you need

In so much misery; and yet finding it
Only in misery, the afflatus of ruin,
Profound poetry of the poor and of the dead,
As in the last drop of the deepest blood,
As it falls from the heart and lies there to be seen,

Even as the blood of an empire, it might be,
For a citizen of heaven though still of Rome.
It is poverty's speech that seeks us out the most.
It is older than the oldest speech of Rome.
This is the tragic accent of the scene.

And you—it is you that speak it, without speech,
The loftiest syllables among loftiest things,
The one invulnerable man among
Crude captains, the naked majesty, if you like,
Of bird-nest arches and of rain-stained vaults.

The sounds drift in. The buildings are remembered.
The life of the city never lets go, nor do you
Ever want it to. It is part of the life in your room.
Its domes are the architecture of your bed.
The bells keep on repeating solemn names

In choruses and choirs of choruses,
Unwilling that mercy should be a mystery
Of silence, that any solitude of sense
Should give you more than their peculiar chords
And reverberations clinging to whisper still.

It is a kind of total grandeur at the end,
With every visible thing enlarged and yet
No more than a bed, a chair and moving nuns,
The immensest theatre, the pillared porch,
The book and candle in your ambered room,

Total grandeur of a total edifice,
Chosen by an inquisitor of structures
For himself. He stops upon this threshold,
As if the design of all his words takes form
And frame from thinking and is realized.

The Poem That Took the Place
of a Mountain

There it was, word for word,
The poem that took the place of a mountain.

He breathed its oxygen,
Even when the book lay turned in the dust of his table.

It reminded him how he had needed
A place to go to in his own direction,

How he had recomposed the pines,
Shifted the rocks and picked his way among clouds,

For the outlook that would be right,
Where he would be complete in an unexplained completion:

The exact rock where his inexactnesses
Would discover, at last, the view toward which they had edged,

Where he could lie and, gazing down at the sea,
Recognize his unique and solitary home.

Two Illustrations That the World Is What You Make of It

The Constant Disquisition of the Wind

The sky seemed so small that winter day,
A dirty light on a lifeless world,
Contracted like a withered stick.

It was not the shadow of cloud and cold,
But a sense of the distance of the sun—
The shadow of a sense of his own,

A knowledge that the actual day
Was so much less. Only the wind
Seemed large and loud and high and strong.

And as he thought within the thought
Of the wind, not knowing that that thought
Was not his thought, nor anyone's,

The appropriate image of himself,
So formed, became himself and he breathed
The breath of another nature as his own,

But only its momentary breath,
Outside of and beyond the dirty light,
That never could be animal,

A nature still without a shape,
Except his own—perhaps, his own
In a Sunday's violent idleness.

The World Is Larger in Summer

He left half a shoulder and half a head
To recognize him in after time.

These marbles lay weathering in the grass
When the summer was over, when the change

Of summer and of the sun, the life
Of summer and of the sun, were gone.

He had said that everything possessed
The power to transform itself, or else,

And what meant more, to be transformed.
He discovered the colors of the moon

In a single spruce, when, suddenly,
The tree stood dazzling in the air

And blue broke on him from the sun,
A bullioned blue, a blue abulge,

Like daylight, with time's bellishings,
And sensuous summer stood full-height.

The master of the spruce, himself,
Became transformed. But his mastery

Left only the fragments found in the grass,
From his project, as finally magnified.

Prologues to What Is Possible

There was an ease of mind that was like being alone in a boat at
    sea,
A boat carried forward by waves resembling the bright backs of
    rowers,
Gripping their oars, as if they were sure of the way to their
    destination,
Bending over and pulling themselves erect on the wooden
    handles,
Wet with water and sparkling in the one-ness of their motion.

The boat was built of stones that had lost their weight and being
    no longer heavy
Had left in them only a brilliance, of unaccustomed origin,
So that he that stood up in the boat leaning and looking be-
    fore him
Did not pass like someone voyaging out of and beyond the
    familiar.
He belonged to the far-foreign departure of his vessel and was
    part of it,
Part of the speculum of fire on its prow, its symbol, whatever it
    was,
Part of the glass-like sides on which it glided over the salt-
    stained water,

As he traveled alone, like a man lured on by a syllable without
    any meaning,
A syllable of which he felt, with an appointed sureness,
That it contained the meaning into which he wanted to enter,
A meaning which, as he entered it, would shatter the boat and
    leave the oarsmen quiet

As at a point of central arrival, an instant moment, much or
    little,
Removed from any shore, from any man or woman, and needing
    none.

II

The metaphor stirred his fear. The object with which he was
    compared
Was beyond his recognizing. By this he knew that likeness of
    him extended
Only a little way, and not beyond, unless between himself
And things beyond resemblance there was this and that
    intended to be recognized,
The this and that in the enclosures of hypotheses
On which men speculated in summer when they were half
    asleep.

What self, for example, did he contain that had not yet been
    loosed,
Snarling in him for discovery as his attentions spread,
As if all his hereditary lights were suddenly increased
By an access of color, a new and unobserved, slight dithering,
The smallest lamp, which added its puissant flick, to which he
    gave
A name and privilege over the ordinary of his commonplace—

A flick which added to what was real and its vocabulary,
The way some first thing coming into Northern trees
Adds to them the whole vocabulary of the South,
The way the earliest single light in the evening sky, in spring,
Creates a fresh universe out of nothingness by adding itself,
The way a look or a touch reveals its unexpected magnitudes.

Looking Across the Fields and
Watching the Birds Fly

Among the more irritating minor ideas
Of Mr. Homburg during his visits home
To Concord, at the edge of things, was this:

To think away the grass, the trees, the clouds,
Not to transform them into other things,
Is only what the sun does every day,

Until we say to ourselves that there may be
A pensive nature, a mechanical
And slightly detestable *operandum*, free

From man's ghost, larger and yet a little like,
Without his literature and without his gods . . .
No doubt we live beyond ourselves in air,

In an element that does not do for us,
So well, that which we do for ourselves, too big,
A thing not planned for imagery or belief,

Not one of the masculine myths we used to make,
A transparency through which the swallow weaves,
Without any form or any sense of form,

What we know in what we see, what we feel in what
We hear, what we are, beyond mystic disputation,
In the tumult of integrations out of the sky,

And what we think, a breathing like the wind,
A moving part of a motion, a discovery
Part of a discovery, a change part of a change,

A sharing of color and being part of it.
The afternoon is visibly a source,
Too wide, too irised, to be more than calm,

Too much like thinking to be less than thought,
Obscurest parent, obscurest patriarch,
A daily majesty of meditation,

That comes and goes in silences of its own.
We think, then, as the sun shines or does not.
We think as wind skitters on a pond in a field

Or we put mantles on our words because
The same wind, rising and rising, makes a sound
Like the last muting of winter as it ends.

A new scholar replacing an older one reflects
A moment on this fantasia. He seeks
For a human that can be accounted for.

The spirit comes from the body of the world,
Or so Mr. Homburg thought: the body of a world
Whose blunt laws make an affectation of mind,

The mannerism of nature caught in a glass
And there become a spirit's mannerism,
A glass aswarm with things going as far as they can.

The World as Meditation

*J'ai passé trop de temps à travailler
mon violon, à voyager. Mais l'exer-
cice essentiel du compositeur—la
méditation—rien ne l'a jamais sus-
pendu en moi . . . Je vis un rêve
permanent, qui ne s'arrête ni nuit
ni jour.*

—GEORGES ENESCO

Is it Ulysses that approaches from the east,
The interminable adventurer? The trees are mended.
That winter is washed away. Someone is moving

On the horizon and lifting himself up above it.
A form of fire approaches the cretonnes of Penelope,
Whose mere savage presence awakens the world in which she
    dwells.

She has composed, so long, a self with which to welcome him,
Companion to his self for her, which she imagined,
Two in a deep-founded sheltering, friend and dear friend.

The trees had been mended, as an essential exercise
In an inhuman meditation, larger than her own.
No winds like dogs watched over her at night.

She wanted nothing he could not bring her by coming alone.
She wanted no fetchings. His arms would be her necklace
And her belt, the final fortune of their desire.

But was it Ulysses? Or was it only the warmth of the sun
On her pillow? The thought kept beating in her like her heart.
The two kept beating together. It was only day.

It was Ulysses and it was not. Yet they had met,
Friend and dear friend and a planet's encouragement.
The barbarous strength within her would never fail.

She would talk a little to herself as she combed her hair,
Repeating his name with its patient syllables,
Never forgetting him that kept coming constantly so near.

An Old Man Asleep

The two worlds are asleep, are sleeping, now.
A dumb sense possesses them in a kind of solemnity.

The self and the earth—your thoughts, your feelings,
Your beliefs and disbeliefs, your whole peculiar plot;

The redness of your reddish chestnut trees,
The river motion, the drowsy motion of the river R.

The Plain Sense of Things

After the leaves have fallen, we return
To a plain sense of things. It is as if
We had come to an end of the imagination,
Inanimate in an inert savoir.

It is difficult even to choose the adjective
For this blank cold, this sadness without cause.
The great structure has become a minor house.
No turban walks across the lessened floors.

The greenhouse never so badly needed paint.
The chimney is fifty years old and slants to one side.
A fantastic effort has failed, a repetition
In a repetitiousness of men and flies.

Yet the absence of the imagination had
Itself to be imagined. The great pond,
The plain sense of it, without reflections, leaves,
Mud, water like dirty glass, expressing silence

Of a sort, silence of a rat come out to see,
The great pond and its waste of the lilies, all this
Had to be imagined as an inevitable knowledge,
Required, as a necessity requires.

Lebensweisheitspielerei

Weaker and weaker, the sunlight falls
In the afternoon. The proud and the strong
Have departed.

Those that are left are the unaccomplished,
The finally human,
Natives of a dwindled sphere.

Their indigence is an indigence
That is an indigence of the light,
A stellar pallor that hangs on the threads.

Little by little, the poverty
Of autumnal space becomes
A look, a few words spoken.

Each person completely touches us
With what he is and as he is,
In the stale grandeur of annihilation.

The Hermitage at the Centre

The leaves on the macadam make a noise—
    How soft the grass on which the desired
    Reclines in the temperature of heaven—

Like tales that were told the day before yesterday—
    Sleek in a natural nakedness,
    She attends the tintinnabula—

And the wind sways like a great thing tottering—
    Of birds called up by more than the sun,
    Birds of more wit, that substitute—

Which suddenly is all dissolved and gone—
    Their intelligible twittering
    For unintelligible thought.

And yet this end and this beginning are one,
    And one last look at the ducks is a look
    At lucent children round her in a ring.

The Dove in Spring

Brooder, brooder, deep beneath its walls—
A small howling of the dove
Makes something of the little there,

The little and the dark, and that
In which it is and that in which
It is established. There the dove

Makes this small howling, like a thought
That howls in the mind or like a man
Who keeps seeking out his identity

In that which is and is established . . . It howls
Of the great sizes of an outer bush
And the great misery of the doubt of it,

Of stripes of silver that are strips
Like slits across a space, a place
And state of being large and light.

There is this bubbling before the sun,
This howling at one's ear, too far
For daylight and too near for sleep.

The Planet on the Table

Ariel was glad he had written his poems.
They were of a remembered time
Or of something seen that he liked.

Other makings of the sun
Were waste and welter
And the ripe shrub writhed.

His self and the sun were one
And his poems, although makings of his self,
Were no less makings of the sun.

It was not important that they survive.
What mattered was that they should bear
Some lineament or character,

Some affluence, if only half-perceived,
In the poverty of their words,
Of the planet of which they were part.

The River of Rivers in Connecticut

There is a great river this side of Stygia,
Before one comes to the first black cataracts
And trees that lack the intelligence of trees.

In that river, far this side of Stygia,
The mere flowing of the water is a gayety,
Flashing and flashing in the sun. On its banks,

No shadow walks. The river is fateful,
Like the last one. But there is no ferryman.
He could not bend against its propelling force.

It is not to be seen beneath the appearances
That tell of it. The steeple at Farmington
Stands glistening and Haddam shines and sways.

It is the third commonness with light and air,
A curriculum, a vigor, a local abstraction . . .
Call it, once more, a river, an unnamed flowing,

Space-filled, reflecting the seasons, the folk-lore
Of each of the senses; call it, again and again,
The river that flows nowhere, like a sea.

Not Ideas about the Thing
but the Thing Itself

At the earliest ending of winter,
In March, a scrawny cry from outside
Seemed like a sound in his mind.

He knew that he heard it,
A bird's cry, at daylight or before,
In the early March wind.

The sun was rising at six,
No longer a battered panache above snow . . .
It would have been outside.

It was not from the vast ventriloquism
Of sleep's faded papier-mâché . . .
The sun was coming from outside.

That scrawny cry—It was
A chorister whose c preceded the choir.
It was part of the colossal sun,

Surrounded by its choral rings,
Still far away. It was like
A new knowledge of reality.

The Sail of Ulysses

Under the shape of his sail, Ulysses,
Symbol of the seeker, crossing by night
The giant sea, read his own mind.
He said, "As I know, I am and have
The right to be." Guiding his boat
Under the middle stars, he said:

I

"If knowledge and the thing known are one
So that to know a man is to be
That man, to know a place is to be
That place, and it seems to come to that;
And if to know one man is to know all
And if one's sense of a single spot
Is what one knows of the universe,
Then knowledge is the only life,
The only sun of the only day,
The only access to true ease,
The deep comfort of the world and fate.

II

There is a human loneliness,
A part of space and solitude,
In which knowledge cannot be denied,
In which nothing of knowledge fails,
The luminous companion, the hand,
The fortifying arm, the profound
Response, the completely answering voice,
That which is more than anything else
The right within us and about us,
Joined, the triumphant vigor, felt,
The inner direction on which we depend,
That which keeps us the little that we are,
The aid of greatness to be and the force.

III

This is the true creator, the waver
Waving purpling wands, the thinker
Thinking gold thoughts in a golden mind,
Loftily jingled, radiant,
The joy of meaning in design
Wrenched out of chaos . . . The quiet lamp
For this creator is a lamp
Enlarging like a nocturnal ray
The space in which it stands, the shine
Of darkness, creating from nothingness
Such black constructions, such public shapes
And murky masonry, one wonders
At the finger that brushes this aside
Gigantic in everything but size.

IV

The unnamed creator of an unknown sphere,
Unknown as yet, unknowable,
Uncertain certainty, Apollo
Imagined among the indigenes

And Eden conceived on Morningside,
The centre of the self, the self
Of the future, of future man
And future place, when these are known,
A freedom at last from the mystical,
The beginning of a final order,
The order of man's right to be
As he is, the discipline of his scope
Observed as an absolute, himself.

v

A longer, deeper breath sustains
The eloquence of right, since knowing
And being are one: the right to know
And the right to be are one. We come
To knowledge when we come to life.
Yet always there is another life,
A life beyond this present knowing,
A life lighter than this present splendor,
Brighter, perfected and distant away,
Not to be reached but to be known,
Not an attainment of the will
But something illogically received,
A divination, a letting down
From loftiness, misgivings dazzlingly
Resolved in dazzling discovery.
There is no map of paradise.
The great Omnium descends on us
As a free race. We know it, one
By one, in the right of all. Each man
Is an approach to the vigilance
In which the litter of truths becomes
A whole, the day on which the last star
Has been counted, the genealogy
Of gods and men destroyed, the right
To know established as the right to be.

The ancient symbols will be nothing then.
We shall have gone behind the symbols
To that which they symbolized, away
From the rumors of the speech-full domes,
To the chatter that is then the true legend,
Like glitter ascended into fire.

VI

Master of the world and of himself,
He came to this by knowledge or
Will come. His mind presents the world
And in his mind the world revolves.
The revolutions through day and night,
Through wild spaces of other suns and moons,
Round summer and angular winter and winds,
Are matched by other revolutions
In which the world goes round and round
In the crystal atmospheres of the mind,
Light's comedies, dark's tragedies,
Like things produced by a climate, the world
Goes round in the climates of the mind
And bears its floraisons of imagery.

The mind renews the world in a verse,
A passage of music, a paragraph
By a right philosopher: renews
And possesses by sincere insight
In the John-begat-Jacob of what we know,
The flights through space, changing habitudes.

In the generations of thought, man's sons
And heirs are powers of the mind,
His only testament and estate.
He has nothing but the truth to leave.
How then shall the mind be less than free
Since only to know is to be free?

VII

The living man in the present place,
Always, the particular thought
Among Plantagenet abstractions,
Always and always, the difficult inch,
On which the vast arches of space
Repose, always, the credible thought
From which the incredible systems spring,
The little confine soon unconfined
In stellar largenesses—these things
Are the manifestations of a law
That bends the particulars to the abstract,
Makes them a pack on a giant's back,
A majestic mother's flocking brood,
As if abstractions were, themselves
Particulars of a relative sublime.
This is not poet's ease of mind.
It is the fate that dwells in truth.
We obey the coaxings of our end.

VIII

What is the shape of the sibyl? Not,
For a change, the englistered woman, seated
In colorings harmonious, dewed and dashed
By them: gorgeous symbol seated
On the seat of halidom, rainbowed,
Piercing the spirit by appearance,
A summing up of the loftiest lives
And their directing sceptre, the crown
And final effulgence and delving show.
It is the sibyl of the self,
The self as sibyl, whose diamond,
Whose chiefest embracing of all wealth
Is poverty, whose jewel found
At the exactest central of the earth

Is need. For this, the sibyl's shape
Is a blind thing fumbling for its form,
A form that is lame, a hand, a back,
A dream too poor, too destitute
To be remembered, the old shape
Worn and leaning to nothingness,
A woman looking down the road,
A child asleep in its own life.
As these depend, so must they use.
They measure the right to use. Need makes
The right to use. Need names on its breath
Categories of bleak necessity,
Which, just to name, is to create
A help, a right to help, a right
To know what helps and to attain,
By right of knowing, another plane.
The englistered woman is now seen
In an isolation, separate
From the human in humanity,
A part of the inhuman more,
The still inhuman more, and yet
An inhuman of our features, known
And unknown, inhuman for a little while,
Inhuman for a little, lesser time."

The great sail of Ulysses seemed,
In the breathings of this soliloquy,
Alive with an enigma's flittering . . .
As if another sail went on
Straight forwardly through another night
And clumped stars dangled all the way.

A Child Asleep in Its Own Life

Among the old men that you know,
There is one, unnamed, that broods
On all the rest, in heavy thought.

They are nothing, except in the universe
Of that single mind. He regards them
Outwardly and knows them inwardly,

The sole emperor of what they are,
Distant, yet close enough to wake
The chords above your bed to-night.

On the Way to the Bus

A light snow, like frost, has fallen during the night.
Gloomily, the journalist confronts

Transparent man in a translated world,
In which he feeds on a new known,

In a season, a climate of morning, of elucidation,
A refreshment of cold air, cold breath,

A perception of cold breath, more revealing than
A perception of sleep, more powerful

Than a power of sleep, a clearness emerging
From cold, slightly irised, slightly bedazzled,

But a perfection emerging from a new known,
An understanding beyond journalism,

A way of pronouncing the word inside of one's tongue
Under the wintry trees of the terrace.

First Warmth

I wonder, have I lived a skeleton's life,
As a questioner about reality,

A countryman of all the bones of the world?
Now, here, the warmth I had forgotten becomes

Part of the major reality, part of
An appreciation of a reality;

And thus an elevation, as if I lived
With something I could touch, touch every way.

As You Leave the Room

You speak. You say: Today's character is not
A skeleton out of its cabinet. Nor am I.

That poem about the pineapple, the one
About the mind as never satisfied,

The one about the credible hero, the one
About summer, are not what skeletons think about.

I wonder, have I lived a skeleton's life,
As a disbeliever in reality,

A countryman of all the bones in the world?
Now, here, the snow I had forgotten becomes

Part of a major reality, part of
An appreciation of a reality

And thus an elevation, as if I left
With something I could touch, touch every way.

And yet nothing has been changed except what is
Unreal, as if nothing had been changed at all.

Reality Is an Activity of the Most August Imagination

Last Friday, in the big light of last Friday night,
We drove home from Cornwall to Hartford, late.

It was not a night blown at a glassworks in Vienna
Or Venice, motionless, gathering time and dust.

There was a crush of strength in a grinding going round,
Under the front of the westward evening star,

The vigor of glory, a glittering in the veins,
As things emerged and moved and were dissolved,

Either in distance, change or nothingness,
The visible transformations of summer night,

An argentine abstraction approaching form
And suddenly denying itself away.

There was an insolid billowing of the solid.
Night's moonlight lake was neither water nor air.

A Clear Day and No Memories

No soldiers in the scenery,
No thoughts of people now dead,
As they were fifty years ago,
Young and living in a live air,
Young and walking in the sunshine,
Bending in blue dresses to touch something,
Today the mind is not part of the weather.

Today the air is clear of everything.
It has no knowledge except of nothingness
And it flows over us without meanings,
As if none of us had ever been here before
And are not now: in this shallow spectacle,
This invisible activity, this sense.

A Mythology Reflects Its Region

A mythology reflects its region. Here
In Connecticut, we never lived in a time
When mythology was possible—But if we had—
That raises the question of the image's truth.
The image must be of the nature of its creator.
It is the nature of its creator increased,
Heightened. It is he, anew, in a freshened youth
And it is he in the substance of his region,
Wood of his forests and stone out of his fields
Or from under his mountains.

Of Mere Being

The palm at the end of the mind,
Beyond the last thought, rises
In the bronze decor,

A gold-feathered bird
Sings in the palm, without human meaning,
Without human feeling, a foreign song.

You know then that it is not the reason
That makes us happy or unhappy.
The bird sings. Its feathers shine.

The palm stands on the edge of space.
The wind moves slowly in the branches.
The bird's fire-fangled feathers dangle down.

NOTES
INDEX OF FIRST LINES
INDEX OF TITLES

For an Old Woman in a Wig

ca. 1916 This poem is found only in manuscript, written in pencil with many lines, phrases, and words erased. In many cases new words have been written over the old, so that the original is illegible. For a discussion of this manuscript, see Robert Buttel: *Wallace Stevens: The Making of Harmonium* (Princeton: Princeton University Press; 1967), pp. 213–16, in which the poem was first published.

Bowl, Cat and Broomstick

ca. 1917 This play has been taken from a typed carbon copy of the manuscript. Although it was performed by the Wisconsin Players at the Neighborhood Playhouse in New York City in October 1917, it was never published by Stevens, and first appeared in print in *Quarterly Review of Literature*, Vol. XVI (Summer 1969), pp. 236–47, with an introduction by A. Walton Litz.

Nomad Exquisite

This poem has, until recently, been dated by its first publication in *Harmonium* (New York: Alfred A. Knopf; 1923). Daryl Hine, editor of *Poetry*, has discovered that Stevens originally wrote it on the back of a postcard to Harriet Monroe, mailed from Florida on January 15, 1919. On the postcard the last line reads "Fruits, forms, flowers, flakes and fountains." I am very grateful to Mr. Hine for this new evidence.

The Man Whose Pharynx Was Bad

This poem was first published in *The New Republic*, Vol. XXVIII (September 14, 1921), p. 74, and appears here as it did in that publication. When Stevens included it in *Harmonium* (Second Edition [New York: Alfred A. Knopf; 1931]), he omitted lines 10 through 13; nor do they appear in *Collected Poems* (New York: Alfred A. Knopf; 1954). While it might seem that this was an oversight, it apparently was intentional: a copy of the magazine in the editor's possession, filed together with a letter relating to new poems for inclusion in the second edition of *Harmonium*, has the lines clearly crossed out in pencil.

The Comedian as the Letter C, Part V, A Nice Shady Home

In *Collected Poems* the penultimate word in the third line is "prickling."

In both editions of *Harmonium*, however, the word is "pricking," which has been restored here.

Anecdote of the Prince of Peacocks
An early version, found in manuscript, reads as follows:

> In the land of the peacocks, the prince thereof,
> Grown weary of romantics, walked alone,
> In the first of evening, pondering.
>
> "The deuce!" he cried.
>
> And by him, in the bushes, he espied
> A white philosopher.
> The white one sighed—
>
> He seemed to seek replies,
> From nothingness, to all his sighs.
>
> "My sighs are pulses in a dreamer's death!"
> Exclaimed the white one, smothering his lips.
>
> The prince's frisson reached his fingers' tips.

Autumn Refrain
The eighth line, as the poem appears here, was included when the poem was first published in *Hound and Horn*, Vol. V (Winter 1932), p. 222. It was omitted in *Ideas of Order* (New York: Alcestis Press; 1935, and Alfred A. Knopf, 1936), and in *Collected Poems*.

Like Decorations in a Nigger Cemetery, Part XXVI
The third word of the first line, both in manuscript and as first published in *Poetry*, Vol. XLV (February 1935), pp. 239–49, is "pastiche." It has not been changed here.

[Prose statement on the poetry of war]
These paragraphs, untitled, appear on the page facing the last page of "Examination of the Hero in a Time of War," as the last page (unnumbered) of *Parts of a World* (New York: Alfred A. Knopf; 1942). When *Collected Poems* was being prepared, Stevens agreed with his editor that they should be omitted.

Notes Toward a Supreme Fiction, Dedication
For a discussion as to whether the opening lines are part of the dedication

to Henry Church, see *Letters of Wallace Stevens* (New York: Alfred A. Knopf; 1966), p. 538, where Stevens says "the first eight lines have nothing to do with Mr. Church: they are by way of an introduction to the poem." The opening, as printed here, restores the order of original publication.

Notes Toward a Supreme Fiction, It Must Give Pleasure, Part VIII

The penultimate word in the second line is "violet" in The Cummington Press editions of this poem (Cummington, Mass., 1942; second edition, 1943). "Violent" first appears as the poem is printed in *Transport to Summer* (New York: Alfred A. Knopf; 1947), and has not been changed here. My thanks to William Burney, Central Connecticut State College, for calling this discrepancy to my attention.

An Ordinary Evening in New Haven, Part IV

Two carbon typescripts in the editor's possession have "writer's" as the penultimate word in line 13, rather than "winter's." It has not been changed here, as it undoubtedly was a stenographic error.

The Old Lutheran Bells at Home

In pencil, on the reverse of his manuscript, Stevens wrote:
> As they teeter and totter in the caterwaul
> As the sextons jangle and dangle and kick their feet
> As they teeter and totter in the belfry [illegible word,
>   may be "earth"]

To an Old Philosopher in Rome

The second stanza, in a carbon typescript in the editor's possession, reads:
> The threshold, Rome, and that more merciful Rome
> Beyond, the two alike in the make of the mind
> Of a common maker, not divine, as if
> In a human dignity two parallels
> Become a single thing, a perspective, of which
> Men are part both in the inch and in the mile.

The first line of the eighth stanza reads:

> So that we feel, in this augustest large

The Sail of Ulysses

A carbon typescript in the editor's possession is glossed as follows in the right-hand margin:

Line	Gloss
Under the shape of his sail, Ulysses	The place of the poem. Its theme.
Part I, line 1	To know is to be.
Part II, line 3	To know is the force to be.
Part III, line 1	The true creator.
Part IV, line 1	The center of the self.
Part V, lines 1 and 2	Except for illogical receptions.
Part VI, lines 1 and 2	Presence of an external master of knowledge.
Part VII, line 1	Truth as fate.
Part VIII, line 1	Shape of the sibyl of truth.

The Sail of Ulysses, Part VII

The original typescript has the word "things" ending line 9. It has been added here, although it was erased on the carbon typescript and does not appear in *Collected Poems*.

Of Mere Being

As printed in *Opus Posthumous* (New York: Alfred A. Knopf; 1957), the last word of the third line is "distance." "Decor" is the word appearing in the original typescript, and has been restored here.

The trade-wind jingles the rings in the nets around the racks by the docks
   on Indian River. 19
The trees were plucked like iron bars 196
The truth is that there comes a time 116
The two worlds are asleep, are sleeping, now. 382
The white cock's tail 47
The whole of appearance is a toy. For this, 285
The wood-doves are singing along the Perkiomen. 277
The wound kills that does not bleed. 282
Then from their poverty they rose, 76
There are no bears among the roses, 85
There are not leaves enough to cover the face 151
There is a great river this side of Stygia, 386
. . There is a moment's flitter 12
There it was, word for word, 374
There was an ease of mind that was like being alone in a boat at sea, 377
There was the butcher's hand. 155
There were ghosts that returned to earth to hear his phrases, 320
These are the voices of the pastors calling 352
These locusts by day, these crickets by night 355
This day writhes with what? The lecturer 301
This is where the serpent lives, the bodiless. 307
This man escaped the dirty fates, 270
This structure of ideas, these ghostly sequences 263
Through centuries he lived in poverty. 283
Tired of the old descriptions of the world, 165
To speak quietly at such a distance, to speak 241
To the imagined lives 17
Today the leaves cry, hanging on the branches swept by wind, 367
Twenty men crossing a bridge, 35
Two figures sit in the circle of a spotlight, on a white bench, before a golden
   curtain. 24
Two forms move among the dead, high sleep 302
Two wooden tubs of blue hydrangeas stand at the foot of the stone steps. 45
Under the eglantine 154
Under the shape of his sail, Ulysses, 388
Unsnack your snood, madanna, for the stars 280
Ursula, in a garden, found 3
Weaker and weaker, the sunlight falls 383
Weight him down, O side-stars, with the great weightings of the end. 368
Well, nuncle, this plainly won't do. 81
What are the major men? All men are brave. 269
What more is there to love than I have loved? 190

Index of Titles

ABOUT THE AUTHOR

WALLACE STEVENS was born in Reading, Pennsylvania, on October 2, 1879, and died in Hartford, Connecticut, on August 2, 1955. Although he had contributed to the *Harvard Advocate* while in college, he began to gain general recognition only when Harriet Monroe included four of his poems in a special 1914 wartime issue of *Poetry*. *Harmonium*, his first volume of poems, was published in 1923, and was followed by *Ideas of Order* (1936), *The Man with the Blue Guitar* (1937), *Parts of a World* (1942), *Transport to Summer* (1947), *The Auroras of Autumn* (1950), *The Necessary Angel* (a volume of essays, 1951), *The Collected Poems of Wallace Stevens* (1954), and *Opus Posthumous* (first published in 1957, edited by Samuel Freud Morse; a new, revised, and corrected edition by Milton J. Bates, 1989). Mr. Stevens was awarded the Bollingen Prize in Poetry of the Yale University Library for 1949. In 1951 he won the National Book Award in Poetry for *The Auroras of Autumn*; in 1955 he won it a second time for *The Collected Poems of Wallace Stevens*, which was also awarded the Pulitzer Prize in Poetry in 1955. From 1916 on, he was associated with the Hartford Accident and Indemnity Company, of which he became vice-president in 1934.

HOLLY STEVENS, the daughter of Wallace Stevens, has edited *Letters to Wallace Stevens* and *The Palm at the End of the Mind*. She is the author of *Souvenirs and Prophecies: The Young Wallace Stevens*.